The Wrecks of SCILLY

Richard Larn OBE

SHIPWRECK & MARINE

ISLES OF SCILLY – TR21 0NQ

G000269098

> **To my wife Bridget,
> with whom I have been privileged
> to share 33 years of marriage and
> adventures. With all my
> love and gratitude**

Distributed by Tor Mark Press, United Downs Industrial Estate, St. Day, Redruth, Cornwall TR16 5HY. Tel: 01209 822101. Fax: 01209 822035. Email: sales@tormarkpress.prestel.co.uk

© Richard Larn. 2010
Reprints 1971, 1979, 1985, 1992, 2010

Larn, Richard
The Wrecks of Scilly
5th Revised edition

All Rights Reserved. No part of this publication may be reproduced, stored in any retrieval system, or transmitted, in any form or by any means, electronic, mechanical, photocopying, scanning, recording or otherwise, without the prior permission of the publishing author.

Richard Larn has asserted his moral right to be identified as the author of this work.

British Library cataloguing in Publication Data:
A catalogue record of this book is available from the British Library

ISBN: 978 0 9523 9719 9

Design & layout by Alix Wood, Launceston; www.alixwood.co.uk

Printed in Cornwall by R. Booth Ltd, The Praze, Penryn TR10 8AA

Front and back cover illustration – Divers at work in 2009 surveying the wreck of HM Fireship *Firebrand*, sunk off St Agnes, October 1707. Courtesy of CISMAS (Cornwall & Isles of Scilly Maritime Archaeological Society), Penzance.

Contents

Introduction

The day I commenced a revision of this book in 2008, the Isles of Scilly were hit by a 105mph NW hurricane, which served to remind me how exposed these islands are, and why so many ships have been lost here. From where Bridget and I live we can clearly see Scilly Rock out to the NW, a 30m tall island of weathered granite, frequently engulfed in huge seas that rear up and often break clean over its peak. When that happens the sea is as rough as it gets, and as much as I love the sea, I for one would not want to be out there in such conditions. At the back of Scilly Rock, a massive three-cylinder triple expansion steam engine which once propelled the steamship *Brinkburn*, wrecked in 1898, has stood upright in some 18m of water for 110 years, defying nature, the sea having long since demolished the rest of the ship. An unusual underwater feature, this upright engine has attracted sport divers for the past five decades, who could swim through the piston rods and around the huge cylinder heads in awe. Covered in marine growth it was a photographers paradise - but alas, no more. Sometime during that hurricane it finally succumbed to nature and collapsed, now lying at an angle of 25° to the seabed, a reminder of the awesome power of the sea.

The first edition of this book then titled 'Cornish Shipwrecks - the Isles of Scilly', the second in a Cornish trilogy I wrote in collaboration with the late Clive Carter, was for me a double first, since it was the only book to record in detail all the shipwrecks of Scilly; also the first book I wrote alone. Inexperience meant it had errors, and in hindsight required more research and perhaps professional proof reading. Now, thirty-eight years and 55 books later, older and hopefully wiser, this is an opportunity to make up for any shortcomings in previous editions.

I would like to acknowledge my debt of gratitude to three individuals who directly or indirectly made this and many other books possible. First the late Joan de Platt Taylor, a professional land archaeologist who founded nautical archaeology in this country in the early 1960's and encouraged me by saying, 'Dick, you have done all this research into lost ships, write a book, do something with it. Do you want a publisher?' She introduced me to David St.John Thomas, who produced books in Newton Abbot. He gave me every encouragement with the reassuring words, 'Anyone can write a book, and I am sure you can.' From there I met the late Theodore Stanhope Sprigg, director and a non-fiction editor of David & Charles Ltd, who gave me a book contract over cucumber sandwiches and Earl Grey tea after only a half hour chat on the subject of shipwrecks. No synopsis, no outline, no schedule. His confidence was not misplaced, since together we produced five books with the company before he died.

We also owe a debt of gratitude to Ivan, Heather and Dan Corbett of Tor Mark Publishing & Truran, St. Day, with whom we have written and published numerous books, have been our distributors for many years, and we are privileged to have become personal friends..

Public interest and the nation's awareness of the importance and potential of ship-wrecks has greatly increased over the past twenty years. We trust this publication will be of general interest to islanders and the many visitors to Scilly who are interested in the island's history alike, and to the ever increasing number of sport divers who come to Scilly to see some of the wrecks for themselves.

RICHARD & BRIDGET LARN, St Mary's, Isles of Scilly, 2010

▲ The wooden ship Minnehaha on the rocks at Peninnis, 1874

For Sale by Auction

WRECK

On WEDNESDAY, the 29th day of APRIL, 1812

by eleven o'clock in the forenoon at

ST. MARYS, ISLES OF SCILLY

the following goods partly damaged and subject to such conditions as shall then and there be produced

3668	Bundles of iron rod	1424	Cast iron pots
63	Iron boilers	11	Iron tea kettles
13	Boxes of tinned plate	160	Sheets tinplate
166	Kegs of round shot	5	Cases of sheet iron
179	Firkins of butter	1	Cask of cudbear
10	Pipes of linseed oil	4	Casks of white lead
2	Cases of English China	47	Dozen files
592	Pieces of woolen cloth	2	Cases, 1 box of hats
550	Pieces of long cloth	80	Pieces barbozettes
24	Pieces of waistcoating	170	Pieces of bindings
449	Bundles and 507 skeins of cotton yard	86	Pieces Manchester Velvet
		3375	Spills cotton yarn
2	Cavalry saddles	23	Matted parcels
1	Case with writing desk	1	Case of cabbage seed

Subject to repayment of drawback and bounty of Excise and Customs 1012 pieces of printed calicoes, and for exportation 16 bags and a quantity of loose coffee. Being part of the general cargo salved from the wreck of the galiot "Maria". Thomas Jones Master, lost on Tresco Island on her voyage from Liverpool to Oporto. A deposit of 33 per cent is to be paid at time of sale and the remainder on delivery in Bank of England notes. For viewing, catalogues or particulars apply four days previous to Woolcock and Edwards, St. Marys.

BY ORDER
this 28th day of March, 1812

▲ The sale of material from shipwreck is nothing new – this is an auction poster of 1812, for wreck goods offered for sale on Scilly

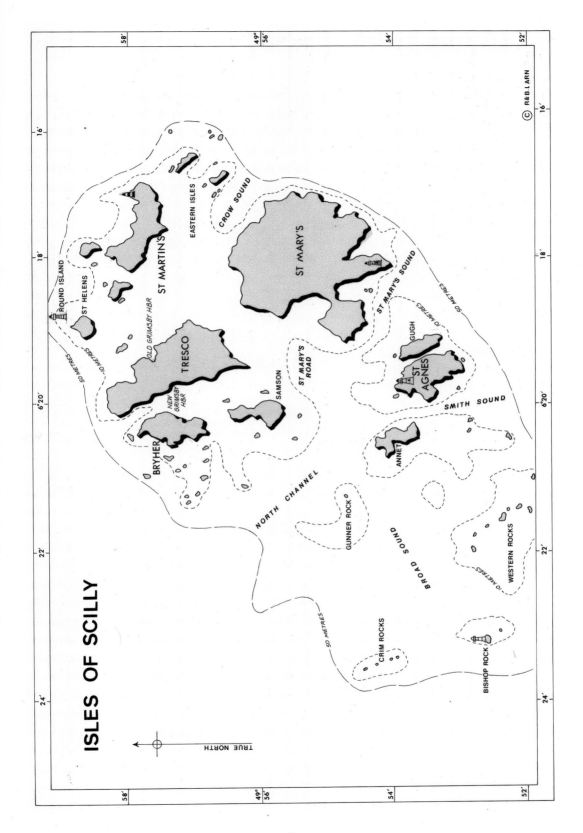

ISLES OF SCILLY

TRUE NORTH

© R & B LARN

1 - Living from the Sea

It is a fact that of all the many islands and island groups around Great Britain, none of equal size or population is as exposed or remote as the Isles of Scilly. Amongst the Western Isles of Scotland, Orkney or Shetland, there are many remote communities, but all much closer to large, well-populated towns or the mainland than St Mary's is to Penzance, in Cornwall. The west coast of Ireland also has its island communities, but they too enjoy a closer proximity to the mainland. Lundy Island in the Bristol Channel probably equates best geographically to the Scillies, but Lundy's population is not even the equal of the tiny island of St Agnes or Bryher, and is roughly only 22 miles from a mainland port compared to the 42 miles between St Mary's and Penzance. Lundy is equally exposed to the weather, lies across a busy shipping channel, was once a haven for pirates, has seen many shipwrecks and a long history of absentee landlords. Both communities have struggled over the centuries, both now almost totally reliant on tourism to remain financially independent, but there any similarities end with one exception, their common heritage, the sea. This is the element that moulded their past, dictated their fortunes, their very way of life, and will dictate their future.

For many people island life might appear idyllic, but island life is dictated by remoteness, access, population, transport and finance. Being remote from the mainland can impose enormous problems which islanders have learnt to live with. Consequently, living on an island presents problems of which visitors are often totally ignorant, and whilst remoteness for some is idyllic, for others it can be insufferable.

Whilst Scilly has been described variously as the 'Fortunate Islands', this is a modern sentimentality, and for much of its early history the 'Unfortunate Islands' would have been more appropriate. Today, the islands are safe in the knowledge that there is now a reliable water and mains electricity supply; a medical service and electronic communication with the outside world. Also, that British International and the Isles of Scilly Steamship company, by a combination of helicopters, fixed wing aircraft and two ships ensure the regular delivery of supplies and the arrival and departure of visitors who now form the island's main economy. Also, in the event of cataclysmic disaster, Government or EEC funding could be called upon. But it has not always been like this. Early occupants of Scilly must often have cursed the sea, for whilst it provided the majority with a living of sorts, and everyone derived some benefit from it, the sea isolated them from the prosperity and progress of the mainland.

On several occasions actual starvation of those living on the off-islands was narrowly averted only by the generosity of others living on the mainland.. In 1818 subscriptions were collected from Methodist congregations as far away as Sheffield and London, to assist 'over 400 distressed off-islanders of Scilly'. In 1825, Bosun Smith, a Penzance Methodist lay-preacher, started the *Isles of Scilly Industrious Society* which sent over fishing boats and equipment to give the men employment, whilst ladies from London came to teach the womenfolk how to make straw hats, weave, plait, knit and make and mend fishing nets. In one instance the much treasured coat of arms from the stern of the wreck of the man o'war Association lost in 1707, in which Sir Clowdisley Shovell and all his crew perished, was allegedly presented to the people of Penzance in appreciation of a ship load of potatoes. That crest still hangs on the wall of the Magistrates Court in the Penzance Guildhall, but all attempts to have it returned to Scilly have so far failed.

Successive monarchs since the time of Edgar and their respective governments and ministers were inclined to forget that Scillies even existed. Only when it was necessary to levy more taxes or in time of war, when there was a chance the islands might be taken by one of our traditional enemies, Spain, France or the Dutch, were they acknowledged as important and garrisoned accordingly. The moment a crisis was over the garrison would be reduced, the number of troops on St Mary's fluctuating between a peacetime garrison of 40 invalid soldiers to an active army of over 1,000 men during the Civil and Napoleonic war periods. The industrial revolution passed Scilly by completely there being no manufacturing capability or natural mineral wealth, the islands benefiting only from a 105 year period of shipbuilding that commenced in 1779. Following his visit to the islands in 1724, Daniel Defoe, the novelist and pamphleteer, in his *Tour through Gt Britain* wrote: *'These islands be so in the middle between the two vast openings that it cannot, or perhaps never will be avoided.'* He referred, of course, to the Scillies' position at the apex of three major shipping routes, the Irish Sea, English and Bristol Channels, and of course its many shipwrecks. The former gave access to Ireland, Liverpool and Glasgow, the English Channel to the south coast ports, the capital and North sea, the latter to the coal ports of South Wales and Bristol, as well as copper and tin from north Cornwall. Defoe in fact should perhaps have written of '-.*three vast openings*', since Scilly is equally the signpost for north and east bound sea traffic coming up from Biscay or across the Atlantic, giving much employment to early Scillonian pilots.

Low lying in the extreme, the highest part of St Mary's is only 55m above sea level and the Scillies' comprise some 145 islands and major rocks, of which only five are now inhabited. Spread out so as to offer a ten mile wide barrier lying NE - SW, they once presented a fearsome barrier to ships, which in the past sometimes claimed several wrecks in a day and continue to claim the occasional vessel, although there has not been a shipwreck on Scilly since the mv *Cita* in March 1997. The fact that the islands have such a low silhouette, and that the majority of the rocks and outlying reefs are covered at high-water, has been the direct cause of the majority of ship losses. When shrouded in fog or rain, the entire island group merges into a back-

▲ The wreck of the barque *Minnehaha* on Peninnis Head, 1874

ground of heaving grey sea, and many a lookout on board sailing ships and steamers alike, lulled into a stupor after several hours of seeing nothing up ahead, saw breakers only when it was too late. 'The three Ls' was the accepted maxim of early sailing masters when instructing juniors, meaning 'Lookout, Lead line and Latitude." Latitude could be readily calculated, so that the master would know how far north or south of the equator his ship was, but determining longitude at sea, ie. their east/west position, defied man's ingenuity until 1765. Even then chronometers were not readily available for sea-going ships until the mid 1800s. Navigation was only as good as the sea chart on which a ship's course would be marked. In the early 18th century, the Isles of Scilly, despite having been surveyed by the Dutch - then considered to be the best chart makers in the world, were shown to be between 15 and 20 miles further north than they actually were, and everyone was ignorant of what today is known as the Rennell Current, which sweeps these waters. As to the lead line, it was necessary to take the way off a ship by reducing sail before a reasonably accurate 'plumb' of the seas depth could be obtained, the minute sample of seabed material brought up stuck in the 'arming' tallow assisting to determine a rough location. But if the chart was inaccurate the whole business was basically educated guesswork. The last resort therefore was the lookout, and around Scilly the dice was frequently loaded against the mariner.

▲ The late Prime Minister Harold Wilson discussing finds from the *Association*, with divers from the late Roland Morris's team on St Mary's Quay

Today, with sophisticated electronic aids to navigation such as GPS, radar and echo sounders, it is difficult to imagine ships wandering the ocean with only a vague idea as to their position, but such was often the case. Two classic examples illustrate the point. A homeward- bound fleet of English East Indiamen in 1703 who 'thought they were in the English Channel making for Portsmouth, sailed so far up the Bristol Channel they eventually sighted Lundy Island before discovering their mistake.' The second concerned a modern motor vessel, the 2,000-ton mv *Shoreham*, which sent out a 'May Day' radio distress signal on 29 June 1979 reporting that she was ashore somewhere near Trevose Head on the north coast of Cornwall. In fact she stranded under the high cliffs of Mullion, on the completely opposite south coast! In the 18th century wrecks around Scilly were so frequent that they were taken for granted, and at that time supposedly no one imagined things would ever change. Exactly how many ships have gone down around Scilly will never be known for certain, but around 1,000 is a fair estimate. Vessels lost at night amongst the Western Rocks might leave no trace by morning, floating evidence such as bodies, timber or cargo being carried away on the tide. One writer debited the islands with 200 wrecks during the past 150 years, another with 75 between 1878 and 1927, whereas more realistic figures are around 365 and 189 respectively for those periods. Early writers made frequent mention of wrecks on Scilly, John Troutbeck in 1796, wrote that:

'Scillonian's are, by their situation, the sons and daughters of God's providence and ac-cordingly are otherwise cloathed and supplied out of wrecks sent in by the sea, the spoil of their rich neighbours'.

Sir Walter Besant in 1860 claimed that 'every rock in Scilly has a shipwreck,' but did not disclose how many he imagined that might total. This book contains an index of wrecks which is as near definitive as anyone could expect, made possible only after exhaustive research into almost every source over many years. However, sur-rounded by deep water well capable of hiding countless wrecks, any such list will forever be 'near definitive' only.

Ships cast ashore 500 years ago were considered of such little importance in them-selves, that their names were seldom if ever recorded, which is strange considering they were not only valuable assets but were far fewer in number than today. Whilst the ships themselves may have been of no importance, their contents most certainly were. It was their cargo, often extremely valuable, which led to 'Rights of Wreck', an exceptionally lucrative and jealously guarded perquisite of rich landowners, usually at the expense of the legitimate owner. 'Right of Wreck', which dates back to before the Roman conquest, had its origins enshrined in Rhodian Law, which refers to the legal beneficiary of shipwreck in a particular area, regardless of whether the item concerned was a whole or part ship, its stores or cargo, including whales, dolphins and porpoise washed up on the foreshore. The fact that this legal expression has survived through our history to the present day, and appears more often in State and legal documentation than any other, demonstrates the great financial benefit and value placed on this ancient and infamous privilege, which was strongly defended. It is interesting that as late as 1992, an A.J. Mildmay-White, of Mothercombe House, Devon, brought a case before the Department of Transport claiming manorial 'Right of Wreck' for his estate which overlooks the River Erme estuary, in Bigbury Bay, south Devon. An historic wreck site had been found on the Mary reef in the estuary by divers, and in the dispute regarding ownership the Crown conceded Mildmay-White's claim to any artefacts recovered.

In Scilly, the 'Right of Wreck', taken as being vested in the English crown in the first place, passed to the church in 1114. Although Scilly is not mentioned in the Doomsday Book, Henry I granted the Abbot of Tavistock 'all the churches of Sully with their appurtenances.' At a later date, Reginald, the Earl of Cornwall confirmed the grant with the amendment 'All the wrecks, except whale and a whole ship.' Although not the first Christians on the islands - there is a legend that Olaf Tryggves-son, king of Norway, came to Scilly in 989AD and was converted to Christianity by holy men already there. The priory on Tresco, then St Nicholas Isle, seemingly having brought some semblance of law and order to the otherwise lawless islands. Piracy was one of their biggest problems, and it is recorded that on Ascension Day 1209, *'pirates were beheaded in St Nicholas Isle in Sully to the number of one hundred and twelve'*. In 1302, Edward I, desirous of obtaining the coveted 'Right of Wreck' of Scilly for himself, challenged the Tavistock abbot, but a jury found that:

> ' - the abbot and all his predecessors had enjoyed wreck from time immemorial, except for whales, gold, scarlet cloth, masts and firs, which were reserved for the king.'

If disputes over wreck arose few if any complaints reached London, and those that did were probably so outdated on arrival there was little point in pursuing them.. After all, the seat of government in London necessitated five days somewhat hazardous journey by carriage or on horseback from Penzance, always provided the weather allowed a boat passage from Scilly in the first place. As late as 1744, passage between St Mary's and Penzance was seldom made more than once a month in summer, and less frequently in winter. To quote Lieutenant Heath in 1750:

> ' - in small boats, amidst the running of several cross tides, the passengers are forced to venture at the extreme hazard of their lives when only the necessity or duty calls them'.

Even by 1822, a crossing could still be an alarming experience, as a very old lady from St Mary's, visiting relatives on the mainland was to discover. After a torturous sea passage lasting over 28 hours allowing her no sleep the boat was forced by stress of weather to divert from Penzance into Mousehole, and the old lady had no option

Sir Clowdisley Shovell's tomb in Westminster Abbey. He lost his life in the wreck of HMS *Association* on Scilly, in October 1707 ▶

but to walk the last three miles to her destination in the dark and pouring rain..

An early case of shipwreck plunder in Scilly which was brought directly to the attention of London occurred in 1305, involving a William Le Poer, the coroner for Scilly. Lieutenant Heath, in his *Natural & Historical Account of the Isles of Scilly*, 1750, quotes a letter from King Edward I which read:

> 'We understand by the grevious Complaint of William Le Poer, our Coroner in the Islands
> of Scilly, belonging to our County of Cornwall, that whereas he, lately for the Preservation
> of the Peace at La Val, Trescaw, in the islands aforesaid, did repair to enquire of
> Manslaughter, Robberies, Incendiaries, and other Felonies: and Receivers of Goods felo-
> niously stolen; and of Wreck of the Sea, as to the said office appertaineth. Ranulph De
> Blackminster; Michael Petit; Edmund Specot; John Gabbere; Robert Abbat of Tavistock;
> Frier, John De Yalineton; Frier, John of Exeter; and Oliver of Scilly, Chaplain, the aforesaid

Coroner, by force of Arms, imprisoned, ill used, and there did maliciously procure him to be kept, at the said Town of de La Val, until such time as the said Coroner paid a fine to the said Ranulph, Michael, Edmund, John, Abbat; John, John and Oliver, and the Malefactors aforesaid, of 100 shillings for his enlargement out of the prison aforesaid'.

In 1337 the Right of Wreck in Scilly reverted to the crown, when Edward III endowed his son Edward, the Black Prince, with the Duchy of Cornwall, a relationship between the county, the islands and the monarchy which continues to this day. Whilst some may imagine that the Duchy embraces all Cornwall, in fact it has only ever owned seventeen per cent of the mainland, but historically 100% of the Isles of Scilly. Currently, all of Hugh Town and some other properties on St Mary's are now freehold. Five years after the initial grant, in 1342, the prince was complaining to his father that *'Certayn persons have helped themselves to my priveleages, to £1,000 worth of goods'*. A similar letter followed a year later, this time the sum being £3,000, and again in 1345 *'goods to the value of 2,000 marks are missing, the rightful perquisite of the prince, stolen on the spot'*. As mentioned earlier, the value of wreck goods was the sole concern, with no mention of the ship's name or consideration for the owner of the vessel or its cargo. So it continued, both on the mainland and amongst the islands, wreck after wreck, for literally centuries, the locals describing their activities on the foreshore or amongst the Western Rocks as *'a-shoring'*, which sounded more refined rather than simply *'wrecking'*.

Wrecking is an expression which has two definitions, related, but infinitely different in execution. A modem dictionary defines a *'wrecker'* as *'a person who*

▲ Another victim of fog, the ss. *Plympton*, carrying a cargo of bagged maize, struck the Lethegus Rocks on 14 August 1909, but remained in this position less than a day before she capsized, drowning two local men

15

◀ Silver serviette rings from the saloon of the ss.*Schiller*. Each bears a table or seating number

purposely causes a wreck or, one who plunders a wreck'. Whilst there is ample evidence of looting and plunder of shipwrecks by Scillonians and Cornishmen alike, there is not one documented case of a ship being lured by false lights whether 'tied to donkey's tails' or not. In fact the only known case in the country to come before a magistrate's court of displaying false lights was in 1773 in Anglesey. That is not to say that Cornishman never deliberately tried to lure a ship ashore, simply that there is no proof either way. For a long time it was generally accepted that no Cornish jury would ever convict a fellow countryman on a charge of wrecking, but the exception was proved in 1767. Mr Justice Yates, either at Bodmin or Launceston, sentenced a wrecker to death and *'improved the occasion by addressing not the prisoner but the court against so savage a crime'*. Every effort was made to save the man's life, the MP for Launceston putting pressure on the Secretary for State, Lord Shelborne, by reminding him that feelings were high in the wrecker's favour and that an election was due soon! Nevertheless, the man was duly hanged, one of the few cases on record of the death penalty being administered for stealing from a wreck.

In 1536 Henry VIII created a Vice-Admiral for both Devon and Cornwall, a position held only by gentlemen or nobles. Seventeen years later the counties were separated into Vice-Admiralties, but Scilly was omitted, leased instead in 1571 to Frances Godolphin of Breage, near Helston, Cornwall for the annual sum of £20. Previously, successive 'Lords' of Scilly, namely Blanchminster, Denver, Whittington, the Coleshill's and Arundell's, had all used the islands for their own ends, whereas the coming of the Godolphin's at last brought to an end what has best been described as *'the islands' awful period'*.

During his visit to Scilly in 1724 mentioned earlier, when Daniel Defoe remarked upon *'- the two great openings'*, he also wrote:

'- the sands covered in people, they are charged with strange bloody and cruel dealings, even sometimes with one another, but especially with poor distressed seamen who seek for help for their lives and find the rocks themselves not more cruel and merciless than the people who range about them for their prey.'

Borlase, in 1756, saw islanders stripping the clothes off the back of a shipwrecked mariner, found half drowned on the foreshore, and the man was probably lucky to have been left alive. Legally, if a man or dog escaped alive from a ship it was not considered a wreck; a peculiar technicality going back to Rhodian Sea Law and the Rolls of Orlean surely that could be interpreted as an open invitation to commit murder? More than one hundred years after Defoe's visit to Scilly, in their report of 15 August 1836, the Government's 'Select Committee Appointed to inquire into the Causes of Shipwreck' reported to Parliament:

'- whilst on other parts of the English coast persons assemble by hundreds for plunder on the occurrence of a wreck, on the Cornish coast they assemble in their thousands'.

In Scilly of course, there was insufficient population to assemble in such numbers, but it was certainly true of Mount's Bay and the St Ives area in Cornwall, where tin miners would congregate literally in thousands, from miles around at the scene of a wreck. When a family was living at near starvation level, or the children were without boots or warm clothing in winter or if a man helped himself to foodstuffs otherwise going to waste in the shallows, or removed the shirt and boots from a corpse to help the living, who could blame them? As far as the 'wrecker' was

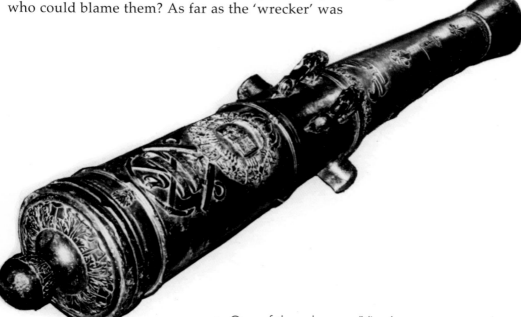

▲ One of three bronze 'Vigo' cannon measuring 9ft 6ins (2.9m) long, and weighing in excess of 2 tons, recovered from the *Association* by the Roland Morris team. The Royal Navy recovered two very similar cannon, one of which remains on Tresco, Isles of Scilly

Silver plate from the *Association*, bearing the personal crest of Admiral Sir Clowdisley Shovell, which is now displayed in Rochester Town Hall, where the Admiral was the local MP ▶

concerned, the dead had no use for clothing, but regrettably, the law had no time for sentiment or personal circumstances.

Wrecks represented gain in many different forms, and no Scillonian could afford to miss an opportunity to make a few shillings, or improve their lot. The variety of goods carried in ships is infinite; food, timber, paint, flour, soap, clothes, iron, wire, leather, even pencils, ink and paper – it could all be put to some use, bartered or sold, and a whole house could be furnished from a wreck, down to carpets, stove, lamps, bedsteads, and occasionally, even a piano! For merely being the first to bring news of a wreck to the Receiver at the Custom House in Well Lane, Hugh Town, earned a reward of five-shillings, and often relatively large sums would be awarded by the owner of a derelict or damaged ship towed in and saved, which would be shared amongst those responsible. One example in 1880 concerned the saving of the schooner *Strathisla* after she had been abandoned by her crew. For getting the vessel into St Mary's, the pilot-gig *Bernice* and the pilot-cutters *Atlantic* and *Presto* were awarded £48, and for saving the crew, the gig *Agnes* received £15. On 24 October 1878, when the ss *Ely Rise* stranded in Crow Sound, some 30-40 pilots were employed to save the provisions and furniture on board, for which they claimed £100. Unfortunately, the event was marred by the theft of £200 worth of property and £80 worth of provisions, and coastguards were put on watch. That night, officer McGillicuddy, patrolling on foot against smuggling on St Martin's, came across a dozen men, laden with stolen wreck goods. They dropped everything and ran, except for James Nance, who lay down and tried to hide but was apprehended. A warrant was issued for his arrest but on hearing of it he jumped into his boat and sailed off to the mainland!

When the ss *Castleford* was lost amongst the Western Rocks in 1887, £12.11s went to St Agnes men for saving eighteen cattlemen, and £500 to Bryher men for the rescue and care of 66 passengers and four stewardesses, plus £5 for every head of cattle saved and £1 for every corpse buried on the foreshore. Such sums were almost untold wealth to Scillonians, and many families literally earned their living from the sea in this way.

Unfortunately, no written account of what it was like to be wrecked on Scilly has survived, unlike Devon and Dorset where quite graphic accounts are to be found. The coast of mainland Cornwall abounds with long sandy beaches on which a vessel could be driven if in distress, with every chance the ship and crew would survive, but not so on Scilly. In even a moderate sea and swell the Western Rocks, by far the most dangerous waters locally, are a quite fearful and dangerous place. In a howling SW gale, with mountainous seas breaking over seemingly endless reefs and shoals, turning the surface into one mass of broken white water with rocks showing their black heads in all directions, a shipwrecked crew must have thought they had sailed into hell. With their ship literally being torn to pieces beneath their feet by the constant heave and surge of gigantic waves, the rigging offered the only remaining sanctuary, at least until the chain plates gave way and the masts fell. The men, already half frozen and near unconscious from exposure, would then be plunged into a gelid sea. Few people at that time could swim, and those that could would be hampered by heavy sodden clothing and leather sea boots, so that the majority drowned. Others would find floating wreckage to which they clung, fighting for air as wave after wave passed over them, doing their best to get away from the rocks that could break limbs and inflict severe lacerations. If they were lucky, a local boat might put out when the weather eased and rescue them, or they might be unlucky, and get swept far out to sea with the tide, to suffer a lonely, pitiless death in the open Atlantic.

Survivors would generally be well received ashore but not always, and if foreign, language difficulties often made communication impossible. Generally shipwrecked seamen probably had no conception as to where they were, they had no money, and no idea of what to do next. A short uncomfortable sea crossing from Scilly to Penzance saw them thrust ashore in another strange country, where times were equally hard and few could afford to help a shipwrecked mariner. How such unfortunates got back to their homes and families in Venice or Lisbon, Ghent or St Petersburg, defies imagination, since they were faced with travelling the width of England, then finding a ship to cross the channel, finally making their way across Europe. They must frequently have been given up for dead, arriving home months, perhaps even years later, their wives having remarried, their children grown up and no longer recognizing their father.

The history of Scilly has been one of constant change, from periods of stability, relative wealth and peace, to extreme hardship, always dictated by the sea. Usually, no sooner did a little prosperity appear than the source or demand would vanish, and the people were reduced once more to hard times. Kelp burning offered the off-islanders a stable living for well over a century, then Spanish Barilla took its place and kelp burning ceased. Smuggling and pilotage lasted for centuries, then the Government 'privatized' the pilotage service to Trinity House as a means of stopping smuggling, which lead to its ultimate cessation. It also led to restrictions as to the number of men allowed on board pilot-cutters and gigs which in turn led to a severe decline in pilotage services. The Quarantine Station in St. Helen's Roads gave the off-islanders income by supplying the *Pandora*, the lazaretto or hospital ship and her consort, HMS *Hornet*, as well as the plague ridden merchant ships, food, water and smuggled spirits, but as with the Sea Fencibles, an early sort of WW2. 'Home Guard', both sources of income collapsed at the end of the Napoleonic Wars. It is remarkable that the islands remained inhabited for certain periods, but the people of Scilly were a hardy breed who knew from bitter experience how to weather a storm in more than one sense. When the price of burned kelp fell, or the pilchards and herrings disappeared, there was always the sea. When Trinity House deprived three-quarters of the pilots their living; when steamships caused the islands the loss the revenue brought by the hundreds of sailing ships which would otherwise have crowded St Mary's Roads; when ship-building ceased because iron was taking the place of wood; and steam replaced sail; when the hopes of a coaling station and then the Royal Navy making St Mary's Roads a heavily defended fleet anchorage came to nothing, there was always the sea. Even today, the current prosperity of the islands can be directly attributed to the sea that isolates it from the mainland, its main attraction to holiday makers being their isolation and unspoilt character. The flower industry may be in decline, unable to compete with flowers grown elsewhere due to high freight charges, but the farmers have adapted to the tourist trade, and life goes on. Seldom does the sea bring a shipwreck these days, although gales lash the islands with the same violence they did 250 years ago, and fog makes their outline just as indistinct.

Little has changed in fact, except that man has learnt better to predict the elements, and master them when at sea.

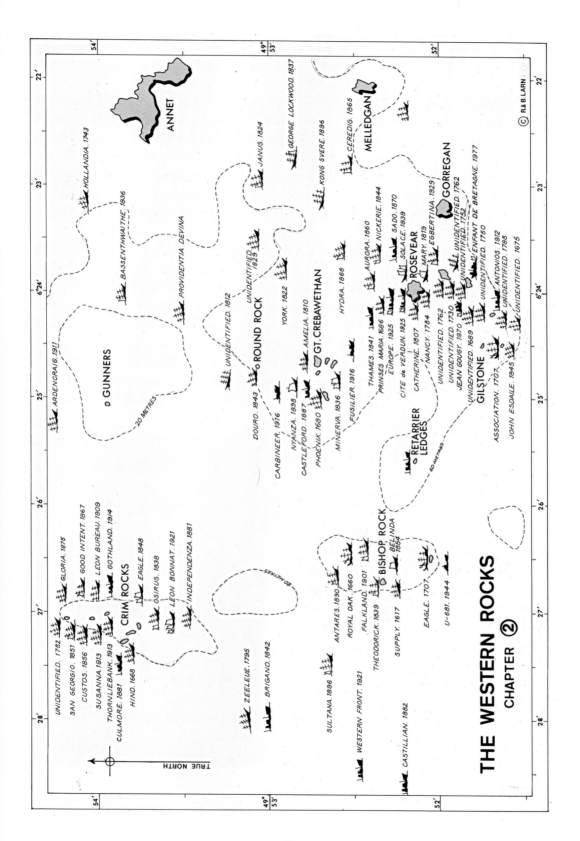

THE WESTERN ROCKS

CHAPTER ②

TRUE NORTH

© R & B. LARN

ANNET

GUNNERS

CRIM ROCKS

ROUND ROCK

GT. CREBAWETHAN

RETARRIER LEDGES

BISHOP ROCK

GILSTONE

ROSEVEAR

GORREGAN

MELLEDGAN

HOLLANDIA. 1743
BASSENTHWAITHE. 1836
PROVIDENTIA DEVINA
ARDENGRAIG. 1911
UNIDENTIFIED. 1782
SAN GEORGIO. 1851
CUSTOS. 1856
SUSANNA. 1913
THORNLIEBANK. 1913
CULMORE. 1881
HIND. 1668
GLORIA. 1875
GOOD INTENT. 1867
LEON BUREAU. 1909
GOTHLAND. 1914
EAGLE. 1848
OSIRUS. 1838
LEON BONNAT. 1921
INDEPENDENZA. 1881
ZEELEUE. 1795
BRIGAND. 1842
SULTANA. 1896
WESTERN FRONT. 1921
CASTILLIAN. 1882
ANTARES. 1890
ROYAL OAK. 1660
FALKLAND. 1901
THEODORICK. 1899
SUPPLY. 1617
BELINDA. 1864
EAGLE. 1707
U-681. 1944
JANUS. 1824
GEORGE LOCKWOOD. 1837
KONG SVERE. 1896
CEREDIG. 1865
UNIDENTIFIED. 1812
UNIDENTIFIED. 1829
YORK. 1822
AMELIA. 1810
HYDRA. 1866
AURORA. 1860
NICKERIE. 1844
SADO. 1870
SOLACE. 1839
MARY. 1819
EGBERTINA. 1929
L'ENFANT DE BRETAGNE. 1977
UNIDENTIFIED. 1762
UNIDENTIFIED. 1752
UNIDENTIFIED. 1750
ANTONIOS. 1912
UNIDENTIFIED. 1788
UNIDENTIFIED. 1675
CARBINEER. 1916
DOURO. 1843
NIYANZA. 1898
CASTLEFORD. 1887
PHOENIX. 1680
MINERVA. 1836
FUSILIER. 1916
THAMES. 1841
PRINSES MARIA. 1686
EUROPE. 1925
CITE de VERDUN. 1925
CATHERINE. 1807
NANCY. 1784
UNIDENTIFIED. 1762
UNIDENTIFIED. 1730
JEAN GOUGY. 1970
UNIDENTIFIED. 1689
ASSOCIATION. 1707
JOHN ESDAILE. 1845

2 - The Western Rocks - a maritime graveyard

It is doubtful if any collection of rocks in the whole of the British Isles has a worse reputation than those to the west of the island of St Agnes. Known collectively as the Western Rocks, this immense area of hidden danger covers almost 10 square miles, and has been the setting for the worst of the many wreck disasters on Scilly. Prior to 1680, when the islands were marked by neither light nor beacon, the toll of shipping between St Agnes and the Bishop and Clerks, as the outer rocks were then known, must have been nothing short of appalling. Even after the wood fired beacon on St Agnes had been erected and lit, the Western Rocks continued to claim ships almost as if they had some magnetic attraction. When it became obvious that a warning light further west was essential, a more powerful and reliable light than St Agnes, there were serious misgivings as to the choice of site. The fact that the Bishop Rock was chosen on which to erect the new lighthouse is testimony in itself to the respect men had for this mass of rock and reef. Of the many available sites on which to build, there could hardly be one more difficult or exposed on which to carry out such a feat of engineering. Only two miles to the east lie the islands of Rosevear and Rosevean, infinitely more sheltered and suitable one might think, but unfortunately neither mark the extreme westerly limit of the Scillies. Between them and the open Atlantic

lie the Gilstone Reef, Retarrier Ledges, the Crebinicks, the Crim and finally Bishop Rock itself, all of which have taken a fearful toll of life and property over the centuries. Exactly how the Bishop acquired its name is uncertain; one explanation suggests the name was derived from an incident which happened 200 years ago, when a fleet of merchantmen coming from Spain were shipwrecked there (the Bishop and Clerks), and only a Miles Bishop and step-brothers John and Henry Clerk were preserved on a fragment of a mast.

The first lighthouse on the Bishop was designed by James Walker and partially assembled by Nicholas and James Douglass between 1848 and 1850, the component parts having been pre-cast in an iron foundry in the midlands, but it

▲ Bishop Rock lighthouse, with maintenance helicopter on the platform

proved n expensive failure. Unlike the present-day lighthouse, with its slender granite structure, the first light was atop an open construction made of cast iron. A central pillar, 3ft 6in in diameter, carried an entrance door and ladder by which access was gained to the keepers' quarters and light platform, 120 ft above, the whole being supported by wrought-iron stays secured to bed rock. The onset of winter in 1849 brought work to an end, it being the intention to complete the light the following spring. But disaster struck during the night of 5 February 1850 when the entire framework was swept away by a severe gale. It was not the method of fastening the column and stays to the rock which had been at fault, but the inadequate tensile strength of the materials used. Ten days elapsed before anyone could approach the Bishop Rock to inspect the damage, which showed that both stays and central column had sheared off between 3 and 5ft above their base. Undaunted, Trinity House remained firm in their confidence in the Douglass's, father and son, and by early 1852 a new structure began to rise above the Bishop rock. This time the tower was constructed of granite, great blocks hewn from the quarries of Carnsew and Lamorna in Cornwall, ferried first to St Mary's to be dressed on St Mary's quay, and then to the Bishop in the sailing tender *Billow*, and later in barges towed by the tug *Bishop*. Rosevear, an uninhabited island, was chosen as a base for the workmen, masons, engineers and blacksmith's, and a number of stone buildings were erected. This was, in fact, the second time Rosevear had been utilised as a base camp, since it was from here that the Herbert salvage expedition of 1709-10 worked the wreck of the *Association* and other vessels in Sir Clowdisley Shovell's fleet of 1707.

Work continued on the lighthouse throughout 1852, often under appalling conditions, and it was not until the solid base had reached a height of 45ft (14m) above sea level that the workmen could relax their vigilance. Whilst the first granite blocks were being keyed into the base rock, the labourers were often completely engulfed by the sea when huge waves broke over them. The stonemasons worked in permanently wet clothes, and on more than one occasion were washed clean off the rock into the boiling surf, saved by lifelines worn for this very reason. By the end of 1852, 44 blocks had been laid, and the vital lower stones securely dove-tailed into the natural rock. It was during this early stage of building that the cutter *Belinda* of Cardiff, on passage from Cork to Falmouth with limestone, hit the Bishop, drifted away and was abandoned to sink on 27 June 1854. A recent local publication claims that the half-naked survivors scrambled into the cofferdam set up on the Bishop Rock, and that 'the workmen witnessed many corpses floating by lifeless on the tide. All these bodies needed to be picked up and stored on Rosevear until the boat came to take them away.' The truth is that there was never a cofferdam used in the construction of the Bishop light, and as for 'many corpses floating by,' there were only three crew on board the *Belinda*, all of whom were saved by a Swedish brig named *Lieutenant Peterson* who landed them safely at Falmouth.

Upon completion, the tower reached a height of 131ft (31m) above high-water mark and, when the light was first displayed on 1 September 1858, it was visible for 14 miles. Four keepers were employed to maintain the light, three on duty at any one time, the fourth ashore in rotation at the Trinity House cottages on the Garrison, overlooking Porthcressa Bay. and their occupation was not one to be envied. The Bishop lighthouse is one of the most exposed in the country, and the damage inflicted on the structure during its first baptism by storm on 30 January 1860 showed the destructive force of the sea to its full. The massive bronze ladder and door which gave access to the interior were swept away, windows 5in (13cm) thick were smashed, glass prisms in the light broken and the tower flooded. The huge fog bell, weighing a little over a quarter of a ton, was washed off its mounting on the gallery and fell onto the rocks below. In falling it may well have smashed, but since there is no record of it ever being found it is assumed it lies on the seabed in fragments. In September 1870, the lighthouse was again battered by a severe gale - if anything, worse than the gale ten years earlier, which sent seas completely over the lantern from eight o'clock in the morning until two in the afternoon. On 20 April 1874 it was subjected to an even more trying test. When that gale was over, the keepers stated that waves had reached the level of the kitchen window 70ft (21m) above the sea and had broken clean over the lantern, bathing the interior of the light in a ghostly green glow. Had the storm continued with equal violence for another 24 hours the entire structure might well have been endangered, possibly even destroyed. As it was, the exterior was considerably damaged and had to be repaired immediately. Subsequently between 1882 and 1887, the lighthouse was enveloped in a new stone casing dovetailed both vertically and horizontally, and the overall height increased by 36ft (11m). This work was so efficiently carried out that the building has required no further strengthening to this day.

There are many fascinating stories connected with the Bishop Rock but none more intriguing than the disappearance of the Principal Keeper. In early November 1889 John Ball said farewell to his wife Teresa and his seven children, who lived in the Trinity Cottages on St Mary's, and departed for the Bishop for his spell of three months duty. On 19 December he completed his daily inspection at 3.30pm, went down the spiral staircase to the base, presumably to get some exercise, smoke his pipe or enjoy some private time. The Bishop light was lit and set in motion at 4.30pm by the other keepers, who wondered why the Principal Keeper had not attended as usual. Two keepers searched the tower from top to bottom, inside and out, but John Ball had disappeared, never to be seen again.

What happened to him will never be known. Did he slip and fall into the sea or suffer a heart attack, commit suicide, or was he pushed? Teresa Ball sent her children to search the Garrison shore every day looking for their father, seeking a definitive end to the mystery and a proper burial, but his body was never found.

◀ Principal Lighthouse Keeper John Ball, of the Bishop light, who disappeared whilst on duty 19 December 1889, and was never found

Apart from its long history of wreck with accompanying loss of life, the Bishop appears to have been the scene of many other deaths, the rock once having been used for the execution of felons. This was in 1284, the twelfth year of the reign of Edward I:

'John de Allet and Isabella his wife, hold the Isle of Scilly and hold there all kinds of pleas of the Crown throughout their jurisdiction and make indictments of felonies. When anyone is attained of a felony he ought to be taken to a certain rock in the sea, and with two barley loaves and one pitcher of water upon the same rock they leave the same felon, until by the flowing of the sea he is swallowed up'.

The earliest recorded wreck on the Bishop itself is probably the brig *Theodorick*, from Mogador to London, which struck in rough misty weather on 4 September 1839, whilst carrying general cargo. In the surrounding waters, the earliest and best authenticated wreck is that of the English East Indiaman *Royal Oak*, lost on 18 January 1665. The original document giving details of this wreck was unearthed in 1966 in the Bodleian Library, Oxford, and states:

' The manner how ye ship Royall Oake, Mr Robb Locke commander, from ye East Indies was cast away upon ye westerne rocks of Scilly called ye Bishopp and Clarks'. The ship

The Bishop Lighthouse Keeper Washed Away.

On Monday night, about eight o'clock, the Bishop lighthouse flashed from its six miles distance from St. Mary's, distress-signals, but that no assistance was wanted until morning. On Tuesday a boat took down relief. The utmost secrecy as to the cause of distress was preserved until the forenoon, when it became known that Mr. Ball, the head-lightkeeper, had disappeared. It is supposed that he has been washed off the rock at the base of the lighthouse. Mr. Ball leaves a wife and family.

▲ Newspaper cutting from the Royal Cornwall Gazette, reporting the loss of Principal Keeper John Ball, 22 December 1898

had sailed from Bantam for England via Cape Bona Sprance and St Helena, and when forty leagues east of St Mary's was beset by gales. On the morning of 18 January, they 'were inviorned with rockes and beaches which terrible sight made us all bestire ourselves, some in ye toppes to see if there were any passage through but could fine none'. The report continues, telling us that the best bower anchor was dropped and the mainmast cut away, but this did not prevent the ship from being driven between two outcrops and foundering within fifteen minutes. Her crew reached some rocks but had to abandon them for higher ground when the tide rose. They remained there from early morning on the 18th until the 20th, not being rescued for fifty-two hours, where wee induced soe much cold yt all our leggs and hands were so swelled yt wee could but few of us stand.'

A packet paddle-steamer was another early victim of the Bishop itself, the 600-ton *Brigand*, carrying 200 tons of bunker coal and patent fuel from Liverpool to London and St Petersburg. Valued at £3,200 she was a very fast vessel for her size, being fitted with a 200hp engine, and had been specially built for the Bristol-Liverpool trade. On Monday, 10 October 1842, the *Brigand* left Liverpool, her lookouts sighting St Agnes light through rain and drizzle at 5am on 12 October. Shortly after, breakers were sighted ahead and she struck the Bishop Rock a mighty blow. Two large plates in her bow were stove in and, seconds later, she struck a second time beam on, so that the port paddle-wheel and box were driven bodily into the engine-room. A 5ft(1.5m) hole appeared in her side and the sea poured in, quickly swamping the boiler fires. Attempts were made to stem the inrush, but with such tremendous damage it was impossible, and on fast failing steam pressure the vessel drifted clear

GOING DOWN OF THE BRIGAND STEAMER, OFF THE SCILLY ISLANDS.

LOSS OF THE IRON STEAMER BRIGAND.

The above sketch represents the loss of the iron steamer Brigand, on Wednesday, the 12th inst., off the Scilly Islands. We cannot better convey an idea of this lamentable catastrophe than by giving the subjoined narrative, written by an eye witness, of the awful event:—"We left Liverpool at two, P.M., on Monday last, and proceeded on our voyage, without any thing particular happening until a quarter before five, a.m., on Wednesday, going from 11 to 12 knots an hour, with a strong current, light wind from the north-east, the morning being hazy, when she suddenly ran foul of the breakers, and struck twice; the first time right abreast of the foremast in the bluff of the bow, and the next blow was of such great force that it carried off her paddle-wheel, and drove it right into the engine-room. We saw the St. Agnes light, but in consequence of the haziness of the weather we considered it was at least 15 miles off. Soon afterwards we saw the breakers, but too late to avoid them. We put the helm hard aport, however, to endeavour to do so, and immediately received the shocks on our broadside. Where she struck was in lat. 49. 56. N., long. 6. 16, W., on the Crim Rock, near the Bishop's Rock, about three miles and a half from the spot where the Thames was lost, and 67 hands, in January, 1841. Both compartments of the vessel were stove in, and she began to fill rapidly. The captain and crew immediately exerted themselves to the utmost to save the vessel. The carpenter placed a board against the side, and placed stays against the cylinder, and stopped up the crevices with "waste" and grease; but these efforts were ineffectual, as were likewise the endeavours to lighten her by throwing the fuel overboard, which we continued to do till the hold filled with water. The engines had become completely useless, and the fires were out, but the crew continued to exert themselves for nearly two hours, when the captain ordered all hands on the quarter-deck, and ordered out the jolly-boats. At this time she had drifted about seven miles from the breaker, and after waiting a quarter of an hour we got into them, the captain and mate still remaining on the quarter-deck; the boats stood by the vessel another quarter of an hour, and then, as she was sinking fast, the captain and mate got into one of them and we shoved off. In about half an hour after we saw her go down by the head, in about 45 fathoms of water. We rowed for the Rock, and got on it, to see how the land lay; the other boat came after us, and we joined in a small bay leading to St. Agnes light, where two boats from the shore came out to us, having seen our lights, and took us in tow for the harbour, St. Mary's, which we reached about three o'clock. The same night we went in the Antelope pilot-boat to Penzance, and from thence to St. Ives, where we got a passage to Bristol in the Herald."

The Brigand has only been built about two years since, by Messrs. Grantham, Page, and Co., of Liverpool, for Mr. Redmond, of Wexford, at a cost of £32,000, and intended to trade from Liverpool to Bristol, calling at Wexford, which she continued to do till a short time since, when she was superseded by the Troubadour, another iron steamer, of 250 horse-power, and she was now on her voyage from Liverpool to London, having merely 200 tons of fuel to carry her to St. Petersburg. She was an elegantly-built vessel, and fitted up in the most elegant style. She was 600 tons burden, and 200 horse power, and built with bulk-heads, having four compartments, and had she not been struck a complete broadside, so as to stave in both compartments, she would have been saved. We understand she was not insured.

▲ The paddle-steamer *Brigand* sinking off the Bishop Rock, 1842 with one paddle-wheel still rotating. Fortunately, her construction was such that she had four watertight compartments and continued to float. Firemen desperately shoveled coal overboard in an attempt to lighten her, whilst others manned the pumps, but inevitably the steam pressure failed completely, and with it all hope of ever reaching land. By 7am her bows were under water and the whole 27 crew took to the two boats carried, both now dangerously overloaded. The *Brigand* finally sank in 45 fathoms, seven miles from where she had first struck. Her master, Captain C.P.Hunt, and his crew landed at St Mary's safely and after taking passage to Penzance in the pilot-boat *Antelope*, went overland to Hayle where they shipped aboard the Cornish packet steamer *Brilliant* for Bristol.

More fortunate was the Liverpool steamer *Castillian*, bound from Oporto to her home port with fruit and wine, which broke down off the Bishop when a piston-rod snapped on 13 September 1882. She would have drifted onto the rock but for the timely assistance of another vessel which towed her clear. Another lucky escape was that of the brigantine *Antares* of Nantes, found in distress just north of the lighthouse on 3 May 1890. Carrying pitwood from France to Llanelly, she was presumed to have struck the Crim Rocks and floated clear in the fog. It was a different story for the Swedish barque *Sultana* which went to the bottom on Sunday, 17 February 1895. She had become unmanageable after springing a leak and was abandoned close to the

▲ The Isles of Scilly packet *Peninnis* standing by the burning American *Western Front*, after she caught fire and drifted to within ten miles of the Bishop Rock before sinking, 11 July 1921.

The body of a drowned seaman from the *Western Front* is brought ashore on the quay at St Mary's ▶

Bishop light, her 18 crew being landed at Scilly from a passing French schooner. There was one ship that actually struck the lighthouse itself; that was on 22 June 1901 at 7.30pm when the four-masted Liverpool barque *Falkland*, Captain Gracie, 135 days out from Tacoma with grain, on passage from Puget Sound to Falmouth for orders, was swept on to the rocks during a strong SW gale after missing stays. She struck beam on, her main yard hitting the light tower; after drifting half a mile to the north she fell on to her beam ends and sank. 31 of the crew, along with the captain's wife and child, escaped in the port boat, the captain and five others remaining on board attempting to launch the starboard boat which was stuck on its skids by years of paint. Eventually the boat fell out of its stowage and the captain led the others over the now horizontal jigger-mast to board it. At that moment compressed air blew out the charthouse roof and the *Falkland*, deprived of its remaining buoyancy, sank like a stone. Captain Gracie and the mate were sucked down and drowned, the mate's body coming ashore in Hell Bay on Bryher, whilst one of the seamen, known only as 'old George', slipped from his lifebelt and drowned, as did the steward and two able seamen. Built in 1889 by W.H Potter & Sons for the Palace Shipping Co Ltd, the *Falkland*, 2,867 tons gross, was sister-ship to the *Holinwood*, lost by fire in the late 1890s.

On 11 July 1921, the Bishop lighthouse-keepers were afforded a grandstand view of the destruction by fire of the steamer *Western Front*, Jacksonville to London, carrying 7,000 tons of naval stores which included naphtha, turpentine and resin, a highly inflammable combination of materials. Registered at Seattle, the 5,743-tons

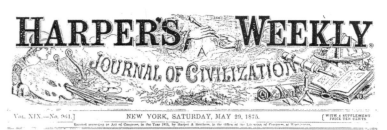

HARPER'S WEEKLY.
A JOURNAL OF CIVILIZATION

VOL. XIX.—No. 961.]   NEW YORK, SATURDAY, MAY 29, 1875.   [WITH A SUPPLEMENT PRICE TEN CENTS.

Entered according to Act of Congress, in the Year 1875, by Harper & Brothers, in the Office of the Librarian of Congress, at Washington.

THE WRECK OF THE "SCHILLER"—BISHOP'S ROCK LIGHT.—Drawn by J. O. Davidson.—[See Page 177.]

◄ The American Harper's Weekly Journal depiction of the sinking of the German liner ss. *Schiller* in 1875

gross steamer had been built in 1917 for the US Shipping Board by the Skinner Eddy Corporation. Fire was discovered on board when some 20 miles W of the Bishop, but by the time the St Mary's lifeboat *Elsie* had reached the scene and rescued forty of the crew from their own boats, the *Western Front* had drifted to within seven miles of the Western Rocks. The steamer *British Earl* saved the rest of the crew, the only casualty being one able seamen. During the First and Second World Wars there were many tragic losses in the vicinity of the Bishop, some of which are mentioned in Chapter 8, but the only inshore incident concerned the German submarine *U-681* which is thought to have struck either the Bishop or the Crebinicks on 11 March 1945. Badly damaged, the enemy submarine attempted to reach a neutral port in southern Ireland, but was sighted and attacked by an American Liberator aircraft, whereupon her crew of 50 abandoned ship after opening her sea cocks, but only 42 survived. The wreck of the *U-681* was found in 2002 by divers, some distance off Bryher, 4 miles N of Mincarlo in deep water, its identity confirmed from a pair of leather overalls and a German navy inflatable raft found outside the wreck.

East of the Bishop Rock lie the Crebinicks and Retarrier Ledges, the latter much in the headlines of British and American newspapers in 1875 when, on 7 May, they were struck by the 3,421 tons gross passenger-steamer *Schiller* of Hamburg, which sank with the loss of 311 lives. The Western Rocks were blanketed in dense fog that night, the worst in living memory, as the German Transatlantic Steam Navigation liner crept ever closer to the Isles of Scilly. By 8 o'clock that evening Captain Thomas had reduced speed to four knots and posted double lookouts. An hour later, with the Bishop lighthouse still neither seen nor heard, volunteers from amongst the male passengers were asked to act as additional lookouts, with the promise of a bottle of champagne to the first man to see the light or hear the Bishop Rock fog bell. The prize was never collected. Shortly before ten o'clock the liner struck the Retarriers with her starboard bow, having passed inside of the lighthouse. Her engine pulled her clear of the rocks, but three huge waves in succession struck her starboard side slewing her round, and the stricken vessel was flung beam on to the reef where her port side plating collapsed. Distress rockets and signal-guns were fired – some of the witnesses later gave the number as at least ten, but these were mistaken by the lighthouse-keepers and locals on St Agnes alike as merely a vessel signaling her arrival off Scilly,

▲ The German liner ss *Schiller*, alongside a berth in Hamburg

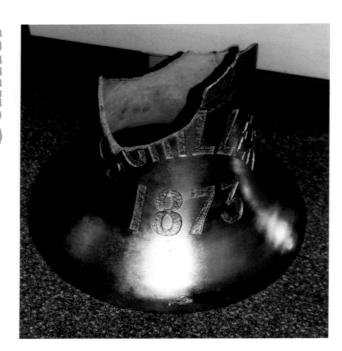

◀ The bell from the wreck of the *ss.Schiller*, found and raised by David McBride, St Mary's

as was the custom, and not a vessel in distress.

Pandemonium broke out on deck amongst the fear-crazed passengers and the captain was obliged to fire a revolver over their heads to retain some order, but there was little hope for anyone. The *Schiller* carried only eight boats, two of which were reduced to match-wood when one of her two funnels collapsed across them. Two others jammed in their chocks due to the ship's heavy list, one capsized as soon as it touched the sea and another smashed against the hull in lowering and hung useless from its davits. Only two boats finally got clear and drifted off into the gloom of the night. For the 320 men, women and children left aboard, it was to be one of mounting horror. The sea boomed all around them, fog closed in from all sides, and they had not the slightest idea where they were or what hope there was of rescue. By midnight the *Schiller* had assumed an even heavier list, and Captain Thomas ordered the women and children to gather on the roof of the deck-house, over the midships saloon. Fifty of them huddled there, weeping mothers and bewildered youngsters, momentarily clear of the seas which swept the length of the flush-decked vessel. Then another succession of giant seas struck the wreck, the first tearing off the roof of the deckhouse, the second hurling both it and its occupants into the sea. By the time the third wave had passed, not one of those who had been clinging to the deckhouse was to be seen. At dawn, a Sennen fishing-boat was first on the scene and rescued seven men, two of whom later died from exposure. Soon a whole fleet of small boats, accompanied by the Scillies packet steamer *Lady of the Isles*, appeared. During the morning, two men were rescued from off rocks, and the two lifeboats from the wreck landed at Tresco with 26 men and one woman aboard.

Of the *Schiller's* original complement of 59 saloon, 75 second-class and 120 steerage-class passengers, plus 101 crew, a total of 355, only 42 men and one woman survived. The *Schiller* had left New York for Hamburg via Plymouth on 27 April, carrying 250 bags of Australian and New Zealand mail, a valuable general cargo, and £60,000 in American $20 gold pieces, 300,000 coins in all. Sometime after she was wrecked, the sea ripped the ship open and the specie became scattered amongst the wreckage. Mail-bags floated up and out on the tide, 30 being found ashore on Samson alone and others as far away as Penzance. Three days after the wreck, on Monday 10 May, the *Queen of the Bay* left the mainland for St Mary's, and between the Longships and Wolf Rock reported she sailed through a sea of wreckage consisting of light woodwork, empty barrels, cigar boxes, cases, tables, portions of agricultural implements, mail-bags, and one male corpse, still wearing a lifebelt with $135 in his pockets. Weather conditions were so bad that no one could approach the wreck to carry out salvage or a survey until 11 May, when the ship was found in seven fathoms (42ft), with only two spars showing above the surface. The first divers went down on the 15th and found the vessel smashed to pieces, with no sign of the bullion. They surfaced with just two sewing machines after two hours underwater! The coin had been shipped in six small kegs, the size of small herring barrels, each containing 50,000 gold pieces. The casks, marked 'F.S.B & Co,' had been stowed amidships between the main and spar decks, but it was soon apparent that it was going to be no easy task to find them, and that a full-scale salvage operation would be necessary. Meanwhile, bodies were being landed at St Mary's which needed immediate attention. 37 internments took place on the Monday following the wreck, 20 the following day, and 90 on the Thursday.

Prior to internment, each and every body had to be searched for identification and valuables, requiring a Salvors Warrant to be made out by a St Mary's Customs Officer

▲ Collection of silver cutlery and artefact material recovered by David McBride, St Mary's, from the wreck of the ss. *Schiller*, lost 1875

◄ Silver dish and cutlery, the personal property of a Louise Becker, a passenger on board the *ss.Schiller*, who died in the wreck. Recovered by David McBride, St Mary's

who acted as the Receiver of Wreck, naming the individual who had found the body, where, when and any personal effects. These warrants survive and make poignant reading:

'Warrant No.1 - 8.5.1875. Quarter Master, Peter ? - dead body, gold ring marked M.M.C.T; few coins; silver watch 1874; paper money, 75 cents; piece of paper, Master H. Martin, Hastings-upon-Hudson. Received the above, Jn. Banfield, Vice Consul. Body picked up near the wreck site and delivered at the store on the Quay. Salvor - signed John George, St Agnes'

'Warrant No.3 - 8.5.1875. Dead body of male Doctor of the ship - Anton G. Sanders. Had 3 coats on, outside contained pocket book which held the passport of George G. Lenkland, Citizen of New York. 17 dollars, 65 cents; found on inside clothing, 90 large gold coins, 23 small gold coins, 113 in total; large silver coins 2, 2 rings, 2 brooches, 1 crucifix, 3 lockets, 10 ear drops, 5 pins, 18 studs, 1 pencil case, 1 silver whistle, 1 pair bracelets, sundry small coins, 2 watches and 3 chains. Received the above T.J. Beeston. Body picked up near the site of the wreck and delivered to the Quay, William Pender and crew of the *Gem*, St Agnes.'

▲ Pair of bone glove stretcher tongs recovered by David McBride from the wreck of the *ss. Schiller*

nb: A young surgeon from Rotterdam who volunteered, whilst his own ship was being repaired, to take the place of Dr. Boll, who was supposedly ill in Philadelphia. Dr. Boll did in fact join the *Schiller* at the last moment, both doctors now looking after the passengers. It appears Dr. Sanders picked up the overcoat of a passenger, George C. Leonhardt, and put it on, which caused the bodies to be misidentified at first. Dr. Sanders initials were W.A. not Anton G. as given in the above warrant. He was buried on St Mary's.

'Warrant No.9 - 8.5.1875. Dead body of Carl Schmidt, passenger. 2 studs, Masonic emblem, 1 diamond and stud, 1 diamond, purse containing 23 paper dollars, 10 gold Marks, 3 large pieces of silver, 1 small piece of silver, pocket book, passport, bills of exchange for 20,000 Francs, 60,000 Rix Marks, gold watch and chain, match box with silver top initials C.S. Received the above Jn. Banfield, German Vice Consul. Body found near the site of the wreck, picked up and delivered to the Quay by Horatio Jenkin, Tresco.'

nb: Carl Schmidt was accompanied by his wife Catherine, who also drowned. He was a prosperous partner in the firm of Fox & Co, Jewellers, 2 Maiden Lane, New York, which explains why he carried so many items of jewellery. His body was embalmed and returned to the USA.

'Warrant No.11 - 8.5.1875. Dead body, male, of Henry Friend, passenger. Gold watch and chain, 25 large gold coins, 13 small gold coins, 1 large silver coin, 80 dollars paper money, 2 pocket books containing letters addressed to Henry Friend Esq.& others, Four letters of orders for 15,000 Francs, 5,000 Rix Marks, pair of eye glasses and frame. Received Jn. Banfield, German Vice Consul. Body found near the wreck site by George George Dove, St Agnes.'

nb: Henry Friend was accompanied by his wife Frances, who also drowned, leaving behind in New York eleven children Both bodies embalmed and returned to the USA.

'Warrant No.13 - 9.5.1875. Body of female, Susan Dimock, MD. Gold watch and chain, 20 paper dollars, 18 cents, £5 Bank of England note, 21 whole and 2 halve foreign gold coins, 2 cuffstuds, seven papers on French Bank. Received the above 14/5, T.J. Beeston. Body found near site of the wreck by Stephen Jenkin, of the *Queen*,

A leather 'bulse' found by David McBride in the wreck of the ss. *Schiller* ▶

St. Martins.'

nb: Susan Dimock, of Boylston Street, Boston, was a general practice doctor. Her body was embalmed and returned to the USA.

The burial of so many bodies presented something of a problem, since there is no great depth of soil at Old Town church to create the necessary mass grave. The bodies were laid to rest in plain deal boxes painted black which were sent over from Penzance. Three mass grave sites were dug using gunpowder in Old Town church-yard, rock having to be blasted in order to create sufficient depth. Fortunately, the identity of each named coffin, marked on pieces of wood above ground, later enabled several to be exhumed, embalmed and forwarded to New York, presumably by ship to Penzance and from there to Plymouth. With no hearse on the island, pony carts with two coffins each were used and the whole of the island's population went into mourning. To quote an account from the *Sherborne Mercury* newspaper: *'The most melancholy spectacle that ever was, or we trust will never be seen again, passed through Helston to St Keverne on Tuesday, 24 May, being several wagons laden with coffins to the amount of fifty.'*

Why coffins were reported as being en route to St Keverne, Cornwall, is something of a mystery. It was not until 11 August that the first gold coin was found, after which

▲ One of two mass graves dug in Old Town church cemetery. This one is the Lower Terrace grave

▲ The Upper Terrace mass grave in Old Town church, dug for the victims of the wreck of the ss. *Schiller*, 1875

large numbers were seen scattered loose around the engine-room. On Friday, 20 August, 561 gold pieces were salvaged, 848 on Saturday and 108 on Monday, so that by the end of August £6,068 had been salvaged. Work continued until 6 May, 1876, by which time the divers had recovered a total of £57,712 out of a possible £60,000. They literally took the wreck to pieces, searching not only for the gold pieces but for valuables lost by the passengers. One American passenger, a Mr Kornblum, a paper manufacturer from New York, had on board with him 85 gold watches, a large quantity of diamond jewellery and £500 in coin. Items of the Schiller's general cargo, such as bags of feathers, casks of resin, flour etc, were picked up all round Cornwall for weeks afterwards. Built by Napiers of Glasgow for Alexander Stephens (Ship-builders), the *Schiller* had been launched in August 1873, and was on her last voyage for her current owners before being incorporated in the Eagle Line. In Old Town churchyard, St Mary's, the largest monument to a *Schiller* victim takes the form of an obelisk high up overlooking the church and bay. It's dedication reads:

> '*In memory of Louise Holzmaister, born at New York, 15 May 1851, who lost her life in the wreck of the ss Schiller on the Scilly Isles, 7 May 1875. Her body rests in the deep, this monument has been erected to her memory as a mark of affection by a sorrowing husband*'.

Close at hand are the graves (No's 1005-6) of Clara & Edward Just, with their children Else and Edward. They had lived at 613 Broadway, New York where Edward Snr. was a shirt manufacturer, travelling 1st Class with his family. The body of Else was never found. The other grave is to Herman Zinkeisen of Milwaukee, born 22.8.1827, his wife Celina Bertha Nataliemor, born 21.7.1828, and their daughter Anna Cecelia Zinkeisen, born 14.9.1862. This family had come from Milwaukee and had left four young sons in the United States. They too were 1st Class passengers.

Suggestions that Scillonian's had robbed the corpses from the *Schiller* were made by a Mr. T. Cornish in a public address delivered at the Abbey Gardens, Tresco, published in the *Cornishman* newspaper of 22 August 1875:

'The islanders pride themselves that for many years there has been no wrecking on the coast; but, when the Schiller *was wrecked, the robbing of the dead was horrible. Men returning from California, wearing belts with pockets containing rows of $20 gold pieces or silver dollars, in every case were robbed, and the bodies were washed or brought ashore with empty belts.'*

This was of course pure fiction, since none of the Warrants reported male corpses with empty money belts, and in any case, not one passenger came from California. The bodies of 66 adult male, five boys, 34 adult females and two girls, were landed by boatmen and buried at Old Town church, with the exception of four males buried on St Agnes and one on St Martin's. J.E. Hooper, shipping agent and Vice-Consul for the German Empire who lived at Tremelethan, Hooper's Hill, now Church Road, responded:

'From my own personal observation - being continually at the dead house when the bodies were brought in - I have no hesitation in stating that there were no belts or signs of any having been on the person of the bodies. I have shown the Register to many strangers, who in every case have praised the boatmen for their honesty in bringing in so much property on the bodies. I trust that this may tend to remove any prejudice against the islanders which may have arisen in any of your readers minds.'

Ironically, the Scillonian boatmen then brought a claim against the salvors of the 'treasure' before the Admiralty Court on 24 April 1877. The owners, masters and crew of the individual pilot boats that had saved ten passengers and some of the crew of the *Schiller* instituted a case of salvage against the owners of the specie, claiming remuneration. The case was complex. The Court of Admiralty were in the habit of awarding a larger sum for salvage where life had been saved, but the Merchant Shipping Act merely confirmed that if the ship or any part was saved, the ship paid salvage. If cargo was saved the cargo paid, but passengers had nothing to do with cargo, and each passenger ought to pay for being saved, or the salvors be paid out of the Mercantile Marine Fund. The case dragged on but in the end the Judge held that the salvors of the cargo, ie. the gold specie, which amounted to over £57,700 were liable to pay salvage, and the boatmen were awarded £500 between them.

Tragic though the wreck of the *Schiller* was, it was by no means the worst amongst the Western Rocks, for the second worst Royal Navy disaster England had known occurred less than half a mile away from the Retarrier Ledges, on the Gilstone Reef. Here, on 22 October 1707, Rear Admiral Sir Clowdisley Shovell and some 1,450 officers and men met their deaths when HM men o'war *Association*, *Eagle*, *Romney* and *Firebrand* all struck within the same area and sank. Technically, only the *Association* was lost on the Gilstone, the *Eagle* being lost on Tearing Ledge, the Firebrand close to Menglow rock near St Agnes, whilst the wreck of the *Romney* has never been found. For ease of narration we can consider them as all lost in the same area. Returning to Portsmouth after a successful summer campaign in the Mediterranean, these ships were part of a fleet of 21, nine of which were of 70 guns or more. They left Gibraltar on 27 September 1707 but a week later, after encountering gales from all points of the compass, they were hopelessly lost. So much so that the fleet hove to in order to take soundings with their deep-leads, which caused them to believe they were due west of Ushant, and that the English Channel lay open before them. Legend has it that a meeting of sailing masters took place on board the flagship, and that only Sir William Jumper of the *Lennox* disagreed with the others regarding their position, insisting they would sight Scilly within three hours – but no such meeting took place. The fleet sailed on, only now the *Royal Anne*, *Panther* and *Firebrand* were the lead ships of the three columns, *Le Valeur*, *Lennox* and *Phoenix* having been dispatched to Falmouth to escort a merchant navy convoy up Channel to the Thames. The great ships lumbered on unaware of the danger that lay ahead. At 8 o'clock on the evening of 22 October, the flagship plunged straight on to the Gilstone Ledges, breaking up and sinking almost immediately, her entire crew of some 650 supposedly lost on the spot, but more of that later. She

Portrait of Sir Clowdisley Shovell, Rear Admiral on board the *Asociation*, when it wrecked in 1707 ▶

was followed closely by the others, and in quick succession the *Eagle*, *Romney* and *Firebrand* all struck and went down. The *St George*, Captain Dursley, 90 guns, was exceptionally fortunate in that she struck the Gilstone but floated clear, with little damage other than a smashed stern gallery.

Unknown to the fleet, the three lead ships dispatched earlier in the day had also blundered into the Western Rocks, leaving the *Phoenix* fireship badly damaged and full of water in New Grimsby harbour, Tresco, where she was to remain for almost four months undergoing repair. Of the 1,673 men aboard the wrecked ships, only 26 survivors were reported, 25 from the *Firebrand*, and just one man from the *Romney*, George Lawrence, a quarter-master, who was found next morning atop what today is known as Carn Lawrence, at the back of Gorregan. There may in fact have been other survivors, since the majority of men in service were 'pressed' and might have seized this heaven-sent opportunity to desert, although the advantages of desertion on 18th century Scilly are doubtful and hanging would have been their punishment if caught. The body of Sir Clowdisley was found washed ashore at Porth Hellick, a

sandy bay on the south side of St Mary's, about seven miles from the scene of the wrecks. Legend has it that he was alive when found, then murdered for the valuable rings he wore, after which his naked body was buried in the fore-shore. Later, his corpse was exhumed, identified, and conveyed on board the *Salisbury* to Plymouth Citadel, then on to his house in Soho Square. He was eventually interred in Westminster Abbey, after Queen Anne had ordered a state funeral. Legend has it that many years after the incident, a St Mary's woman made

◀ Terracotta bust of Rear Admiral Sir Clowdisley Shovell, 1695-1707

▲ Carved stern crest from the wreck *Association*, presented to Penzance Borough Council, c1834, in return for a shipload of potatoes to help relieve the starvation on the off islands of Scilly

a death-bed confession to the crime and produced one of the rings, set with a fine emerald and diamonds. Another more credible version states that a soldier found the body and removed the rings. When Lady Shovell enquired as to their whereabouts, they were handed over, in return for which both he and his wife received a pension for life.

The whole story of Sir Clowdisley's supposed murder is highly questionable. A surviving letter states that after Shovell's body was exhumed it was found:

'His ring was lost from his finger, which last however left the impression on his finger as also a second. His head was not at all swelled with the water, neither had he any bruises nor scars upon him, save for a small scratch over one eye as if by a pin.'

It is now known for certain that the bodies of Sir Clowdisley, his greyhound dog named 'Mumper', Captain Loades, Shovell's two stepsons, Sir John and James Narborough, as well as the son of the Bishop of Winchester, all washed ashore in Porth Hellick together. This suggests they escaped from the *Association* in one of the ship's boats, which was a possibility, but begs the question as to why they failed to land

St. Cloudesly Shovel

on St Agnes rather than St Mary's, which was much closer and whose lighthouse would have guided them ashore? All except the Bishop's son and Sir Clowdisley were buried within the chancel of Old Town church. Unfortunately the exact location of the three graves has become lost over time, since much of the original church has since been demolished, leaving their graves somewhere outside the church on the eastern side.

There would have been great activity around the Gilstone after the wrecks which continued for several months, producing one of the richest harvest the islanders have ever enjoyed. It is known that the wreck of the *Association* went to pieces in a very short time, her entire stern section drifting away to sink in deep water. A book about the *Association* published in 1985, 'Admiral Shovell's Treasure & Shipwreck on the Isles of Scilly,' has revealed why the flagship was carrying such a vast amount of gold and silver coin. Much of this would have been the residue of funds from the Government to support the Toulon siege, plus the regimental funds of the Coldstream Guards, and possibly gold belonging to Portuguese bankers. A small scale salvage attempt was made on behalf of the Admiralty by Deputy-Paymaster Herbert in 1709/10, who ordered a base camp set up for the purpose on Rosevear, and Herbert's notebooks tell us that using a wooden diving bell they recovered a buckle and silver coins, but did not stay on the islands very long.

An underwater search for the wrecks of the four men o'war was initiated by the author in 1963, then serving in the Royal Navy as a Chief Petty Officer Mechanician-Diver. Teams of navy divers, supported by minesweepers from the Penzance Royal Naval Auxiliary Service, searched the Western Rocks for two week periods for four years, the *Association* itself finally located in 1967. The site yielded ten bronze cannon of varying sizes from 28-pounders down to miniature, almost toy signal-guns weighing only 50lbs. Other artefacts included silver spurs, gold 'posy' rings, uniform buttons, eating utensils, pewter plates, human bones, candlesticks, lead inkwells, dividers, and, of course thousands of coins, both gold and silver. Exactly how many coins will never be known. In 1969, one of the many civilian diving teams working on the wrecks, located a cannon site in deep water off Tearing Ledge, recovering a large ship's bell bearing a broad arrow mark and the date 1701, as well as a navigational slate and artefacts. According to the Gostello map in the British Library, which purports to show the location of all four ships lost in the 1707 disaster, this is where the *Romney* sank, with the *Eagle* somewhere on the Crim. However, there is good reason, based on a survey of the number of cannon and their size carried out by Peter McBride, to confidently say that the two sites were incorrectly identified at the time, when only their topmasts showed above the surface, a genuine mistake compounded by Gostello's quaint and historic map. If so, then the wreck on Tearing Ledge is the *Eagle*, now a Protected Wreck, but either way, the remains of the third largest warship in the 1707 disaster has yet to found. A cannon site with some 30 guns which lie in

▲ An early lithograph showing the 4th Rate man o'war *Romney* wrecked and going to pieces amongst the Western Rocks. The wreck has as yet not been found.

135 ft (41m) of water close to Zantman's rock, on the seaward side of the Crim, from which a small bell and artefacts have been recovered may well be one of the East Indiamen wrecked amongst the Western Rocks. As for the two fireships which struck near the Gilstone, the *Phoenix* managed to reach the shallows of Tresco Channel and was run ashore at New Grimsby on Tresco. An account of what happened to her can be found in Chapter 5. As for the *Firebrand* fireship, the wreck was not located until 1974, when local diver Mark Groves came across it between Annet and St Agnes, near Menglow Rock. He was fortunate in finding the ship's bell, which bears a government 'broad-arrow' and the date of her last refit, 1701. More details can be found in a full account of the wreck in Chapter 3.

1969 also saw the recovery of a unique bronze cannon from the *Association* site., now on permanent display in the Isles of Scilly Museum. Recovered from beneath a boulder weighing at least 100 tons, this gun carries an inscription which loosely translated reads, 'Charles of Devonia ordered this gun made by Thomas Pitt in the year 1604.' It is not a naval gun but rather a very early military piece, probably retained on board as a trophy. It was unfortunate that neither the Isles of Scilly nor the National Maritime Museums were able to retain a greater cross-section of the items found for posterity, but following three public auctions of the artefacts and coins, one would have to travel to the four corners of the world to see them all. One of the 24pdr bronze cannon was donated by the navy divers to Tresco Garden, where it

▲ Two divers recovering the bell of the man o'war *Eagle*, on Tearing Ledge.

A collection of local, national and international newspapaer and media cuttings commenting on the successful location of the 1707 wreck of the *Association*, by a team of Royal Navy divers. These alone prove that it was the Navy and not Roland Morris who first found the wreck ▶

stands on a replica carriage in the Valhalla figure-head collection; another was sold to the Tower of London Armouries by the Royal Navy team for £3,000. Two guns raised by the Roland Morris team were purchased by Holland & Holland Ltd, of Bruton Street, London, one of which was later stolen. On 15 July 2009 the other was offered for sale at auction by Dreweatts of Donnington, Berkshire with a suggested price of £15,000 to £25,000, but in fact reached £55,000, plus auctioneers fees, well beyond all expectations. This particular gun is of significant historical importance since its breech is incised with the word 'Vigo', indicating that it was captured by Sir Clowdisley Shovel after the Battle of Vigo Bay and taken on board the *Association* as a trophy. The wrecks were again visited by divers during the Herbert Expedition in 1709-10, then in August 1847, the same month that Queen Victoria & Prince Albert made an unscheduled visit to St Mary's, the *Royal Cornwall Gazette* recorded:

'Interesting discovery in the Scilly Islands. Sir Cloudesley Shovell's guns, about 30 in number, and several round and cross-bar shots, were seen on the 17th instant near a rock called the Gilstone, to the westward of the islands, by a diver belonging to the cutter Argyle of Jersey, Captain Masters. He states that two of the guns could be raised with ease, but the remainder are covered over by a rock apparently of about 30 tons weight, which must have fallen upon them. He recovered two round shot of about 24lbs, and a cross-bar shot of the same weight.'

The site was also looked at by Trinity House divers working on the Bishop Rock in 1852, and again in 1857 by divers recovering gold from the *Schiller*, after which it was left alone until Royal Navy divers relocated the site on 4 July 1967.

Sir Clowdisley's ships were not the only losses in and around the Gilstone area; a large unidentified sailing vessel was lost here in 1750, and a tobacco-laden Virginian on 7 June 1788 on Pednathise Head. The 347-ton barque *John Esdaile* of North Shields, from Green Island, Quebec, to London, also struck on the Gilstone Ledges on 1 December 1845, but despite being towed into Smith Sound, went to pieces a week later. Her cargo of deals was salvaged from the beaches of Annet and St Agnes, all her crew being saved, unlike the unfortunate Greeks aboard the steamer *Antonios* wrecked on Old Bess 8 December 1912. The first local knowledge of this wreck came when pieces of lifeboat, wooden derricks, hatch covers and literally thousands of oranges were washed ashore on St Agnes three days later. Only one body was ever found, badly disfigured by the sea and still unidentified. An oar blade marked *Greta Holme* led to identification, proving the vessel to be the 2,626-ton steamer *Antonios* of Andros, Greece, ex-*Greta Holme*. Built in 1894 by J.L. Thompson of Sunderland, she was on passage from Fiume, Algiers, to Liverpool, having left there on 2 December. Black Rock to the east of Pednathise Head still holds a secret, the identity of a 16th century shipwreck that has yielded not only a large number of gold and silver coins, but also a valuable bronze astrolabe. Regrettably the salvor, a local builder, disposed of it on the mainland before anyone had an opportunity to examine, photograph or draw it.

▲ Detail of the ornamental crests and lettering on one of the French bronze cannon captured at Vigo Bay, and taken on board the *Association* as a war trophy

▲ French bronze cannon in Tresco Abbey gardens, as part of the Valhalla collection. From HM. man o'war *Association*

▲ Bronze signal gun from the wreck of the *Association*

The last shipping loss of any significance amongst the Western rocks took place on or around 13 February 1977, in bad visibility and heavy weather on Pednathise Head. The St Mary's lifeboat was launched at 2.15am on 14 February, to search for the French trawler *Enfant de Bretagne* of St Malo, Captain Chilou. By the light of a parachute flare, the crew of the lifeboat eventually saw the bow of the wreck, and heard voices shouting, but then the wreckage disappeared beneath the surface. A navy helicopter from RNAS Culdrose later recovered one body, the lifeboat a second, divers confirming the identity of the wreck from which there were unfortunately no survivors out of her crew of five. Swinging north from the Gilstone and Pednathise Head, there lies a semi-circle of rocks which are a natural trap for east-bound ships. Starting at the southern end, they are Daisy, Dry Splat, Rosevean, Rosevear, Jacky's Rock, Great and Little Crebawethan. The three earliest wrecks on Rosevean, which occurred in 1730, 1752 and 1762, cannot now be identified since their names are not recorded, although some details are known. The first of these was a ship laden with wine from the Canary Islands, whose master, Captain Roberts, at first refused to leave his vessel because of a large sum of money held on board. A worsening of the weather eventually forced him to abandon his ship and, after reaching Rosevean, he and another survivor remained lashed to a rock for three days before rescue. The wreck in 1752 was that of a Dutchman carrying cotton from Smyrna, and from this there were no survivors, unlike the French vessel lost in 1762 from which six of the crew escaped by clinging to floating timbers, although twelve others drowned.

▲ A collection of gold coins found on the wreck of the *Association*

At midnight on 26 February 1784, the same night that a transport vessel from New York came in at the back of Bryher in a SW gale, the East Indies dispatch vessel *Nancy* is thought to have first struck the Gilstone and then driven ashore on Rosevear Ledges, close to a small bay now known as Nancy Porth. Her passengers, twelve in number were mostly army officers returning from Madras, but there were two woman on board, an infamous and well known actress, Mrs Ann Cargill (nee Brown), and an African nanny to a Mr Page who was travelling with his young son. Ann was accompanied by her husband John and their twenty month old son, still a babe-in-arms. There was also a British Army prisoner on board, a Sergeant Tooley, who had led a mutiny in December 1784 on the island of St Helena, where the *Nancy* had called homeward bound.

The *Nancy* was an old East India Company vessel having been built in Bombay in 1774. Decommissioned from the Bengal Marine she had been laid up in Cork, Ireland,

◀ A macabre artefact from the *Association*, a leather shoe holding human ankle and foot bones

awaiting sale, then taken back into service and refitted in Bombay. Of 240-tons, two-masted and armed with ten 6pdr cannon, she was commanded by John Haldane and carried a crew of 36. With no survivors there is no factual account of what actually happened, and lurid descriptions of events such as Ann Cargill singing to her baby as the boat she was in capsized are conjecture if not pure fiction. The morning after the wreck mailbags found ashore on St Agnes caused local boats to put to sea, who found a mass of wreckage on the west side of Rosevear, and an upturned ship's boat. When this was righted, they found the bodies of Ann Cargill and her son, still tightly clutched in her arms. Only 17 corpses were found which were landed on Rosevear, then buried in the shallow soil and rock crevices of the island. When news reached St Mary's that the dead had been buried on an uninhabited island, a Captain Scott took it upon himself to investigate. He went out to Rosevear and exhumed all of them, but only three were in a condition suitable to be brought back to Old Town Church. One was Ann Cargill and presumably her child, the other two were male. Exactly where Ann Cargill was buried in Old Town churchyard is not known, although the *Times* newspaper reported that *'a neat monument has been erected at St Mary's, one of the Isles of Scilly, in memory of Mrs Cargill. It is said to have been paid for out of the produce of some jewels that were found upon her.'* Unfortunately that monument no longer exists, and even the 'Memorial Inscriptions of Cornwall - the Parish of the Isles of Scilly,' which lists every gravestone and monument on all the islands in detail, makes no mention of Ann Cargill. One author has discredited the reference to 'jewels that were found upon her' as paying for the monument on the grounds that when found she was wearing only night attire, but she could well have been wearing several rings, one or more necklaces and bracelets in bed which she took with her into the ship's boat.

The summer of 1784 saw the arrival in Scilly of John Braithwaite and his two sons, William and John, jnr. They brought with them their diving 'machine', to work on the wreck of the *Nancy*, no doubt attracted by the easy target of small cannon in shallow water, and Ann Cargill's cash and jewellery. There were two other contestants for whatever 'treasures' lay underwater in the wreck, a Mathew Cox, who advised the East Company that he had 'copper diving dresses,' possibly similar to that of Captain Rowe, who had copied John Lethbridges 'barrel' made of wood, and a John Harriett. He appears to have been a Lieutenant in the employ of the East India Company, since his application to salvage read:

'As a servant duty bound to render any and every service in his power to those from whom he receives his principal support, your humble servant, a Lieutenant on half pay, takes this liberty of informing you that on perusal of the loss of the Nancy packet from Bombay, he is humbly of the opinion that his judgement, grounded on experience relative to raising sunken vessels, or if too much wreck'd to be raised entire, in getting up the goods etc from the broken parts of the wreck, may be of service by going down and examining the above mentioned Packet.'

The exact nature of the Braithwaite apparatus is uncertain, having been variously described as a 'machine', a diving bell and a chamber. Whatever its form:

'The nature of this artist's apparatus is peculiar unto himself; his general practice is to remain underwater for six hours consecutive. He declares he could without inconvenience remain in his chamber underwater for six weeks, or any length of time.'

▲ Customs Officer 'Bill' Saundby with a bronze cannon and other artefact material from the *Association*, handed in to the Receiver of Wreck on St Mary's

John Braithwaite, who came to Scilly
with his two sons in 1784 to dive on
the wreck of the packet vessel *Nancy*,
to recover treasure ▶

What, if anything of value was recovered remains unknown, but there is an anonymous hand written account of one of Braithwaite's dives on the wreck: *'Everything is at present very scarce here, of account of the long drought, as we have not had any rain since the beginning of May (nb: it was now the end of July). What provisions we get are brought from Land's End, and when it arrives here, it is almost stinking. There is a sloop in the harbour with the ingenious Mr Braithwaite and his two sons on board, who sometime ago took up an anchor to the Royal George (nb: lost at Spithead, Portsmouth).*

We went with them about four leagues to the westward of this place, to a small uninhabited island called La Roche Verde or Green Rock (nb: Rosevear) where the Nancy packet was lost on her return from the East Indies, where the unfortunate Mrs Cargill perished. Some distance from the shore the younger Mr. Braithwaite went down in his machine, and remained two hours underwater, but could not meet with anything although the inhabitants of the islands have at different times found many valuable articles driven on there. Whilst on the island we saw great quantities of bones of the Nancy's crew, covered with small trusses of grass. This was a melancholy spectacle to us, on recollecting the sudden fate of our unhappy countrymen who, in the moment they were comforting themselves with the prospect of returning to their friends, were, alas, suddenly sent to that undiscovered country from whose bourne no traveler returns.'

The lack of a memorial to the *Nancy* incident was put right in 2008, when a dedication service was held in Old Town churchyard and a memorial plaque erected by the diving team who re-located the wreck site, researched the story and published the book *'Ghosts of Rosevear - and the Wreck of the Nancy Packet.'*

The sloop *Mary* of Fishguard, Captain Harris was equally unlucky, being wrecked on 20 March 1819 whilst carrying a cargo of oats from Youghall to Southampton, whilst thick fog caused the loss of the Plymouth ketch *Solace* carrying wheat from Lisbon to Plymouth, Captain Barrett, on 27 April 1839. She struck a shallow reef and went to pieces the following day in a ground swell, but her crew of five managed to save their personal belongings before taking to her boats. Another Dutch owned vessel lost in the area was the *Nickerie*, a barque, registered at Rotterdam, Captain Haweg. On passage from Samarang in Batavia to her home port with coffee and sugar, she struck a rock SW of Rosevear during the night of 21 November 1843 when, in fact, her captain thought he was well up the English Channel.

The *Nickerie* is one of only a handful of wrecks of which a full account survives: '*Early in the morning of Thursday, the 22nd ult., several broken pieces of timber and bundles of rattan, being found on the shore, it was supposed that some unfortunate vessel had been wrecked, which supposition subsequently proved to be correct. The following particulars are from the lips of the two survivors, the sail maker and a seaman, who state that the vessel was the Dutch barque* Nickirie, *Captain J. Haweg, from Batavia, laden with coffee and sugar, for Rotterdam; they left Batavia in October last, and St Helena about the 1st of January. On the 21st instant, about one am, when they supposed the ship had entered and was running up the English Channel, they suddenly & unexpectedly made the St Agnes light, and in about five minutes afterwards the ship struck, but went on without having received much damage; about ten minutes after she struck a second time, and almost instantly went to pieces when eight of the crew, including the doctor and chief officer, were drowned. The remaining eleven, among whom was the captain, clung to the wreck until day-light, when they were in a most exhausted state from wet, cold and want of food. The wreck lay very near the island of Rosevear, but, unhappily, so situated as to be hid from St Agnes, and the hopes of the poor men of being seen were therefore very slender. They, therefore, set about making a large raft, which, before it was finished, became so entangled with the wreck, that they could not possibly clear it.*

About this time, the boatswain, in endeavoring to reach the shore, was drowned, and the carpenter died on the wreck. At eleven am, the sail maker, with great danger and difficulty, succeeded in reaching the shore on a small raft of two spars and two planks; and in an hour or two

Corroded silver and copper coins found on a wreck site by the author, believed to be the *Nickerie*, lost in 1843 near Rosevear ▶

after, the seaman, with the assistance of the sail maker, also got safely on the islet of Rosevear, where they narrowly escaped perishing from cold and hunger during the Wednesday night. On the following morning, Thursday, nothing but loose fragments of the wreck were to be seen, the raft with their unfortunate shipmates having been swept away during the night. The two survivors were shortly after taken off the islet amidst great danger from the tremendous sea that was running, and conveyed to first St Agnes, where they received every attention, and subsequently to St Mary's, there the Consul and other benevolent persons furnished them with what they needed. The bodies of three of the seamen have since been found and buried on St Mary's. This is another loud call to the Trinity Board to lose no time in erecting the long talked of lighthouse on the islet of Rosevear; for had this light existed, we should not have had to record this melancholy event.'

The remains of this private East Indiaman may well lie just to the W of Rosevear Ledges on a site which has been claimed to be that of the packet *Nancy* lost in 1783. Both ships were armed, hence cannon(2) remain on the seabed, and shards of Chien Lung and Qing dynasty pottery found could equally well have come from either wreck. A more convincing aspect is that the *Nancy* was 'country built' in Bombay, in 1774, and carried six cannon, and would be most unlikely to have been built with iron hanging knees, whereas the *Nickerie* is known to have been built with iron knees at Rotterdam.

In 1925, two steam trawlers went ashore on Rosevear although only one was actually wrecked on the island. The first stranding occurred at midnight on 21 March 1925, when the lookouts on board the French *Cité de Verdun* of Boulogne, caught only a brief glimpse of the Bishop light through a blinding snowstorm before their ship struck the rocks. Her crew of 30 got ashore, built a shelter and lit a fire before sending up signals of distress, in answer to which the St Mary's lifeboat *Elsie*, coxswain Lethbridge, went out amongst the Western Rocks and within 45 minutes had them all safely aboard. The RNLI crew responsible for their rescue later received awards from the French government, and amongst the many souvenirs of the wreck which found their way to St Mary's were the ship's name boards, which can still be seen in the Atlantic and Mermaid inns. The second incident concerned another French trawler, the *Europe* of Boulogne, which went ashore during fog at 2.42am on 12 June in almost exactly the same spot as the *Cité de Verdun*. A coastguard on St Mary's spotted her distress flares and alerted the lifeboat crew but, as their boat was laid up at the time for repairs, privately-owned craft went out to search W of Annet. They found the 119-ton steam trawler stranded on the rocks with only her captain and four men aboard, the remainder having already taken to the boats which now lay some distance off. They were convinced that the *Europe* was doomed and were waiting for her to sink. As the tide rose, so the trawler was worked off the rocks, her crew re-embarked, and at 5.15am she radioed Land's End that she was clear and making for Dunkirk, only slightly damaged.

◀ A collection of porcelain shards from the wreck of the paddle steamer, *Thames*, 1841, found by the author

The Western Rocks have witnessed so many tragedies that their individual enormity, although dreadful at the time, were soon forgotten or overshadowed. A total of seven East Indiamen have found themselves in difficulties in the Scillies, all in this quarter of the islands, only one of which, the smallest and least valuable, was saved. This was the *Supply*, Captain John Tottin, an English East India Company pinnace homeward bound to London from Bantam with dispatches, which went ashore in 1617. Less fortunate was the EIC *Phoenix* of 450-tons, also homeward bound from Bantam with a valuable cargo of white pepper in bags, and cloth, which was lost somewhere amongst the Western rocks on 11 January 1680. Armed with 30 guns, under Captain William Wildy and a crew of 90, she was on her 4th voyage to the Far East, her cargo valued at £10,177.18s. Much of the pepper and textiles were sold on Scilly to a Thomas Abney who paid '£202.8s.1d for 269 pieces of Peerlongs'. This sum was minuscule compared to the value of the 'treasure' - presumably all silver specie, which went down on board the Dutch VOC (Verenidge Oostindische Compagnie) ship *Prinses Maria* in February 1686. She sank in shallow water close to Silver Carn, just north of Santaspery Neck, very close to where the ss *Thames* was lost 155 years later. Carrying 46 guns and a crew of 250, the value of silver on board this Dutch East Indiaman was so great that King James II sent his personal yacht to Scilly, along with retainers and soldiers, to recover as much treasure as they could for the king's coffers. Relocated in 1973 under deep sand by a diving team led by Rex Cowan, the site yielded numerous artefacts, a small quantity of Reale coins, iron cannon and timbers. She had obviously been heavily salvaged at the time she sank. A most unusual artefact found by divers was a ceramic Bellamine jar full of mercury, which would have been used for the refining of gold in China.

Typical of the many smaller vessels lost amongst the jumble of rocks west of Annet was the 50-ton lugger *La Virginia de Carmen*, of St.Sebastian's, Captain Manuel. She

Remains of a small china bowl from the wreck site of the ss *Thames*, showing the crest of the City of Dublin Steam Packet Company ▶

was on passage from Vera Cruz to Cadiz and was hopelessly off course carrying a cargo of indigo, cochineal, cocoa, jolap, silver, and other valuables, the property of her passengers, all of whom were lost along with the cargo, only the captain and one sailor were saved. and only four bodies taken up and buried.

One particularly tragic wreck, thought to be the earliest steamer lost on Scilly, was the 500-ton ss *Thames* on 4 January 1841. Owned by the City of Dublin Steam Packet Co, the 14-year-old composite built vessel left the River Liffy for London on 2 January with 26 crew and 36 passengers, of whom some 30 were young recruits for the British Army. Early on 4 January, while battling against a full westerly gale accompanied by rain squalls, snow and thunder, one particularly heavy sea came aboard, flooding the hold, cabins and boiler-room, putting out the fires. Almost simultaneously breakers were sighted to leeward, and Captain James Grey ordered sail to be set on the main and foremasts in an attempt to work her clear, but water-logged and helpless, the little *Thames* fell beam on to Jacky's Rock, between Rosevear and Crebawethan. A worse situation for those on board could hardly be envisaged as seas swept the upper deck, the steamer up against a reef of rocks on her starboard side, illuminated only by flashes of lightning. Distress flares were burnt but went unseen by those on shore, and it was not until daybreak that the first islanders noticed the wreck. Ten of them put out in the gig *Thomas*, followed by the *Bee* and the *Briton*, the pilot-cutter *Active* and the St Mary's lifeboat which, incidentally, was still un-named. The gig *Thomas* was the first to reach the wreck now lying with her bow under water and with the survivors crowded on to her small poop deck. Female passengers were the first to be taken off, a distraught and near-hysterical Celia Morris having to be forcibly pulled from her father's arms. A wave then filled the little gig almost level with her gunwales and while half the crew bailed furiously, the others pulled Mary Meyler and Mary Gregory, both stewardesses, through the sea on a line to safety. With some of her crew still bailing, the gig was rowed to Gorregon, where the three women, now in desperate straits, were transferred to the *Active*. The gale then shifted into the east preventing any further boats from reaching the wreck of the *Thames*. which by now was surrounded by huge seas and almost engulfed in breaking water as her iron framed hull covered with wooden planking, went to pieces.

Meanwhile, on board the cutter *Active*, all three women who were suffering from exposure but still alive, were landed at St Agnes. The Irish recruits attempted to save themselves by launching a lifeboat, but it quickly filled and sank, as did a second. Five of the steamer's crew then managed to construct a raft but once in the sea it capsized and was later thrown ashore on Rosevear, only one of its five occupants reaching safety. All alone on the rock he searched the foreshore, calling out in the hope of finding others alive, but found only useless wreckage and a barrel of porter. This he pulled to higher ground, broached it by knocking in one end, then drinking some of the contents, after which he emptied it, lined it with grass and climbed inside to fall asleep in an improvised shelter. A search party found him the following day, still asleep, and along with bodies recovered from the sea, he was brought to St Mary's. 60 lives, including Captain Grey, were lost in the wreck of the *Thames*, classed as amongst the worst disasters in the islands. Six weeks after the wreck during a period of fine weather, James Deane's diving apparatus, the forerunner of all helmet-diving equipment, was employed on the *Thames* and her anchor cables were salvaged during the first day's work.

Behind Rosevear and Jacky's Rock, to the east, is an area known locally as the Brow-of-Ponds, which was the scene of two wrecks, that of an Austrian brig and a steamship. The brig *Aurora* went ashore at 2am on 19 August 1860 while carrying wheat from Ibrail for Falmouth. Captain Alessio Merlato and his crew got away in the ship's boat only with great difficulty, finally landing at St Mary's. Little of her cargo and only a few spars were saved, and the wreck itself was sold on 23 August. Poor visibility due to fog put the *Aurora* ashore, and exactly the same conditions

An almost intact tea cup found on the wreck of the *Thames* ▶

caused the wreck of the steamer *Sado* of London some ten years later on 20 April 1870. She had left Oporto for Liverpool on the 17th with a general cargo of wine, wool, oranges, minerals, eggs and 30 bullocks, and all was well until a little after midnight on the 20th when fog was encountered. The *Sado* however continued at full speed, about nine knots, until 2.40am, when the 2nd Mate saw broken water ahead. Her helm was put hard over, but more rocks appeared and as her engine was put to full astern, she struck. The 325-ton vessel, built in 1866 became a total loss and at the enquiry her master, Captain Robert Hoodless, had his certificate suspended for three months for not using the sounding lead, and for failing to reduce speed in fog.

Crebawethan, north of Jacky's Rock, has claimed at least seven ships, one of the earliest being the *Amelia* of London on 1 September 1810. Of 349-tons gross, built in 1785, under Captain Craige she was bound from Demerara with rum, coffee, cotton and sugar for London from Gibraltar. She went ashore and was abandoned to the sea along with her cargo, a box of silver coins and another of American dollars. A St Ives schooner, the *Minerva*, Hicks master, was also lost here on 13 October 1836 with only one survivor, and another victim of nearby Round rock was the 200 ton Liverpool schooner, *Douro*, Captain Gowland, on 28 January 1843. Bound from Liverpool to Oporto with a cargo described as 'baled goods, armoury and brass stops', she struck and sank in fog, her entire crew being lost. Six bodies and the ship's figurehead were later recovered, but little else. Built at Sunderland in 1839, when located by divers accidentally in the early 1970's, the 'brass stops' in her cargo proved to be thousands upon thousands of brass manillas, bracelet-type tokens used in the West African slave trade, but this is not proof that the *Douro* was herself engaged in the slave trade.

Two pounds per head was the price offered for every live steer landed on Annet from the wreck of the Liverpool steamer *Castleford* on 8 June 1887. This 3,044 tons gross vessel, launched at Sunderland in 1883 for the Sunderland Shipbuilding Co, had left Montreal for the Thames on 27 May, carrying a general cargo, 450 prime steers on deck, eighteen cattlemen, one passenger and 32 crew. Dense fog around the islands forced

◀ Brass Manilla slave tokens, found by the author on the wreck of the slave trader *Douro*, wrecked in 1843 on Round Rock

Castleford

▲ The wreck of the ss. *Castleford*, lost on Crebawethan in 1887, whilst carrying a general cargo and 450 prime steers

Captain McLean to reduce speed and when a sounding showed 56 fathoms, the ship's engines were stopped in order to listen for the Bishop Rock fog-signal. While the captain was in the chartroom attempting to work out his position, the chief officer ordered the engines to slow ahead again, and before the captain could regain the bridge to countermand the order, the *Castleford* was aground on Crebawethan. Both No's 1 and 2 holds flooded immediately and when the boiler-room bulkhead collapsed flooding the engine-room, her crew abandoned ship. During the subsequent salvage work, cattle were roped by the horns to gigs which towed them to Annet, where they roamed around for ten days consuming what little grazing the island offered before being roped and shipped to Falmouth. Many of the beasts drowned and two local gigs fell victims to the animals. The *Gipsy* was holed by the horns of one frantic animal and the *O & M* had her bow smashed when a steer fell into her off the deck of the ship. The *Castleford* finally broke in two forward of the bridge on 19 July and dead steers washed out of the holds, some reaching as far as Lelant and Penzance on the mainland.

Eleven years later, on 26 May 1898, a small Newlyn fishing lugger, the *Nyanza*, skippered by Alfred Richards, struck the Crim and sprang such a serious leak that she had to be run ashore on Gt Crebawethan to save her. The St Agnes lifeboat, *James & Caroline*, was able to save four of her crew and some of the fishing gear, while an island boat saved a fifth man. One drowned, but nothing could be done for the

lugger, which went to pieces where she lay. An armed auxiliary naval trawler, built in 1915 at Kingston-upon-Hull, having been fitted with a 12pdr gun on her forecastle, HMS *Carbineer*, No.1164, was the last victim of Crebawethan, having struck the Crim on 18 May 1916. A Scillonian crew member, William Trenear, knowing the waters, advised the captain to run her ashore on Crebawethan where she became a total loss rather than have her sink in the deep waters of Broad Sound. Reference has already been made to the Crim, the most seaward of the Western Rocks and an extremely dangerous reef which has terminated the career of something like 30 vessels. In 1782, a Venetian ship named *Providentia Divina*, Captain Pascal Molena, was wrecked here while carrying shell-fish, white clay, Castille soap, wine, almonds and oil from Marseilles to Ostend and London. Eleven of her crew saved themselves by clinging to a mast which carried them to St Agnes. Many were cut and brusied, especially a passenger who, being in his bunk when the ship struck came up on deck stark naked, and left the wreck without time to put on any clothes. Three of the crew were blown into Tresco Channel on a mast and landed at New Grimsby. A French barque, the *Osirus*, was lost on 29 May 1838 during an easterly gale, also the Glasgow schooner *Eagle*, which struck first on the Crim in fog on 18 January 1848, then several other rocks and finally the Bishop Rock before sinking. She was bound from her home port to Charante with iron and coal, and Captain Scott and his crew had a narrow escape when the mainyard fell down while they were abandoning ship, almost sinking their longboat. Another victim of the Crim was the Neopolitan brig *San Giorgio* which, badly damaged slowly sank. Cries for help from the crew were answered by the schooner *Galway Ark*, which took them off and landed them at St Mary's within an hour of the incident. The wreck then drifted out to sea and was later found sixty miles offshore. It took the combined efforts of 15 local pilot-cutters and a schooner to get the brig back to Scilly with her entire cargo of wood and olive oil. After being repaired locally at Edward's shipyard on St Mary's, the brig sailed again renamed the *Lion*, of Scilly.

The first of many such large sailing vessels to fall foul of the Crim was the Liverpool full-rigger *Custos*, lost on 28 August 1856. Outward bound for Bonny in Nigeria with a general cargo and obviously in the slave trade, she sank within ten minutes, and according to the Customs Officer only a small quantity of soap and eighty casks of spirit were salvaged. Her crew of 17 landed on St Agnes in their own boats. The notice of an auction to be held on 2 October, nailed up on St Mary's, tells a different story:

'For sale by auction by order of Francis Banfield, Shipping Agent, St.Mary's. 31 pipes and 55 casks of rum; 25 bales of cotton goods, 49 small boxes of soap,191 muskets, 2 casks of gun-flintsr, 136 barrels of gunpowder, 4 bags of manillas, 3 sails and some spares.'

At the Board of Trade inquiry it was revealed that Captain Daniel Shaw had been drunk for three whole days prior to her stranding. The *Aurora*, an Austrian registered vessel on passage from Ibrail to Falmouth with wheat, struck a rock on 19 August 1860, one mile from the Bishop at 2am, believed to be the Outer Gilstone, where she foundered. Sacks of wheat were salvaged at low water and her captain, Alessio Meriato, sold the wreck on the 23rd. The ss *Sado* of London, 325-tons gross, carrying wool, wine, oranges, minerals, eggs and 30 head of cattle, ran ashore on the Brow of Ponds, Rosevear Ledges, on 20 April 1870. Her three boats took the 20 crew and four passengers, which included Mrs Hoodless, the captain's wife, and child, first to St Agnes and then on to St Mary's. An auction of wool and wine was held on the 10th May, the latter fetching from 4s.6d to 16s a gallon, but no one wanted the water soaked wool. The wreck took place close to where the ss *Thames* was lost in 1841.

A barque named *Glori*, of Genoa, after hitting the reef on 26 August 1875, managed to stagger on to St Mary's, assisted by the ss *Lady of the Isles*, where her cargo of ore and grass from Pomeron was saved. When the Liverpool steamer *Culmore* of 540-tons gross hit the rocks in fog on 7 May 1881, she went down so quickly that Captain G.P. Coble, the chief and second engineers, and a steward went down with her out of her crew of 17. Although the captain and steward surfaced, both died sometime later. Her cargo spewed out across the width of the Western Rocks, and Valencia oranges, pepper and onions came ashore throughout the Scillies. Owned by Edward Paul of Liverpool, the *Culmore* was reported as sinking in deep water, beyond hope of salvage.

Although the *Indipendenza*, a Genoan barque was lost as a result of hitting the Crim on 24 September 1881, she finally sank on the Barrel of Butter rocks overlooked by Star Castle, St Mary's, so that her story has been included in Chapter 4. Next of the big full-riggers to fall foul of the area was the steel-hulled *Ardencraig* of Glasgow which hit the Crim in thick fog then went on to strike the Gunners Ledge whilst her crew were sat down having dinner, Captain Thomas Dunning under the impression she was at least 20 miles WSW of Scilly. The men of St Agnes were alerted by the boom of the Bishop Rock signal gun, which brought out both the *Charles Deere James* and *Henry Dundas* lifeboats from St Agnes and St Mary's on 8 January 1911. Thirty minutes later they had found the huge three-master wallowing in the swell of Broad Sound, all her sails set with her foreyards aback. Shortly afterwards, she rolled over and sank bow first in deep water. The *Ardencraig* was one hundred days out from Melbourne with wheat for Calais via Queenstown for orders, and had in fact, left Ireland only the previous day. Despite her crew of 31 being all saved either in their own boats or by the lifeboats, a court of enquiry found the captain guilty of improper navigation and unseamanlike behaviour and suspended his certificate for three months. The ship had been built in 1886 by Russell & Co of Greenock for the Port

▲ The full-rigged ship *Ardencraig*, half full of water and wallowing in Broad Sound, January 1911

Ship's bell found on the wreck of the full-rigged ship Thomliebank, lost in 1913 on the Crim, recovered in 1988 ▶

Line and was 2,153-tons gross..Two Cape Horners fell victim to the Crim during the latter part of 1913, the same year in which both the *Cromdale* and the *Queen Margaret* were lost on the Lizard. Bound from Iquique to Falmouth with nitrate, the 1,975 gross tons *Susanna*, a ship of Hamburg built in 1893, was sailing in dense fog on 14 August when her lookouts heard the Bishop minute-gun, but were unable to determine the precise direction from which the sound was coming. A few minutes later the ship struck heavily on the southern side of Zantman's Rock and commenced to fill. After the ship's boats had been lowered, the crew remained aboard to see if she could be saved, but by midnight there were signs she was breaking up and they abandoned ship. No sooner had the last of the 22 crew taken to the boats than the *Susanna* rolled over, broke in two and foundered. The wreck still lies close to the south-western side of Zantmans Rock in 90ft (27m) of water, reduced to scrap metal by ground seas over the years. When last visited by the author, only pieces of broken china marked 'Villeroy and Boch. Dresden' identified the vessel, but since then her bronze bell has been located and raised.

The second loss on the Crim three months later that year was the Glasgow ship *Thornliebank* of 2,105 tons gross. On her outward voyage she carried a cargo of coal from Port Talbot to Iquique, then went on to Pisagua, in Chile, where she loaded nitrate of soda worth £30,000 for Falmouth. At the mouth of the Channel heading for Falmouth for orders, she ran into fog off the Scillies, but it cleared sufficiently for the deck watch to identify the Bishop Rock light and the master set a course due SW. At 5 am next morning, 28 November 1913, just as the port watch was tacking ship, there was a grating rumble, the vessel brought up sharply and began to roll heavily. She assumed a heavy list to starboard, so that only the boats on that side could be lowered, and less than five minutes later she fell on her side until the topsail yards touched the sea, then rolled right over and sank, less than 500ft (150m) from the wreck of the *Susanna*. Her crew of 25 having watched their ship go down from the comparative safety of their boats, then rowed towards the Bishop where they saw one of the keepers on the gallery but for some reason were unable to attract his attention. They then decided to row to St Agnes, but were met off Melledgan by the lifeboat *Charles Deere James* and escorted into St Mary's. Later, wreckage from the vessel, a cork lifebelt and a name board, came ashore on the north coast of Cornwall between Perranporth and Watergate Bay.

The 2,105-ton *Thornliebank* was the last sailing ship built for the Bank Line (Messrs A Weir and Co of Glasgow), having been launched by Russell's of Port Glasgow in September 1896. At the Board of Trade inquiry it transpired that Captain G.E. Crosby was unaware of alterations to the pattern of flashes of the Scilly and Wolf Rock lights and, thinking he was close to Ushant, had accidentally steered his vessel onto the Western Rocks. The sole comment of the crew upon leaving the islands for the mainland was: 'Scilly is a wonderful place to be shipwrecked', a tribute to the hospitality they had received. The ship's bell engraved with the name *Thornliebank*, was found by a diver in 1988 then taken to the mainland. The rusting remains of the *Susanna* and the *Thornliebank* were very nearly joined by the 7,660 tons gross Red Star liner *Gothland*, (ex-Gothic, ex-Gothland, ex-Gothic) at 4.30 pm on 23 June 1914, but fortunately the steamer was saved. Launched in 1893 by Harland & Wolff of Belfast, this four-masted, 490 ft-long vessel was on passage from Montreal to Rotterdam with a general cargo which included wheat and 500 tons of frozen meat. In addition to her 131 crew, she carried eighty-six passengers, of whom forty-eight were Belgian refugees deported from Montreal. After striking the Crim, it was possible to climb down into her No's 2 and 3 holds and see the glimmer of sand and light through the holes in her bottom. Captain Young of the Liverpool Salvage Association set about refloating her, and his first action was to build a false floor in No 3 hold, after which the level of water inside was reduced by compressed air and she floated clear. As she was pulled away from the rocks by tugs at 7.15am on 27 June, her foremast literally fell out through the bottom of the ship! She was taken to St Mary's Roads and anchored near Nut Rock, after which she went on to Southampton under tow of the tugs *Linnet, Triton* and *Ranger* and lay at anchor off Netley for many months before being broken up.

◀ Porcelain sherds found by the author on the site of what is believed to be wreck site of the *Zeelilie*, on Crebawethan.

A French three-masted wooden schooner, the 437-tons gross *Leon Bonnat* of Bayonne, whose original name was *Thomas L James*, was the last wreck to occur on the Crim to date. Homeward bound from Cardiff for Bayonne with 600 tons of coal in February 1921, she started to leak during a gale in the Bristol Channel. Captain Robert Chaigre sought shelter at Lundy but the gale swung round to the north and he was forced to run for Scilly. Round Island light showed up ahead and there was every hope the ship would successfully round the Bishop light and reach Mount's Bay, but a westerly gale set in, the tide took her inshore, and at noon on 2 February she struck the Crim, then floated clear. The captain went below to investigate a peculiar tearing noise and saw her cargo literally falling out through an enormous hole in the ship's bottom, the inrush of water being only partially stemmed by the outgoing coal. Though the vessel sank within five minutes of hitting the rocks, her crew of 12 were able to lower and man the lifeboat. Just before the captain left the ship he threw a box containing his papers, sextant, chronometer and valuables into the boat but missed, and it fell into the sea and sank.. A week later that box, now empty, washed ashore near Tresco. Meanwhile, the Bishop Rock keepers had seen the wreck occur and soon afterwards the lifeboat *Elsie* arrived on the scene and took the twelve men aboard.

The Gunners, already mentioned in connection with the *Ardencraig*, claimed HMS *Hind*, a 6th Rate eight-gun ketch, Captain John Withern RN, on 11 December 1668, and is also said to have been struck by the Dutch East Indiaman *Hollandia* in July 1743, before she went on to sink near George Peter's Ledge, just west of Annet, an incident mentioned in Chapter 3. Due south of Gunner's Ledge and north of Rosevear lie a collection of reefs and rocks known as the Great and Little Crebawethan, with another Round Rock to the north. It was here on Great Crebawethan that one of the most valuable East Indiamen wrecks in Scillonian history is thought to have struck in October 1795. A letter written by the local Collector of Customs, Mr.A.A. Leggatt to his superiors in London, tells some of the story:

Pottery shards from the Zeelilie site, showing their Chinese blue and white porcelain origin ▶

'I have a moment allowed me to inform you that one of the Dutch East Indiamen, prize to the Sceptre, a large China ship which left the Shannon last Friday under convoy, was yesterday morning at 3 o'clock totally lost and gone to pieces having struck on the most Western Rocks of the Isles. The accident is said to have been wholly occasioned by the obstinacy of the person having the command, said to be the Mate, who was in high ijine, and appraised of the immediate danger, told what the light was and that the land and breakers were run ahead. He himself drowned, said to have jumped overboard as soon as the ship struck; about 24 others are lost and 45 saved who were taken on board Sir Edward Pellew's ship the Inde-fatigable *which with the* Quebec *and* La Revolution *frigates, were lying in the Road waiting to be joined by the* Cestene. *The Dutch East Indiaman is laden chiefly with tea and china which is all gone to the bottom, the cargo being valued at £140,000.'*

The ship was the *Zeelilie* or *Sea Lily* of Middleburg, 1,500-tons, 54-guns, and the largest vessel in what proved to be the very last homeward bound convoy of the Dutch East India Company (VOC) before it went into liquidation. Built in 1789 and having made her second voyage to the far East, she was returning in convoy with 19 other ships, escorted by a small Dutch naval frigate, when they were captured by HMS *Sceptre*, a 3rd rate man o'war commanded by Captain Essington, part of Admiral Pellew's South Atlantic fleet. The Dutch ships were escorted into Limerick, where the *Zeelilie*, having the most valuable cargo, was immediately sent with an English crew of 69 to London. Off the Scillies she met with a gale and was wrecked with the loss of 24 men, as the letter above explained. What made her so special was that she carried the largest consignment of nine different types of tea ever brought to Europe in a single ship, which was of immense value at the time. Beneath the tea, protecting it from bilge water was 100-tons of the finest Chinese porcelain in crates, representing a phenomenal 2,400,000 individual pieces - again, because this was to be the last VOC convoy, this represented the largest porcelain shipment ever carried. She is also known to have been carrying ingots of zinc. It all went to the bottom and the seabed NW of Little Crebawethan is littered with thousands of fragments of the finest blue Chinese porcelain, but there is something is not quite right about the site. 2.4 million items of porcelain smashed to pieces would represent many, many millions of broken shards, and divers generally agree that there are nothing like that quantity - in which case is this another, unidentified Indiaman and the *Zeelilie* has perhaps yet to be found?

A 300-ton Maryport brig named *Bassenthwaite*, a four-year-old uninsured vessel, struck a partially submerged wreck at the entrance to Broad Sound on 7 April 1836 during a full north-west gale and sank immediately. She was on passage from Liverpool to Quebec with a general cargo, and though ten of her crew were able to escape in the ship's boats, the cook and the cabin boy were both lost in the wreck. A schooner from Surinam to London, the *Challenger*, Captain M. Jones, struck either the Nundeeps or the Gunners and was wrecked on 21 November 1843. Her crew of eight landed on Bryher, as a result of which the complete island was put in quarantine for fear one of the sailors might be carrying cholera. At various times since, several small vessels have met with a similar fate, for the Gunners lie dangerously close to the surface at the entrance to Broad Sound.

Understandably, in an area with so many hazards as the Western Rocks, there have been innumerable wrecks about which little or nothing is known. Oranges floating amongst the Western Rocks in large numbers on 21 February 1812 were the sure signs of a wreck, thought to be Spanish, but her identity remains unknown since there were no survivors. The *York*, Captain James Farthing, another fruit-laden ship, Seville to London with oranges, was lost on 5 February 1822. Duchy records reveal that,

'On Tuesday morning (5th) a dead body and several pieces of wreck were driven ashore on the island of St Agnes, and on the following day three more bodies with a quantity of oranges were thrown ashore at the same place. The bodies from the wreck were decently interred in St Agnes churchyard in coffins provided by the direction of John Johns Esq, agent to the Duke of Leeds. Great praise is due to the islanders of St Agnes for the promptitude with which they exposed themselves to a most violent sea, in a fruitless endeavour to discover any survivors of this melancholy catastrophe.'

Other losses included an unidentified ship known to have been registered in Newfoundland, from which only three bodies were recovered in the November of 1829. A Scarborough-owned brig, the *George Lockwood* of 290 tons, laden with timber from Quebec for London, got amongst the Western Rocks on 19 December 1837 but managed to reach Penzance safely, where she was beached in a waterlogged condition. The *William Preston*, a South Shields vessel of 160-tons, built in 1841, was lost on 12 February 1842 near Melledgan, and whilst neither Captain Couper or any of her crew survived, her figurehead, described as 'a man's head and bust, painted white, with a spy-glass under the left arm' washed ashore, but what happened to it is not recorded. On her maiden voyage from Odessa with wheat, it were two water-casks bearing the ship's name, found ashore on St Agnes, that gave the first indication of her loss. Today, these shipwreck incidents are nothing more than names with little meaning to anyone, yet, at the time, many were major disasters to those concerned, leaving families bereaved of father or sons, and if, as was often the case, the master was sole or part owner, the loss often brought financial ruin as well. The list of ships which have struck on the Western Rocks is almost endless; a 540-ton Bergen brig built in 1871, the *Ceredig*, Captain J. Trumpy on 22 September 1865, which was eventually saved; the Norwegian barque *Kong Svere*, Captain Thomas Petersen, carrying coal from Cardiff to Kingston, Jamaica on 21 August 1896, and many others. Truly, these dangerous rocks have claimed more than their fair share of victims.

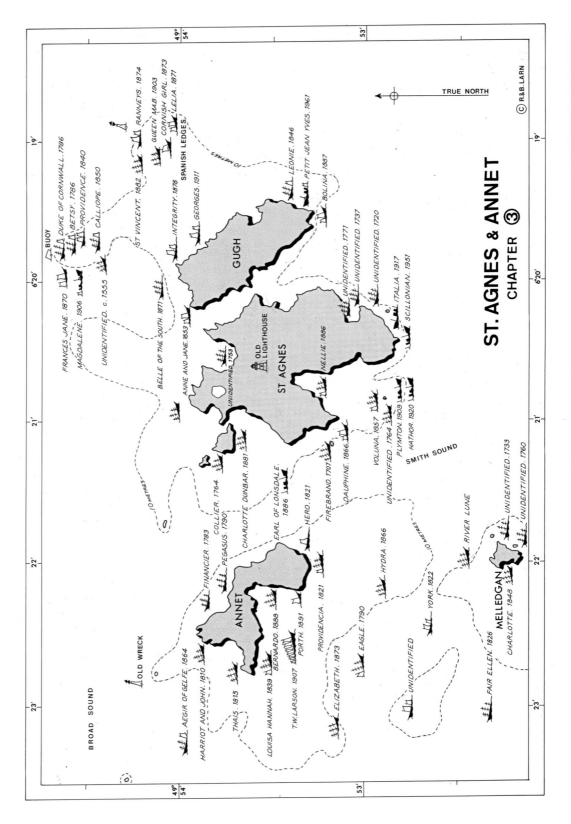

ST. AGNES & ANNET

CHAPTER ③

© R&B LARN

TRUE NORTH

66

3 - The Islands of St Agnes & Annet

St Agnes island children when saying their prayers at night 150 years ago were taught: *'Good night father, good night mother, Good night friends and foes, God send a ship ashore before morning.'*

Due to their physical and intimate connection with the Western Rocks, St Agnes was once the centre of wreck activity at Scilly. The pilot-gigs, cutters and lifeboat of St Agnes were usually the first to reach any wreck in the area, and there was once a time when few mornings passed in succession before the 'wrecker's prayer' was answered and some unfortunate vessel was found ashore. Children learnt the prayer from an early age, for a good wreck would support the entire community throughout a winter, always a time of shortages and desperate want amongst the islanders in those days. Such prayers, inhuman though they may seem today, were by no means peculiar to the island of Scilly. On lonely Tristan da Cunha for example, way down south in the Atlantic, infinitely more isolated than Scilly, the young maidens were taught:

> *'Please God send us a good shipwreck so we can get married.'*

St Agnes's association with shipwrecks goes back a very long way, well before the reign of Richard I (1189-99), when the island was named Hagness, or Hagenes. According to legend, which so often has an element of truth, it was here that St Warna landed having reached Scilly from Ireland in a coracle. St Warna is said to have been the islanders' patron saint of shipwrecks, and if this is true he could not have landed at a more appropriate spot. A cove on the southern side of the island still bears the saint's name, and the remains of a wishing-well survive into which the islanders once dropped pins or coins when they could afford the luxury, before making a wish. If wrecks were asked for in return for their offerings, then the occupants of St Agnes were in little doubt as to their saint's influence. Even the island church came about as a result of a wreck, said to have been built from the proceeds of a French vessel lost near Gorregan, but the bell which still calls the faithful to prayer tells a different story, its moulded inscription reading:

> *'Guten af a Billsten 1 Norrkopping - Fregate Skeppet Grefwe Lillieberg Bygt Pa.Halgerum - AR1781'.*

A literal translation of the original Swedish is something close to:

> *'I was moulded by A.Billsten of Norrkopping for the frigate ship Count Lilleberg, built at Helgerum in the year AD 1781'.*

The expression 'Fregate' does not imply a frigate warship, but an ordinary ship. There is a record in Sweden of this ship being built at Westerwik in 1781 and wrecked near

67

Stockholm that same year. How the bell reached St Agnes is unknown, possibly purchased second-hand by a Scillonian sea captain and brought to Scilly to be hung in the belfy of the St Agnes church, '- *built a few years since and completed internally in 1821'*, hence the bell was 40 years old when first rung on the island.

Offshore from the two islands can be found many reefs and rocks which reach up to the surface from deep water, some with names associated with wrecks long forgotten. Northwest of Annet lies an outcrop called Old Wreck, whilst off St Agnes can be found the Bristolman, Barrel of Butter, Spanish Ledges, Beady Pool and Boy's Rock, all of which have been the setting for some maritime disaster. The latter two are associated with the same wreck, though these names are not to be found on any chart or ordnance survey map since Beady Pool is really Wingletang Bay and Boy's Rock only an outcrop in the shallows. Long ago a large Venetian ship, carrying a general cargo which included glass and pottery beads for the natives of Africa, went ashore here and was lost with all hands. The body of a young boy, a member of her luckless crew, was found wedged against this particular rock, hence its local name. To this day, patient digging in the sandbanks above high-water mark may uncover some of the dark-brown, red and clear beads which were once part of this cargo. Over the years, sufficient have been recovered for the St Mary's museum to string into a necklace and put on display, and Old Town Café also has a good collection. From afar, the most prominent feature of St Agnes is the old lighthouse, now disused after two and a half centuries of continuous service. A squat, circular structure painted white, it showed a warning light to mariners from October 1680 until September 1911, when it was rendered obsolete by the Peninnis

▲ Beads found on the beach on St Agnes made into necklaces

18th century African trade beads found in Beady Pool, St Agnes, from an unidentified shipwreck. ▼

◀ St Agnes lighthouse, the 2nd oldest in Gt.Britain, built in 1680

beacon on neighboring St Mary's. The first proposal for a light at Scilly is thought to have been submitted in 1665 by Sir John Coryton of Newton Ferrers, but was denied him following strong opposition by the Trinity Brethren, This application by Sir John was refuted by the Lighthouse Commissioners in 1861, who insisted that the first was a three-fold application submitted in 1679 by a Sir John Clayton, the East India Company, and prominent merchants of the Port of London. Whatever the truth of the matter, Trinity House obtained the first patent, the three-storied building was erected, with surrounding keeper's houses, exhibiting its first light on 30 October 1680. The light was originally an open wood fire, then coal, burnt in a huge iron grate, or 'cresset' over a brick platform, to which was attached a pair of leather bellows to create the necessary draught. When lit the light was visible from Land's End, but there were many occasions when the fire was barely discernible from St Mary's, or went out completely, either by design or neglect on the part of the keeper.

In later years, the coal fire was replaced by oil burning Argand lamps, and the massive 'cresset' found its way to Tresco, where it can still be seen in the abbey grounds, unfortunately mounted upside down! Surprisingly, by 1790 the St Agnes light was altered to rotate, as the following newspaper account of 6 September shows:

'The improvement lately made in the light upon St Agnes, one of the islands of Scilly, is spoken of very highly by nautical men who have seen it, as very well calculated to answer the ends proposed; namely to give a stronger light, and to be distinguished from any other light in the Channel. The light makes a revolution once in a minute, and consequently shows itself like a brilliant star, or flash of lightening in every direction once in that period; a distinction that cannot be mistaken.'

The earliest wreck authenticated on St Agnes was that of a Dutch vessel, lost on Great Wingletang Rock in December 1720, along with her entire crew and cargo, after which it was not until 1917 that the Wingletang claimed a vessel of any note. This was the steamer *Italia* of Spezia, which went ashore the same dark, foggy night that sent another steamer, the *Lady Charlotte*, crashing on to the rocks at Porth Hellick, St Mary's, less than four miles to the E. Although the *Italia* went down under the Italian flag, she had for the greater part of her career flown the red ensign as the ss *Gulf of Florida*. Built for the Greenock Steamship Co by Hawthorn Leslie & Co of Newcastle in 1891, this 2,792- tons gross vessel joined a fleet of seven Gulf ships which included the *Gulf of Ancud* and the *Gulf of Panama*. Rigged as a two-masted schooner, the *Italia* was designed to carry six passengers and 63 crew, a phenomenal number for a relatively small ship. In 1910 she was bought by the Dall Orso Co of Genoa, who changed her name and port of registry. As the *Italia*, under Captain Aicaroi, she left Cardiff for Taranto with coal on 9 May 1917. Whilst groping around the Scillies on 11 May in dense fog, she went aground at 3.30pm in such a position that her stern almost touched the Great Wingletang Rock, her bow to the south-west. There was only one witness to the sinking of the *Italia*, a young girl on St Agnes picking wild flowers on Wingletang Down, who saw the dim outline of the wreck during a break in the fog. By the time the weather had cleared, the steamer had sunk and no one believed her story. Wreckage seen was presumed to have come from the *Lady Charlotte* and when finally the *Italia*'s crew, none of whom spoke English, reached St Mary's, it was assumed that their ship had been torpedoed offshore. Thereafter, the wreck lay undisturbed until 1964, when it was located and purchased by the author. Positive identification came from the evidence offered by the serial number of the ship's Walker log, an instrument which records the distance a ship has travelled through the water, and the name plate on her stern gun and live ammunition scattered around its mounting, which was salvaged by Royal Navy divers.

Brass name-plate from the stem gun of the ss.*Italia*, an Italian steamship lost on St Agnes in 1917, found by the author in 1964 ▶

▲ The 75mm stem gun, complete with mounting and barrel from the *Italia*, is loaded onto the *Scillonian* for transport to RNAS Culdrose, in Cornwall

Had the sea been anything but flat calm on 10 September 1951, the Wingletang Ledges would certainly have claimed the islands' packet steamer *Scillonian*. Feeling her way across from Penzance on a day excursion trip in thick fog, the packet missed the entrance to St Mary's Sound and went aground. Her 54 passengers were taken on to Hugh Town by the company launch *Kittern*, which also went ashore, this time on Rat Island, at the entrance to Hugh Town harbour. Fortunately, they managed to get off again with nothing worse than a badly damaged rudder, whilst the *Scillonian* floated clear at high water, none the worse for the incident, her second stranding in nine years. East from Wingletang, the sea shallows as it swings round into Wingletang Bay and on towards the sandbar linking St Agnes with the island of Gugh.

Apart from the early Venetian wreck already mentioned, the only other incident here was that of an unidentified Dutch vessel which stranded and sank during a SE gale in 1737, with the loss of her master and one seaman. On Gugh itself, another unidentified ship was lost with all hands in 1771, probably on Cuckolds Ledge, which the local wreckers got at, since one of her anchors was later found by a Customs Officer on Salakee Downs, hidden under a pile of stones. The brig *Leonie* went onto the Bow on 4 January 1846; a Caernarvon schooner struck south of the island in 1887 and a French trawler, the *Petit Jean Yves*, went ashore in 1961. The *Leonie*, laden with brandy for Liverpool and the Clyde, missed stays when entering and struck so heavily that her masts had to be cut down in order to get her off. The Caernarvon schooner was the *Bolina*, carrying 180-tons of slates from Port Madoc to London, and she became a total wreck on 12 January 1887 during an easterly gale, her crew being saved. The trawler *Petit Jean Yves* went aground near Cuckolds Carn on 9 March. The St Mary's lifeboat rescued her crew of five at night, returned them on board the next day and completed the service by successfully refloating the trawler on the next high water. Less than half a mile offshore from Gugh, to the east, lie the Spanish Ledges, marked with a bell-buoy since 1873 to ensure that ships pass them on the correct side. The proposal made by Benjamin Tucker in 1810 to make a large anchorage at Scilly would have linked Drop-Nose on Gugh with Round rock and Spanish Ledges by a huge breakwater, but nothing ever came of the idea. It is assumed that the reef derived its name from some early wreck connection, but surprisingly enough in view of its exposed position there are few recorded incidents here and only one total loss. On 13 October 1871, the French schooner *Lelia*, Neath to Rochelle with coal, went onto the ledges but managed to get clear.

The Fowey-owned schooner *Ranneys*, with coal from Cardiff for Palermo, also struck Spanish Ledges on 10 March 1874 and was saved, as was the *Queen Mab*, the largest of all these vessels, on 20 September 1903. The *Queen Mab* was a steel barque of 1,027 tons gross and the valiant efforts made to save her rank high among the many outstanding feats of salvage performed in Scilly. 105 days out from Punta Arenas, Chile, with fustic log-wood, this Glasgow-registered barque passed the Wolf Rock light-house during the early hours of 18 September 1903, tacking southward into the teeth of a strong south-easterly. By dawn the following day, the anticipated time of her arrival at Falmouth, the crew were still having to wear ship every watch and she was some 24 miles from her destination. By midnight the wind freshened to a full easterly gale and, having made no further progress towards Falmouth, Captain Boxhall turned towards Scilly. As they neared the islands, a pilot jack was flown but

◀ Artefacts from the ss *Italia*, the ship's log and spinner whose serial number identified the wreck; a 75mm shell case, oil lamp and pottery sherds

▲ After striking Spanish Ledges and only narrowly avoiding Bartholemew Ledges as she entered St May's Sound, the barque *Queen Mab* anchored off Samson on 20 September 1903 but was fast taking in water. She just made the shallows of Hugh Town harbour, watched by a great crowd

no gig came out in answer so the captain decided to make for the roads unaided. Approaching the deep channel between St Agnes and St Mary's with only her topsails set, the vessel failed to weather the Spanish Ledges and passed inside of the buoy, her crew all unaware of the extent of the underwater damage she was sustaining as she bumped and ground over the shoal.

As they cleared the reef, they were met by the St Agnes gig *0 & M*, whose coxswain saved the vessel from almost certain destruction on Bartholomew Ledges, another set of rocks just ahead of the Spanish Ledges. Captain Boxhall was advised to anchor his ship off the Tail of Samson in nine fathoms, and only then was it noticed that the sea was pouring into her hold. By 8am the water level inside the vessel had reached 8ft, and she was abandoned by all except her master and pilot Hicks. Shortly afterwards, the St Mary's lifeboat arrived alongside, whereupon the barque's crew reboarded and, assisted by the 13 local men, began pumping. The St Agnes lifeboat, *James & Caroline* also came out, having been launched with great difficulty by islanders wading waist deep at Periglis. Her crew also boarded the *Queen Mab* and with their assistance a second pump was got going. To encourage the men, Captain Boxhall offered them £2.10s per head if his vessel sank, but £56 if she could be kept afloat until beached. In the meantime, Mrs Boxhall and small son had been landed, along with valuables and the ship's papers, and a request had been made for the assistance of the island packet-steamer *Lyonnesse*. Unfortunately, she was aground in the harbour but as soon as the tide served the packet left Hugh Town and reached the distressed barque, now with 13ft of water in her hold. By now, the men aboard had been pumping continuously for five hours and were exhausted, but still kept the pumps going while Captain Tiddy of the *Lyonnesse* took the barque in tow and brought her into Hugh Town harbour where she went aground near the entrance. Men were put to work on her day and night, patching two holes and repairing underwater damage, while others recovered the anchors and cable she had slipped when taken in tow. Mr Banfield, the Lloyd's agent, inspected the vessel after she had been pumped dry and valued her hull at £4,500, her cargo at £2,729, with additional freight and materials at £1,070. All concerned were well rewarded for their services, and a notable feat of salvage happily ended on 7 October when the Falmouth tug *Triton* towed the *Queen Mab* away to Falmouth and then on to Le Havre.

Another incident involving Spanish Ledges occurred on 24 April 1882, when the barque *St Vincent* of London, Captain G.Melhuish, carrying 17 crew, struck heavily on the westward side of the reef but bore away for Crow Sound, only to sink at anchor in 12 fathoms off Tolls Island, near Pelistry. On passage from the West Indies and St Vincent for London with sugar, the 479 tons gross *St Vincent* had been built in 1867 by Clarke of Jersey, for a Mr. Sorulton of London. Mid-way between Gugh and St Mary's lie the Bartholomew Ledges, a rock outcrop with 40ft of water on three sides, but dangerously sited in the centre of an otherwise unobstructed fairway. The names of at least seven vessels which struck the ledges are recorded, but there must have been dozens of others whose names are forgotten. Amongst the fragments of

One of over sixty lead ingots, c1555 found on Bartholomew Ledge in 1974. ▶

Lead Ballast Weight From The Historic Wreck Site
On Bartholomew Ledge

wreck around the Ledges are the remains of what is the oldest known shipwreck in the Isles of Scilly. Discovered in 1978 by Michael Pirie, some 60 boat-shaped lead ingots weighing around 80lbs each were recovered, along with five tons of bronze bell fragments and other artefacts, before the site was protected by the Secretary of State as being of historic importance. The remains are of a small armed Spanish or Spanish/Netherlands cargo vessel, the evidence being 15 small breech loading cannon, several anchors, a number of silver two Reale coins of the reigns of Ferdinand & Isabella (1474-1504), Ferdinand and Johanna (1504-1506) and a silver 'Karolus-guilden' (Charlesguilder) of Charles V (1506-1555), sounding lead, shards, a lead gun apron, a pewter spoon and other artefacts.

There has been much speculation that the name of the still unidentified ship must have a connection with the name of the reef, ie:. Bartholomew. It has even been linked to a known vessel in the second Spanish Armada, the *San Bartolome*, but the Spanish archives confirm that whilst this vessel was indeed lost, it was no where near Scilly at the time. A vessel the size of this war galleon would have carried numerous heavy cannon, not the size and number of small breech loading guns found on the Bartholomew Ledge site. In 2004, Wessex Archaeology, on behalf of English Heritage, carried out a full underwater survey of the wreck remains and history, publishing a comprehensive report, a copy of which is available in the St Mary's Museum library, which also has a display of artefacts from the wreck site.

▲ As well as lead ingots, the wreck on Bartholomew Ledge, c1555, carried about 5-tons of bronze bell fragments, of which these are a small sample on display in St Mary's museum

The French steel trawler *Magdeleine*, which struck Bartholomew Ledge and sank in June 1906 ▶

On Christmas Eve 1788 two vessels were lost here, the Penzance brigantine *Duke of Cornwall* and the Chester brig *Betsy*. The former was the Duke of Cornwall's private tin ship, Captain Hoskin, carrying a general cargo from London to Falmouth. She had to be run ashore on St Agnes, where 'very little of her cargo was saved for the proprietors'. Shortly after her loss the following advertisement appeared in the Sherbourne Mercury newspaper:

'*Advertisment - Brigantine* Duke of Cornwall, *belonging to Penzance. All such persons as have goods on board the said vessel at the time she was wrecked on the Island of Scilly on her voyage from London to Falmouth and Penzance, and have not yet made their claims to the parts thereof which were salved from the said vessel, are desired to make and prove the same to William Carne, Penzance grocer, by 20th September 1788.*'

The *Betsy*, Captain Williams, Chester to London with lead ingots and empty casks, struck and carried on for a short distance, finally sinking between Bartholomew and Perconger. *Providence*, Captain Hoare, was a 99 ton Dartmouth schooner that hit the ledges on 29 December 1840 and had to be run ashore on St Agnes, whilst the Greek brig *Calliope*, Captain Consalapulo, Odessa to Falmouth, had to be put on the Garrison shore near Woolpack Battery in order to save the vessel on 30 October 1850. With her cargo ruined and hull badly damaged, the wreck of the *Calliope* was sold for £22.10s. An Irish schooner of Carrick-Fergus, the *Frances Jane*, Runcorn to Plymouth with salt, was another victim on 28 May 1870 but got off. Only the seventh and last victim left her hull plating to rust on the seabed around Bartholomew Ledges, this being the Boulogne steam-trawler *Magdaleine*. She entered St Mary's Roads in search of medical assistance for an injured seaman on 2 June 1906, and unwittingly passed the wrong side of the Ledges buoy. Fortunately, the tide being full, she cleared the rocks and reached the anchorage safely. The following day, on leaving for sea, Captain N. Gence made the same mistake again, took her inside of the buoy, between Bartholomew and St Agnes, and this time she struck heavily and foundered two hours later, her crew of 14 being saved, leaving her boilder and plating scattered across the reef. Closer inshore to Gugh and St Agnes, a London barque, *Belle of the South*, Davis master, struck Perconger Ledges during a heavy rain squall on 7 July 1871. Fortunately for the owners, there was a pilot aboard at the time that got her off and she ran for St Mary's making water fast. Beached near Hugh Town with 10ft of water in her, she was pumped out and laid alongside the pier where a piece of Perconger rock, 2ft long, was found embedded in her hull. On passage from London to Algoa Bay she was carrying a general cargo.

Other wreck incidents in the vicinity include the schooner *Anne & Jane* of Caernarvon, Captain Pritchard, which struck a rock north of St Agnes on 3 March 1853 while carrying slates from her home port to Perth. Local pilots assisted her to safety, a service for which they received £30. The *Integrity*, an Aberystwyth schooner of 98 tons net (sometimes quoted as the *Integrite*) was also aided by pilots who beached her in the vicinity of Perconger on 10 October 1878 after she had lost her foremast and longboat in heavy seas off the Bishop. Bound from Lisbon to Wicklow with lime phosphates, she became unmanageable in Smith Sound and drifted round the back of Annet before going ashore. Captain Evans and three of the crew were saved, but a fourth man was swept overboard and drowned. She floated off on 12 October and was taken to St Mary's pier. Whilst derelicts were not uncommon at sea, the crew of the St Mary's lifeboat, *Henry Dundas*, called out at 7.35pm on 12 January 1911, were surprised to find the French ketch *Georges*, of Auray, at anchor in the roads near St Agnes, with a light burning but no one aboard. Closer examination showed that the sea had flooded the cabin to floor level, and a smashed bulwark and broken rudder told their own story. The *Georges* had left Swansea on 10 January with 170 tons of coal for Trinite, but encountered a gale which carried away all her canvas and started a severe leak. After reaching St Mary's Sound in a sinking condition, her crew abandoned ship and landed safely on St Agnes, except for one man left behind who had a broken leg. Whilst at anchor overnight the ketch slowly filled, and by morning had gone down.

In 1753 a large unidentified vessel went ashore in Porth Killier the same day that the *Johanna* of Topsham, from her home port to Swansea to load coal, was wrecked on Little Smith. Another ship with a similar name, the *Lady Johanna*, Captain David Giston, is also believed to have been wrecked on the same rock on 2 February 1782. Burnt Island, which offered some protection for the old St Agnes lifeboat station from NW gales which howl straight down the north channel, has been the site of two losses. A collier with fuel for the lighthouse was totally wrecked here in 1764, and on 18 January 1881 an 82-ton French brigantine was found ashore abandoned. She was the 42-year-old wooden-hulled *Charlotte Dunbar* which had sailed from Newport for

Audierne with coal, then ran into a NE gale which reached hurricane force. Nothing more was ever heard of Captain Guillon or his five-man crew.

It is difficult to imagine a more unlikely place for a steamship to be wrecked than the narrow channel separating St Agnes from Annet, but it was here that the ss *Earl of Lonsdale*, Captain Llewellin Davis, was stranded at 3am on 8 June 1885. Owned by Thomas Dunford of Newcastle, the vessel's port of registry, the *Earl of Lonsdale* was carrying beans and cotton seed from Alexandria to Portishead. While steaming recklessly at full-speed in dense fog, the lookout on her forecastle sighted breakers ahead but no sooner had her course been altered than she struck a submerged rock and remained fast, her engine-room filling rapidly. Shortly after, the fog lifted and no one was more surprised than the captain to see the Troy Town maze and St Agnes lighthouse close at hand. He imagined his ship was at least ten miles S of the Bishop when she struck in Smith Sound. With her hull pierced in several places, salvage was out of the question and the 1,543-ton vessel, built at North Shields in 1872, had to be abandoned as a total loss. Four days later the wreck was sold by Mr J. Hooper, a shipbroker on St Mary's for £67 to a London purchaser, whilst 900-tons of her bean cargo was sold to a local, W. Rogers, for 22 shillings, who in turn sold them to local farmers. Within the month the wreck itself changed hands, bought by Vasey & Co of Newcastle, who were able to salvage such of the machinery as was worth removing

▲ The steamship *Earl of Lonsdale*, lost between St Agnes and Annet in June 1885

before the vessel broke in two on 27 August.

When the *Earl of Lonsdale* sank close to Long Point on St Agnes, it could easily have gone down on top of the wreck of the fireship *Firebrand*, one of the Royal Navy vessels lost on 22 October 1707 disaster. Of 268-tons, 92ft long and carrying eight cannon, she had been built at Limehouse, on the River Thames, in 1694. Near the head of the westernmost column of eight ships sailing in formation, as the three columns of ships blundered into the Western Rocks, the *Firebrand* struck a rock but managed to sail on despite massive underwater damage and leaking badly. Captain Francis Piercey successfully navigated past the islands of Gorregan and Trenemene, Melledgan and Muncoy Neck, heading for the welcoming St Agnes lighthouse. In Smith Sound, between Western Rock and Menglow she filled completely and went down in 75ft of water. Of her crew of 48 only 17 were saved, the master of the *Salisbury* which had sent out boats looking for survivors reporting:
'- the Romney *with one man saved, the* Firebrand *fireship with captain, lieutenant, boatswain, carpenter, surgeon and 15 men and boys saved.'*

This report suggests there were 20 survivors, whereas the ship's Neat Book states 17 who were eventually paid off by the Admiralty. Perhaps three survivors succumbed ashore? To Mark Groves' credit, the finder of the wreck, and Mark Horobin, who between them 'protected' the site of the *Firebrand*, it was little dived until 2007-8 when a proper survey was instigated. In truth, because of its condition, with timbers surviving and her complement of cannon complete, it was in better condition than any of the other 1707 wrecks, and should have been made a Protected Wreck. In 2007 a team of Bristol University Archaeological Department students led by their tutor, Kimberley Monk, commenced a full survey of the wreck. The same team under the guidance of Kevin Camidge of CISMAS (Cornwall & Isles of Scilly Marine Archaeological Society), carried on with the survey work in 2008, and in 2009 with an all CISMAS team, the survey was completed. Two particularly valuable artefacts were found on the wreck in the early days apart from the bell. These were an intact wooden nocturnal navigation instrument, which remains on Scilly, the other a silver porringer bowl, bearing the initials 'WP', once the property of Lieutenant William Probyn, one of the survivors of the wreck. This was auctioned by Christie's in 1998 with a guide price of £500-800 but realized £3,105. It was sold as a silver bleeding bowl, but this description is believed to have been incorrect.

South of St Agnes on the verge of Smith Sound, lie the Lethegus and Shooting Rocks which guard the entrance to St Warna's Cove. This area is littered with wreckage from ships two relatively modern steamers, whilst offshore possibly lie the remains of three large French men o'war and. The tactical value of Scilly as a base in French, Spanish of Dutch hands has fortunately never been put to the test, although Scillonians had repeatedly petitioned successive governments to increase the size of the Garrison in order to better defend the islands. Scilly has in fact only once been 'invaded,' which was during the Civil War. It may have come close to it on 10 October 1781 when it would appear that the French sent a small fleet of troop laden men o'war to capture the islands. The incident is shrouded in mystery and has received little prominence. If the known details are true, then in fact the Scillies witnessed a second naval disaster, equal in terms of lives lost if not worse, to that of Sir Clowdisley Shovell's disaster in 1707. Despite there being no tangible evidence of the event, a legend persists in Scillonian history that a French warship sank close in to the western most point of St Agnes in 1800. Escorted by a frigate, the larger vessel, said to be of 74 guns sank, leaving only a *'tricoloured pennant attached to a mast or staff showing above the surface to mark the grave of over 600 men'.*

Bodies are said to have been buried in mass graves on St Agnes, and the ship identified as *L 'Apollen*, but French records state she was probably lost off Land's End in May 1773, with all hands. A *Sherborne Mercury* newspaper report in March 1781 states clearly that the French *Conquerant*, 3rd rate, 74 guns and 700 men; *Le Priarus*, 3rd rate, 74 guns, 600 men, and the 5th rate *Julie*, a 44 gun frigate with 340 men, were lost off the Isles of Scilly, with all on board, a total of 1,640 seamen. Leading up to this statement, are a number of intelligence reports and sightings of the French fleet in the Channel, and these three ships can be found frequently included in ship lists of the enemy, yet strangely research into French navy records in the Bibliotech Nationale in Paris, suggests two of those ship names were not in use at the time, and the *Conquerant* still in service post 1781. There is probably some truth in all this, in which case there could be French bronze cannon and artefacts lying on the seabed awaiting discovery.

Although re-location of the wreck sites of the *Association* and *Eagle* in 1967 with their gold and silver excited the imagination of those interested in treasure hunting, an even greater prize remained undiscovered off Annet until 1971. The evidence had long been in print. Lieutenant Robert Heath, a military officer at the Garrison of St Mary's wrote in his book, *'An Account of the Islands of Scilly,'* published in 1750:

'About the year 1743, a Dutch East India-man, outward bound was lost off St Agnes in about twenty or twenty-two fathoms of water, with all the people. Their firing of guns, as a signal of distress, was heard in the night; but none could give them assistance. Many of their bodies floated ashore at St Mary's and other islands, where they were buried by the inhabitants, and some were taken up floating upon the tide and buried. A Dutch lady with her children, and servants, going to her husband, an East India Governor, was prevented seeing of him by this unhappy accident. A diver thereupon was sent, by the Dutch merchants, to discover and weigh the plate of considerable value. But the tide running strong at bottom, and the sea appearing thick, the diver could not see distinctly through the glass of his engine so returned without success. This wreck remains as a booty for those who can find it.'

A brass military cartridge case, issued by the Dutch East India Company to their soldiers, found on the wreck of the *Hollandia*. Also a naval cap badge and uniform brass button ▶

It is quite remarkable that Heath, writing the above account only seven years after the event, was seemingly unaware of the ship's name or the date of the wreck. The ship was in fact the *Hollandia*, Captain Jan Kelder, which sank on her maiden voyage on 3 July 1743, with the loss of all on board. She carried 276 crew, passengers and troops, plus a valuable general cargo of lead and trade goods, as well as military stores and silver specie. Heath stated that she had been lost off St Agnes, whereas the Rev. Woodley insisted she struck the Gunners and sank nearby. In fact both men were very close to the truth. However, a third reference implied that the 'mystery' Dutchman sank much closer to St Mary's, which reads:

'We spread our sails to the wind and ran gaily through St Mary's Pool, a little further on is the rock on which the Dutch East Indiaman struck and went to pieces with 250,000 in silver guilders, many of which have been and still are, picked up.'

One possible explanation is that the author of this reference mixed up the East Indiaman wreck with that of the *Triumph* on the Steval, St Mary's, in 1736. Her specie treasure was gold, not silver, and had literally been found in the shallows, and certainly no one had picked up any of the silver guilders from the *Hollandia*, she lay far too deep.

Whilst many thousands of people must have read Heath's account of the wreck, only Rex Cowan, assisted by his wife Zeldie, believed in it sufficiently

◀ Brass military mortar weapon, one of a pair carried on board the *Hollandia* as cargo, destined for Batavia.

◀ Five carved and decorated eating knife handles from the *Hollandia*

to research the incident in the Hague archives of the Netherlands, and ultimately to locate and salvage that vast treasure. Possibly the most unlikely candidate to ever become a seeker of sunken treasure, Rex Cowan was at the time a solicitor in a London practice, with no professional sea experience, was not a diver, and had never been involved with shipwreck before. To his credit, he never once gave up the long and expensive search which he funded over the best part of three years before the wreck was found, the first of four successful projects for him in the Isles of Scilly and

elsewhere. In point of fact, the team's metal detecting magnetometer sensor or 'fish' passed over the *Hollandia* site in 1969/70 but the signal trace was considered too small to be a shipwreck and was ignored. After failing to find the wreck over a long period, a re-run over all the minor targets on 16 September 1971 gave a pronounced reading in the vicinity of George Peter's Ledge, west of Annet. A diver went down, and the elusive Dutch East Indiaman was found, which more than justified Heath's comment, *'This wreck remains a booty for those who can find it'*. A small display of material from the *Hollandia* can be seen in the Isles of Scilly Museum in Hugh Town.

▲ Glass onion bottle, used for wines or spirits, found on the wreck of the *Hollandia*

The *Hollandia* had been built in Amsterdam in 1742, displaced 700-tons and carried 32 cannon. Outward bound for Batavia, modern day Jakatra, her cargo included 129,700 guilders in silver coin, a mix of Pillar Dollars, Silver Riders and Reales. She carried several important passengers including the brother of Gustaaf Willem Baron van Imhoff, the Dutch Governor-General of the East Indies, with the former's wife and sister-in-law, who belonged to the aristrocratic Bentinck family of Bevervoerde. Amongst the many items recovered were bronze cannon bearing the monogram VOC (Dutch East India Company) on the breech surmounted by the letter

▲ The original salvage team examining silver coins and pewter plates from the wreck of the *Hollandia*. The team leader, Rex Cowan, is in the centre touching the coins

'A' indicating the Amsterdam chapter of the company from whence the ship originated. One of these guns, a 6-pdr with an inscribed band marked 'CLAUDY FREMY ME FECIT AMSTELODAMIA.1694' and the engraved number 1640, probably its weight in Dutch pounds, complete with scrolled dolphin handles, was sold in April 1972 by Sotherby & Co at auction to the late James Close for £2,000, who added it to an already extensive collection. On his death the same cannon was offered for sale by Dreweatts in July 2009. With an estimated price of £4,000-6000, it was sold for £15,000. Other major items of armament found in the wreck included two bronze 16pdr land service mortars cast by Ciprianus Crans of Amsterdam, and a bronze 2pdr breech-loading swivel gun.

A Padstow brig, the 336-ton *Valuna*, Captain James Vowden, went ashore on the S side of St Agnes during dense fog on 1 June 1857 (the Board of Trade Wreck Register gives the date incorrectly as 8 June) whilst in ballast from Falmouth for Quebec. Bosun Hodgson was on watch when she struck, and he and the rest of the crew managed to struggle ashore, leaving the *Valuna*, owned by Thomas Seaton of Padstow, built in 1826 at Nova Scotia, to go to pieces in the surf. Another sailing ship to be lost here was the Danish brigantine *Nellie*, of Elsinore, which struck first on Jacky's Rock, out amongst the Western Rocks on 26 March 1886. Part of the vessel drifted onto Annet, the remainder into St Warna's cove. Launched at St Johns, New Brunswick, in 1870 as the *Julia Lingley*, this 316-ton wooden vessel had been in collision west of Scilly and had driven helpless before a full SW gale into the Western Rocks. The 2nd mate and four seamen, who managed to reach Melledgan after three hours on a raft, were forced to quench their thirst with puffins' blood until rescued by a local gig. Later, one seaman and the ship's carpenter were saved after having clung to part of the wreck for 16 hours. Commanded by Captain M. Svendsen, who lost his life in the wreck along with his chief officer, the *Nellie* was on passage from Bordeaux to Cardiff with pit props. Lethegus rocks, which claimed a wine-laden Dutch galliot in 1764 is best known for its steamship wrecks, the first of which occurred in 1909. This led to the remarkable coincidence referred to in Chapter 1, two steamships sitting on the seabed, piled one upon the other like broken toys in a nightmare of twisted steel.

The ss *Plympton* of London, a Commercial Steamship Company vessel, was the first of the two to sink, after going ashore in thick fog on 14 August while carrying maize in bags from Villa Constitution to Dublin, via Falmouth. Her arrival was not exactly unannounced, since she steamed head-long onto the rocks with her fog siren going full blast. An old gig, the *Dolly Varden*, was launched from Porthcressa and after searching around Gugh and the Wingletang area found the *Plympton* with her bows hard and fast ashore, listing heavily to port. After her crew of 23 had been landed, the islanders set about the age-old practice of stripping the wreck. That

▲ The ss *Plympton*, sinking on the Lethegus Reef on 14 August 1909. She later capsized drowning two local men

afternoon, whilst work was still in progress, the flood tide gently lifted the steamer off the rocks, and without warning she fell on her port side and sank, leaving only the bow section above water. Two local men, Charles Mumford of St Mary's and Charles Hicks of St Agnes, were sucked down by the wreck and drowned, several others having lucky escapes; one in particular, a visitor to Scilly named Ormrod, was actually inside the deckhouse when the steamer capsized. He went down with her but managed to escape through a porthole and reached the surface still clutching his trophy, the saloon steward's dinner bell! It was said at the time that his hair turned completely white as a result of the experience. Built for Furness, Withy & Co of West Hartlepool in 1893, the *Plympton*, 314 ft in length and of 2,869 tons gross was declared a total loss, her value for insurance purposes being set at £ 16,000, her cargo an additional £25,000. A Cornish newspaper report of the incident stated that:

'The position is bad and it is doubtful if any further salvage will be possible,. Her after part lies in 15 fathoms, her bows sticking up almost perpendicular and very dangerous'.

The final act in this drama occurred on 2 December 1920, when the big German steamship *Hathor*, of 7,060 tons gross, sank right across the wreck of the *Plympton* at the base of Lethegus Rocks. Built by J.C. Tecklenborg & Co, at Geestemunde in 1912, the *Hathor* of Hamburg had been interned in a Chilean port for the duration of World War I, during which time her machinery suffered badly from neglect. After the war she was released, loaded with nitrate of soda and oil cake at Arica and sailed for

▲ The bow of the ss *Plympton* photographed shortly before she turned completely over and disappeared

◀ A deck winch lying in 30m depth on the deck of *Hathor*, which sank on top of the ss.*Plympton*

Portland but broke down off the Azores. Whilst under tow of two German tugs, she was abandoned in a gale off Scilly after the towing hawsers parted. The St Mary's lifeboat *Elsie* went out in response to her distress call and found the steamer with both anchors down, dragging towards the shore. Only her five officers were still on board, the other 19 members of the crew having taken to the boats. After she had drifted on to the Lethegus, the officers were taken off in a difficult and dangerous rescue, one of them having a very lucky escape after falling between the ship's side and the lifeboat. He was saved from certain death by the prompt action of Bob Ellis, a member of the lifeboat crew, who thrust the first thing to hand into the fast narrowing gap. The improvised fender turned out to be a personal bundle belonging to the *Hathor*'s captain, who thereby lost his clothes, papers, instruments and the ship's chronometer. Forty-six years later that same chronometer was found and brought to the surface by a Royal Navy diver, its gold-plated hands stopped for eternity at three minutes to eleven. The *Hathor* took her cargo to the bottom and little or no salvage was ever carried out on either of the two ships. Underwater the scene is indescribable, with a propeller and huge sections of ships rearing up from the seabed, boilers garlanded with anchor cable, shafting and connecting rods crossed with masts and derricks. The bow section of the *Plympton*, which in a photograph taken just before she sank clearly shows her bell hanging behind the windlass, now lies upside down and still intact, whilst the stem of the *Hathor* remains upright in 100ft (30m) of water, a single kedge anchor davit overhanging the rusting deck rail.

Due west from Priglis Bay

Scrap copper and brass, including the ship's compass binnacle and an engine-room telegraph from the ss. *Hathor* ▶

across Smith Sound, lies Annet, uninhabited except for vast numbers of seabirds for whom the island is a sanctuary. Whilst St Agnes and Annet are very much a part of one another, it is the latter which offers the visitor the first real foretaste of the Western Rocks. The *Financier*, John Lobec master, Charlestown to London with rice, tobacco and indigo, was lost here on 5 September 1783; also the Admiralty 6th rate, 28 gun *Pegasus* of 594 tons, went ashore on Annet on 8 July 1790 but got off on the flood tide undamaged. Hellweathers, an aptly named area and the scene of many small wrecks, claimed the 150-ton Spanish brig *Providencia*, Captain Telerman, a wool ship from St Andero for Bristol, on 2 October 1821 during a NW gale accompanied by rain whose cargo worth £10,000 was valued at only a third of that amount. The very next day, the Bryher owned boat, the *Hero*, with 21 men aboard, was smashed to pieces by heavy seas whilst working cargo out of the Spaniard. Almost every able-bodied male and boat at Scilly was employed in recovering and landing the bales of wool, originally valued at £10 a ton but reduced to only £3 after a soaking in salt water.

Around dawn on 22 February 1839, in response to urgent signals from the St Agnes lighthouse, local boats went out amongst the Western Rocks and found a vessel wrecked on the Ranneys, half a mile W of Annet. Oranges and casks of wine lay thick on the surface, but only 25 casks and a small quantity of fruit were recovered before the tide turned and swept the remainder out to sea. Papers recovered from amongst the wreckage showed the ship to be the 165-ton brig *Hannah Louisa* of Poole, Captain H.Moore. Homeward bound from Lisbon, she was lost with all hands.

▲ Lost in fog in July 1879, the iron barque *River Lune* was wrecked on Brothers Rock, without loss of life

Muncoy Neck, the channel between Melledgan and Annet, is no place for a large vessel even in fine weather, let alone dense fog. On 27 July 1879, the 1,172 tons iron barque *River Lune* of Liverpool, in ballast from Lorient to Ardrossen in Scotland, was groping her way past the islands when the lookouts sighted rocks ahead and then on both sides. Captain George West ordered the helm hard down but she struck on Brothers Rock in coming round and began to sink. Her crew of 20 hastily abandoned ship when her stern went completely underwater, but re-boarded later to collect personal belongings and some ship's fittings. At the subsequent Board of Trade inquiry, the master blamed his chronometer for inaccurate navigation, his calculations and log-book entries showing his position as being at least ten or fifteen miles west of the Bishop light. Built at Wallsend in 1868, the *River Lune* was owned by John Hargrove of Chapel Street, Liverpool, and when sold the wreck fetched only £55. Her figurehead was recovered intact and can be seen in the Valhalla collection of figureheads on Tresco.

Another barque, also in ballast, the *Bernardo* of Genoa, went ashore at the back of Annet on 11 March 1888. This 701-ton Italian vessel in ballast had lost all her sails during a WNW gale and completely helpless, was blown ashore. Although one boat was launched, it quickly capsized in the heavy sea drowning all its crew. Captain Andrew Dapelo, who had remained on board, was forced to swim for his life when the vessel broke up beneath him, and managed to reach Old Woman Rock, to which he clung until rescued by fishermen. The 13-year-old *Bernardo*, owned by G.B Degregori of Camogli, Italy, quickly went to pieces and nothing of value was saved. The 34-ton smack *Porth* of Padstow, Captain John Billing, although much smaller was another wreck in the same area on 10 March 1891, the night of the 'Great Blizzard' that caused so much havoc in the West Country, the worst storm for 200 years. With a crew of three, she had sailed from Swansea on 2 March with 60 tons of culm destined for St Colomb Minor. After wasting six days sheltering in Mumbles, she sailed at 4pm on the 8th, but during the following night both gangways, the cookhouse and water-closet were washed away in the gale, her only boat was stove in and the ship's bulwarks damaged. Whilst entering St Mary's Roads via Broad Sound, she ran ashore on the Minmanueth Rocks. The 10 oared St Agnes lifeboat *James & Caroline* rescued the master and his son, but the third member of the crew, Charles Boxer, was found frozen to death high above the tide line.

In 1907 there occurred a wreck which has become a legend amongst seafarers and certainly amongst the islanders of Scilly. This was the gigantic steel schooner *Thomas W Lawson*, one of the largest pure sailing vessels the world has known and certainly the largest vessel to be wrecked here, until comparatively recent years. The *Lawson*, to use the name by which she became known locally, began her relatively short career on the slipway of the Fore River Engineering Co of Quincy, Massachusetts in 1902. Built at a time when sail was battling with steam for survival, she was an attempt to prove that huge sailing vessels with small crews were both practical and more economical, in comparison to their dirty, smoke-belching rivals. Her tonnage and other statistics were impressive to say the least. She was 395ft in length and carried 25 sails totaling 40,612 sq ft of canvas on seven masts when under full spread. Her tonnage, 5,218 tons gross, 4,914 net and 5,006 under deck – combined to give her a deadweight cargo capacity of 7,500 tons and an overall displacement of over 10,000 tons, the vessel being entirely wind-driven. Any steamer of comparable size would have carried a crew numbering between 35 to 50, whilst a conventional full-rigged ship would certainly have had 28, yet the *Lawson* managed with only 18! Designed to be worked by a minimum crew, there were many mechanical aids on deck, including donkey engines at the foot of each mast. This made it unnecessary for men to go aloft to work sail, and greatly facilitated the handling of yards, sheets and braces.

Her last voyage began on 20 November 1907 when, under the command of Captain Geoffrey Dow, the huge vessel left Philadelphia for London with almost 2,250,000 gallons of paraffin oil in drums, valued at £40,000. In crossing the Atlantic, two bad gales in succession were encountered, so that upon sighting Scilly not a single boat remained intact on its chocks and she had only six serviceable sails left. On Friday, 13 December 1907, a traditionally unlucky day, the *Lawson* reached the

▲ The largest sailing schooner ever built, the *T W Lawson* was lost on 14 December 1907 off Annet

▲ All that could be seen of the 5,218-ton *T W Lawson* the morning after she parted her anchor cables and drove ashore

Bishop Rock but due to a tidal set, found herself well inside of the lighthouse and virtually trapped within the Western Rocks. The schooner was brought to anchor in Broad Sound, where it was anticipated she would ride out the NW gale. Ashore, her plight had not gone unnoticed, since the St Agnes lifeboat was launched and reached the sailing vessel at 5pm. To the surprise of the lifeboat's coxswain, Captain Dow refused his offer of assistance and only reluctantly accepted the services of William Cook Hicks, known locally as Billy Cook, a Trinity House pilot. The St Mary's lifeboat also put out, but broke her mast under the stern of the *Lawson* when going alongside and had to return, taking with her orders to telegraph Falmouth for tugs. As the wind freshened from the N, so the seas increased, and soon the St Agnes lifeboat was forced to leave, not only on account of the weather conditions but also because one of the crew had collapsed and was in urgent need of medical attention. As they pulled clear of the pitching schooner, the final instructions given to Billy Cook were for him to burn a flare if the situation deteriorated further or the services of the lifeboat were again required. Between 2.30 and 2.50am on Saturday, 14 December, it was noticed that the schooner's lights had vanished, but since no flare had been lit it was assumed that all was well on board. In fact, the *Thomas W Lawson* had already become a total loss but no one ashore knew that, and in complete darkness the watchers on St Agnes could only maintain their anxious vigil.

Daybreak revealed a mass of floating wreckage around St Agnes and Annet, the fate of the world's largest schooner very apparent. Regardless of personal danger in the appallingly high seas which were then running, a volunteer crew speedily launched the six-oared gig *Slippen* to search the outlying rocks and islands for survivors. Manned by eight men from St Agnes, five named Hicks, the gig put out and soon men could be seen on Annet, but the sea was far too rough to reach them. Later when a landing was possible, only corpses were found at first, but a further search found a seaman, George Allen of Battersea, injured but alive, and he was quickly taken to St Agnes. That afternoon the *Slippen*, still manned by the same crew put to sea again, rowing as far as Hellweathers. where two more survivors were found. These proved to be Captain Dow and the *Lawson's* engineer, Edward Rowe of Boston, both of whom were saved after a heroic rescue by Frederick Cook Hicks, the eldest son of the pilot who had lost his life in the wreck. Freddie Cook swam a line to the injured men through raging surf, bringing them back one at a time. Jack Hicks, the last survivor of the crew that manned the *Slippen* that day until his recent death, was presented with a gold watch by the United States government for his service in the St Agnes lifeboat. Each member of the gig's crew received a gold medal, and it is fitting that the old *Slippen* herself has not been forgotten. Refitted, the gig has found a permanent home on the mainland at Newquay, where it is held in trust. The full story of the wreck was pieced together from the two survivors.

After the St Agnes lifeboat had left the moored vessel, the gale increased until it reached 90 mph. At about 1.15am, first the port cable parted, then the starboard and the *Lawson* was adrift and being blown towards Annet. Captain Dow, the engineer, the mate, a steward and pilot Hicks all took to the mizzen rigging. Less than fifteen minutes later the vessel struck west of Carn Irish. She then broke in two between No's 4 and 5 holds and collapsed on her starboard side on Shag Rock, throwing all

◀ A wooden tub once filled with petroleum carried as cargo on board the T W Lawson, along with light lubricating oil and paraffin

Gold medal awarded by the President of the United States of America to William Cook Hicks of St Agnes, for saving three men from the *T W Lawson* shipwreck ▶

on board into the sea. Until recently it was accepted that the wreck occurred on the outside of Minmanueth, to the west of the Haycocks, but this was not the case. The wreck of the *Thomas W Lawson* was successfully relocated in 1969, when her two sections were found almost a quarter of a mile apart, the bow section to the NE of Shag Rock, the stern to the SW, both in 45ft (15m) of water.

Melledgan, a small uninhabited island one mile south of Annet, has claimed three vessels. One was a ship whose name is unrecorded, carrying mahogany from the Bay of Honduras to London which went ashore here in 1733, the only survivors her captain and one seaman. They drifted around on a raft for two days before getting ashore on Kitten Rock, north of Gugh, where they were found days later. The second was a Dutchman, loaded with wine and paper, which was lost on the Biggal of Melledgan in 1760, while the third, the 350-ton Swedish brig *Charlotte*, foundered on Christmas Day 1848. Loaded with deals and balk timber from Gothenburg for Montevideo, the *Charlotte's* captain named Stanwitz,, the mate, two seamen and a passenger all lost their lives when she struck. The ten survivors erected a rough tent on the rock where they spent a bleak and cheerless night before the flag they had hoisted on a spar was sighted, and they were rescued by a passing boat. Whilst the wreck locations of the fifty or so ships already mentioned are reasonably well documented, as in other parts of Scilly, there have been many incidents with only a vague geographical location. Reports in local newspapers or Customs Records of such incidents state merely 'lost off St Agnes', or, 'ashore amongst the Western Rocks', but since this book seeks to be a faithful record they too must receive a mention. One such vessel was the brigantine *Eagle* of Charlestown, USA, Captain John Rosseter, laden with tobacco, rice and staves, ashore near St Agnes on 5 June 1790. Others include the *Harriet & John*, sloop of 69 tons, Captain Baker, who was also her owner, ashore November 1810, and the *Thais* of Penzance, 29 October 1815, both of which were saved. A schooner, the *York* of Chichester, Captain James Farthing, carrying a cargo of oranges from Seville to London, was lost with all hands on 4 February 1822; the *Fair Ellen* went ashore, but was saved later on 7 September 1826, and two local

◀ Anchors lie scattered on the seabed amongst the Western Rocks, on an unidentified wreck site

pilot boats were wrecked in the same area early in January 1831. An unidentified schooner was lost on St Agnes on 2 April 1841; the Swedish brig *Aegir*, of Gelf, Malaga to St Petersburg with olive oil, struck on 1 May 1864, but was refloated the same day, and the *Hydra*, a barque, was another victim on 6 February 1866. On the 13th of the same month, the French schooner *Dauphine* sailed from Scilly but caught fire two hours later and became a total loss, her hulk eventually drifting onto St Agnes, not far from the spot where seven years later, on 15 March 1873, the *Elizabeth* was lost with all hands. Details of her loss were given in the *Cornish Telegraph* newspaper, which read:

'A quantity of wreckage was washed ashore on the island of St Agnes on the 16th consisting of cabin doors, cupboard doors, tables etc; also some pieces of deck planking, a broken oar, and a small piece of a ship's boat, resembling the wreckage of an English coasting vessel. Part of a name board was also washed ashore on the island of St Martin's about the same time with the name ELIZABETH carved in and gilded on a blue back-ground, leaving no doubt that a small coasting vessel has been lately wrecked near the islands. Jetsam picked up near Mount Todden, St Mary's, includes part of a ship's headboard with the letters ELI- on it'.

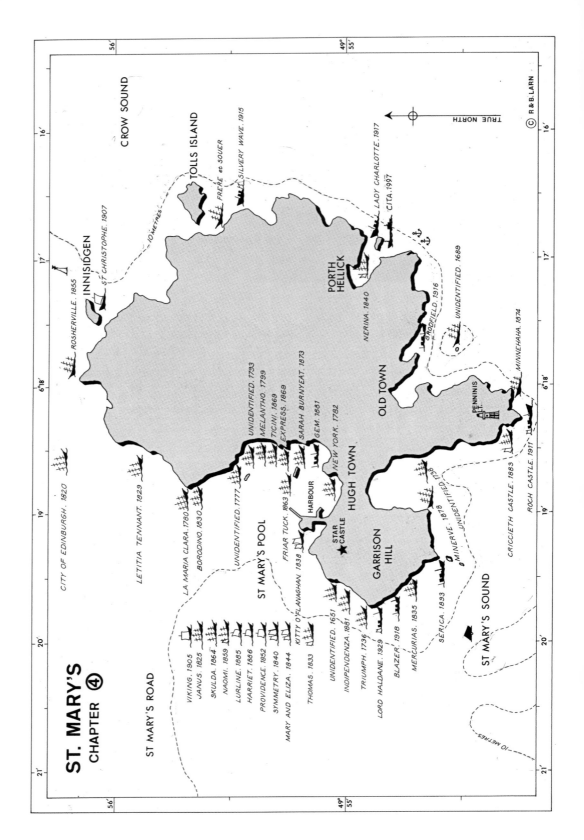

ST. MARY'S
CHAPTER 4

CROW SOUND

TOLLS ISLAND

INNISIDGEN

ST MARY'S ROAD

ST MARY'S POOL

HUGH TOWN
HARBOUR
STAR CASTLE
GARRISON HILL

OLD TOWN

PORTH HELLICK

ST MARY'S SOUND

PENNINIS

TRUE NORTH

© R & B. LARN

ROSHERVILLE. 1855
ST CHRISTOPHE. 1907
CITY OF EDINBURGH. 1820
LETITIA TENNANT. 1829
LA MARIA CLARA. 1780
BORODINO. 1830
UNIDENTIFIED. 1777
UNIDENTIFIED. 1793
MELANTHO. 1799
TICINI. 1869
EXPRESS. 1869
SARAH BURNYEAT. 1873
GEM. 1881
NEW YORK. 1782
FRIAR TUCK. 1863
KITTY O'FLANAGHAN. 1838
VIKING. 1905
JANUS. 1825
SKULDA. 1864
NAOMI. 1859
LURLINE. 1885
HARRIET. 1886
PROVIDENCE. 1852
SYMMETRY. 1840
MARY AND ELIZA. 1844
THOMAS. 1833
UNIDENTIFIED. 1651
INDIPENDENZA. 1881
TRIUMPH. 1736
LORD HALDANE. 1929
BLAZER. 1918
MERCURIAS. 1835
SERICA. 1893
MINERVE. 1818
UNIDENTIFIED. 1736
CRICCIETH CASTLE. 1883
ROCH CASTLE. 1911
MINNEHAHA. 1874
UNIDENTIFIED. 1689
BRODFIELD. 1916
NERINA. 1840
LADY CHARLOTTE. 1917
CITA. 1997
FRERE et SOUER
SILVERY WAVE. 1915

56'   16'   17'   6°18'   19'   20'   21'

49° 55'

4 - St Mary's – 'a meatley strong pile'

The largest of all the islands, St Mary's became the centre or 'capital' of Scilly not solely on the merits of physical size but because it offered the best anchorages. It receives a measure of protection on three sides from other islands in the group, making St Mary's Roads and Pool sheltered havens for shipping, with easy access to the open sea. Another anchorage, known as Old Town Bay, which is completely open to the SE, was for centuries the chief landing place and main settlement on St Mary's, then known as Hencastle or Heyugcastle. A sod battery with cannon on Tolman Point, backed up by Ennor Castle overlooking the town, offered protection from a seaward attack, and it was to the latter fortification that Leyland referred when he commented: *'St Mary's, a five mile or more in cumpace, it is a poore town and a meately strong pile, but the rofs of the buildings in it be sore defacid and woren'.*

The gradual decline of the old town in favour of the newer Hugh Town was brought about by the building of Star Castle in 1592-3 and the need for a larger and better protected anchorage, though legend says that it was the result of a curse placed upon Richard, Earl of Cornwall, for murdering a man of the church. Monks residing at Holy Vale were said to levy a toll on all boats and persons landing, and controlled a chain boom from Tolman across the entrance. The Earl of Cornwall, upon hearing of this, disguised himself as a pilgrim and when refused permission to land unless he paid the fee, leapt over the barrier and struck the prior a mortal blow. Whether by curse or circumstances, Ennor certainly did fall into disuse. Two of the sod-battery guns were removed in 1767, the third about 1820, and Old Town gradually dropped into the background of events. There are, unfortunately, no reliable records of very early wrecks in this area, though dozens of small sailing vessels must have been lost on the headlands, on either side or merely been blown ashore. The Reverend Troutbeck briefly dismisses wrecks by saying *'Church Ledge Bay and Church Ledges, many vessels lost here, deep water all round'.* An unidentified transport vessel, outward bound, was lost on or near the Old Town Gilstone in 1689, having struck the Woolpack, south of Star Castle, and iron cannon and anchors have been located by divers on the seabed to support the story. One of these cannon was raised in 1964, but no identifying marks remained and due to its poor condition disintegrated shortly after for want of conservation treatment.

A mystery 'wreck', if indeed this was a 'cargo' in the first place relates to a unique collection of 'anchor stones' found by Mark Groves of Old Town, off Gull Rock at the entrance to Old Town Bay. There are several different names for these, including 'sea-stones' and 'killicks' which are not uncommon items but have never been found in such proliferation at one location. These stones totaling some 28-30 in number are

◀ A stone anchor of indeterminate age, found with a large number of anchor stones in Old Town Bay

a mixture of granite, slate and basalt, all with a deep hand worked 'groove' around them to take a rope or line. The same site also yielded two triangular anchor stones sufficiently large to hold a vessel of some 15-tons, but why a craft would have been carrying so many 'anchor stones' is unclear, and unfortunately it is impossible to date them. However, the triangular anchor stones on the site suggest it could be medieval, and hence at least 5-600 years old.

One of the better-known wrecks on St Mary's occurred at Peninnis, between the Point and Pulpit Rock. This was the 845-ton wooden ship *Minnehaha* of Liverpool, Captain Jones, which had reached Falmouth on 16 January 1874 from Callao in Peru with a cargo of guano, then sailed for Dublin to discharge the following day. The weather deteriorated badly after she left, and soon a hard NW gale was blowing. At 3am on Sunday, 18 January, a light seen ahead through the murk was assumed to be the Wolf Rock, and the captain ordered the helm to be put

◀ Stone 'killick' or anchor, with groove to take a rope, one of dozens found by Mark Groves, on what may be an early wreck site in Old Town Bay

▲ The 845-ton ship *Minnehaha* of Liverpool, wrecked under Peninnis Head on 18 January 1874

down. The Channel pilot, Captain David Volk of Falmouth, shortly afterwards countermanded this order without the captain's knowledge, and within minutes the vessel struck on the SE corner of Peninnis, amongst the Jolly Rocks. She went ashore with all sail set, almost on top of the tide, and thumped the rocks so hard that a large hole appeared in her port bow, into which the sea poured. Within two minutes she was under water, and those who had not been swept away took to the rigging. Captain Jones undressed in the mizzen-top and shouting *'With God's help I will save your lives'* jumped into the sea and was last seen swimming for the shore. Robert Thomas, the first mate, led the nine remaining survivors from the mizzen to the main shrouds, down the forestay and over the jib-boom onto the rocks. Shortly afterwards they met one of the islanders, Israel Pender, in King Edward's Lane and told him of the wreck, the islands first knowledge of the tragedy. The pilot, Captain Volk, who had survived a narrow escape in the Austrian brig *Slaven* under Pentire Cliffs, Padstow, in March 1869, was drowned, along with the captain of the *Minnehaha* and several members of the crew. Had they followed the mate's example and waited in the rigging until daybreak, all would no doubt have been saved. Owned by Messrs Hughes of Menai, and built at St Johns, New Brunswick, in 1857, the *Minnehaha* had been 14 months on passage from South America and was uninsured. Almost two months after the wreck, on Sunday 15 March, Captain Yolk's body was recovered from the sea off St Eval cliffs, near Padstow. His funeral in Falmouth was attended by a large number of fellow Channel pilots and local officials. On 3 April that same year, the *Belle*, a Plymouth barge, dragged her anchors when a gale blew up whilst she was salvaging timbers from the *Minnehaha* and was driven ashore, but managed to get off again. The *Minnehaha's* bell has now found a permanent resting-place in the Isles of Scilly Museum, having been located and raised by a diver in 1964.

Another tragic loss close at hand was that of the Port Madoc brig *Criccieth Castle*, 233-tons, built at Port Madoc by Morris Owen in 1876, which struck on the SW corner of Peninnis between the Murrs and the Inner Head on 9 February 1883. Bound from Fray Bentos to Liverpool via Falmouth with patent guano, she left Carrick Roads on 2 February, only to hit the rocks on Scilly and sink leaving no survivors out of her crew of six. Three bodies were later found; that of the 17 year-old black Santa Cruz cook, James Ruban, her master James Morris of Barmouth, and her Falmouth pilot. Identification of the wreck was made from a lifebelt marked 'CC. Port Madoc', and some papers found floating whilst her timbers were strewn the width of Portcressa beach. A considerable amount of wreckage still lies on the seabed hard up against the steep cliff-face between the Murrs and The Chair, and although it has not been possible to identify them with certainty, a number of items raised by divers in 1964, including sounding leads, copper hull fastenings, brass fittings and an anchor, were probably from this particular wreck.

A more modern vessel, the Swansea steam trawler *Roche Castle*, also struck Peninnis on 14 April 1911 in fog. Loaded with 30- tons of dried fish from Morocco for Hull, she was refloated and taken into port the following mornmg. At the mouth of Porthcressa lies an outcrop known as Nicholl's Rocks, which took their name from the captain of a vessel bound to Le Harve with wheat, which was blown ashore here and wrecked on 28 April 1738. An earlier wreck, still unidentified under Morning Point, the location of the sewer outfall for St Mary's, left a number of iron cannon scattered in the shallows, amongst which have been found many lead and iron ingots. A French lugger, the *Henri Letour*, Newport to Basac Indre, also went ashore in Porthcressa Bay, but was towed off by pilots, as was the Whitehaven brigantine *Emily Burnyeat* in fog on 23 May 1873, while carrying copper ore from Lalasa for Swansea. Initial attempts by the tug *Guide* to refloat her that day were unsuccessful, but she was got off next day on the top of the tide. Previously, her sister-ship, the *Sarah Burnyeat*, a Whitehaven barque had gone aground in Porth Loo under Harry's Walls, the site of an unfinished 16th-century fortification. On passage from Madras to London with cotton, hides and skins, the *Sarah Burnyeat* was ashore for two days before being refloated by the *Queen of the Bay*. In 1880, a ship's name-board bearing the word *Voltri* in gilt lettering on a blue background was found on Porthcressa beach one morning, assumed to have come from a wreck out in the Western Rocks. Gigs carried out a search of the islands, but nothing more was ever found.

On New Year's Eve, two years prior, on 31 December 1878, a particularly severe SW gale caused the anchor cables of the French brigantine *Minerve* of St Malo, Captain

Jean Budiguet, to part and she drove ashore. All seven crew were saved, six by the local Coastguard LSA crew and one by boat. By morning the vessel, bound from Swansea to Cadiz with coal, had gone to pieces 150 yds off Morning Point. Going back to Old Town Bay, the long stretch of coast on the north side between Church Point and Porth Minick, holds not only the remains of several small sailing ships but also the rusting plates of the ss *Brodfield*. Owned by the Brodfield Steamship Co of Holland House, London and 3,567-tons, she was employed as an Admiralty auxiliary supply ship and had left Le Havre for Barry in ballast on 11 November 1916 with a crew of 70 under Captain Hubert Rowland of Birkenhead. Despite the German U-boat campaign being at its peak she sailed alone without escort, following a route recommended by the local naval authorities, making her best speed until she encountered fog off Start Point, south Devon, which dictated a reduction to seven knots. Shortly after dark, soundings were taken and showed 42 fathoms with a sandy bottom and a second at midnight showed 49 fathoms. At 2.50am on 13 November the fog thickened and speed was further reduced, the ship's siren blaring out its mournful warning. On the bridge were the captain and the 2nd Mate, whilst a seaman had been posted in the foremast crow's nest and two apprentices stood lookouts on the forecastle head; it was the latter who first sighted cliffs dead ahead.

Although their warning shout came in time for the engine to be put to full-astern, it was too late to stop the ship driving ashore and grounding heavily on the rocks beneath Blue Carn. Her boats were lowered and the crew mustered, while the carpenter went round sounding the double-bottom tanks, finding the forepeak and No 1 hold leaking badly and slowly filling. Soundings around the hull showed five fathoms towards the bow and 15 astern. A radio message was sent asking for immediate assistance from tugs, after which the tank-top covers on No's 3 and 4 holds were removed so that they could be flooded to counterbalance the bow section and lift the ship clear of the rocks. By 6am the fog had lifted, and at 7.30am on the top of the tide, the engine was re-started in an attempt to pull the ship off. As the water boiled around her thrashing propeller, she began to swing slowly to port and even a hastily-rigged kedge anchor failed to check the swing, and the ship ended up beam on to the shore, bumping and rolling heavily in the surf. By 8am several naval patrol vessels arrived on the scene and attempted a tow, but without success and later, even with assistance from five other vessels and her own engine she remained fast aground. A salvage crew arrived from the mainland and worked on her for three days until a gale forced them to leave. It freshened rapidly and during the night of 16-17 November the *Brodfield* broke in two and became a total loss. A steel-hulled, schooner-rigged steamship, she had been built at Hawthorn Leslie's yard at Hebburn in 1899 as the *Surrey*, then sold to the Blue Star Line in 1915 and renamed. At the enquiry held on 17 November her captain was cleared of all blame, the stranding being attributed to bad visibility as the result of fog.

Continuing east towards Porth Hellick Point, Porth Loggos is known to have been the scene of a wreck in 1771, an unidentified ship carrying salt. Wreckers got to work on her and the Customs Officer was hard pressed to stop looting. Later, one of her anchors was found half a mile away buried under stones on Salakee Down. There is also evidence to support the story of another, larger shipwreck in the vicinity, since two huge anchors, their wooden stocks long since eaten away, lie embedded in the sand bottom between Church Porth and Newfoundland Point. Even so, two anchors do not necessarily mean a shipwreck, and may have simply been abandoned when their cables were cut in some long-forgotten incident. The quiet sheltered waters of Porth Hellick, where the body of Sir Clowdisley Shovell came ashore and was buried in 1707, may seem remote from disaster but in fact it was here that a large steamer, the ss *Lady Charlotte* was lost in 1917, also the French brig *Nerina* came ashore here in 1840, bottom up with three men and a boy still alive inside her hull. The 114-ton *Nerina* of Dunkirk had sailed from her home port on 31 October 1840, commanded by Captain Pierre Everaert. She was bound for Marseilles with a cargo of canvas and oil, and carried a crew of six in addition to the captain's 14-year-old nephew, Nicholas Nissen.

During the early hours of Monday 16 November, a gale forced her to heave-to about 30 miles SW of Scilly. Four hours later, still under only a close-reefed main topsail and mainsail, she was struck by a very large sea and turned completely over. Only one man was on deck at the time, a seaman named Bourneard, who disappeared. Meanwhile, inside the forecastle, two seamen, Vincent and Vantire, were able to hang on to the windlass bitts, draw themselves up to the keelson and keep their heads above water. A third man with them, Jeanne Marie, somehow got entangled and drowned after thrashing about violently for a time. In the capsize, the cargo had fallen towards the inverted deckhead, distorting the bulkhead between forecastle and hold, so that Vincent and Vantire were able to work their way aft the length of the vessel, towards the sound of voices they could hear. Captain Everaert, the mate Jean Gallo, and young Nicholas were all below in the cabin when the ship turned turtle and became trapped inside. The mate opened a hatch in the deck, cleared away some empty casks which enabled them to scramble into the narrow space, where they were joined shortly afterwards by the two seamen from the forecastle. There was no light in their shallow prison other than that reflected dimly through the sea and cabin skylight and, forced to sit waist-deep in water with necks bent, their only relief was to take it in turns to stretch full length and relieve cramped and frozen limbs.

For two days and nights they endured this awful torture, without food or water, quenching their thirst by chewing bark from the casks. As time wore on and the air became more foul they were threatened with suffocation, and the mate, who had been working on the hull with a knife, re-doubled his efforts to make a hole. Fortunately, the knife blade broke before he could succeed, otherwise the trapped air would have escaped and the vessel would have sunk. During the night of Wednesday 18 November, it came on to blow and the inverted hull was tossed around like a cork. Vincent, caught by an upsurge of water, lost his hold and fell out through the cabin hatch and drowned, whilst the remainder scrambled towards the bow. Shortly afterwards, it was noticed that the water level had fallen, then rocks were seen underwater through the cabin roof and the *Nerina* became fast onshore. Unbeknown to the survivors, the brig had drifted ashore at Porth Hellick about midnight and lay there until 7am on the Thursday, when an islander found her high and dry. Approaching the hull, he pushed his hand through a hole in her quarter and was terrified when he felt it grasped and held firm from the inside. Local farmers cut her hull open with axes, liberating the survivors who had by then been trapped inside for three days and nights. Later, it was learnt that the *Nerina* had in fact been sighted about a mile offshore the previous afternoon and taken in tow by two pilot-boats. However, the lines had parted in rough seas and she had been abandoned with little more than her keel showing. Had the wreck not been taken in tow and brought that much closer to the islands, the ebb tide would almost certainly have carried her out into the Atlantic.

The other wreck incident connected with Porth Hellick concerned the 3,593-ton steamer *Lady Charlotte* (ex.*Aphrodite*) of London. Carrying coal from Cardiff to Alexandria, she went ashore in dense fog only a matter of hours before the ss *Italia* struck the Wingletang, both on the same day, 11 May 1917. Owned by the Redcroft Steam Navigation Co of Newcastle, the *Lady Charlotte* had originally been named *Aphrodite*, built by the Tyne Iron Steamboat Co in 1905. The wreck broke up and her coal cargo was abandoned, a welcome 'gift' to the people of Scilly in wartime. An enterprising sport diver decided there was money to be made out of the remaining coal in 1987-8 when the price of fuel shot up, and laboriously recovered many tons and sold it by the sack full. The trouble was it was not domestic coal but 'steam' coal intended for ship use, which burns at a much higher temperature, resulting in several domestic fire grates and stoves being badly damaged!

The last shipwreck on Scilly to date was the mv. *Cita*, on 26 March 1997, which made more than a lasting impression on the islands since it carried a general cargo the like of which no one could remember - not even the ss *Minnehaha* which stranded on Scilly Rock on 18 April 1910, carried such a variety of goods. After this liner went aground, remaining ashore for 23 days before being refloated, it was said that there had never been such a bounty of general cargo. However, there were two important distinctions between these two wrecks, apart from the time scale. In 1910 there would have been a diligent Customs Officer/Receiver of Wreck stationed on St Mary's, who would have made every attempt to stop any pilfering of wreck goods, backed up by Coastguards and the local constabulary, all attempting to ensure that everything that came off the wreck was declared. Hence any sewing machines, carpets, pencils, shop-tills, motor cars etc. from the *Minnehaha* that found their way into local homes illegally would have been kept well hidden, otherwise they would be seized, followed by possible prosecution. With the *Cita*, things were entirely different. With neither Customs nor a Receiver of Wreck resident on Scilly and only one regular Coastguard Officer, who had recently retired and left the islands, enforcement was minimal. In 1910 wreck goods had to be actually handed to HM. Customs who locked them up in the 'Queen's Warehouse' on St Mary's, whereas today salvors have only to complete a form, ROW/1, and post it off to the Receiver's office in Southampton, undertaking to hold the goods until otherwise instructed. Hence there was no legal enforcement, nor were properties searched for undeclared goods. Anyone could recover anything and sit on it at home, provided it was declared on paper.

▲ The container feeder ship *Cita* ashore and half submerged on Newfoundland Point, St Mary's, on 26 March 1997

The mv. *Cita* was built in Germany in 1977 as the *John Wulff* then changed her name and flag in 1983, becoming the *Lagarfoss*, registered at St John's, Antigua and Barbuda, then in 1996 became the *Cita*. A container feeder ship capable of carrying 128 units, she was 3,083-tonnes gross, 90.53m long, fitted with a single 3 x cylinder engine, and single variable pitch stainless steel propeller, with an additional bow thrust propeller. She carried an all Polish crew of seven under Captain Jjerzy Wojtkow, and was on passage from Southampton to Belfast. It transpired that the crew were exhausted after working very long hours, and were all in their bunks asleep as the ship reached Land's End, except for the Mate, on watch on the bridge alone. He switched off the radar alarm, engaged the ship's automatic pilot then promptly fell fast asleep in the watch chair, to be rudely awoken when she drove ashore at 14 knots.

The very nature of the *Cita's* general cargo which was worth some £10 million, was greatly reduced following immersion in the sea. Leaf tobacco in huge zipped up bags worth about £1 million and wine in bottles were the only dutiable commodity in the cargo, the tobacco being collected by HM. Customs, transhipped to Plymouth on a barge and burnt, the container of wine sinking and has seemingly never been found. A large quantity of butane gas cylinders, unaffected by immersion, were shipped back to the owners. Thousands of items of Marks & Spencer's clothing floating in the sea, could never be recovered and sold hence was of no use to the company; similarly trainer shoes, Ben Sherman shirts, Big Bertha golf-bags, computers, Action man toys, fridge magnets, work overalls etc. had no second hand commercial value. Only the thousands of vehicle tyres, fork-lift trucks, memorial grave stones and the like had any value after recovery. The manufacturer's of the golf bags and a few other manufactured items bought them back for a nominal sum, to prevent them finding their way onto the market, but in general the insurance companies appeared disinterested.

Some of the general cargo items carried on the *Cita* when she was wrecked. Other items included grave stones, fork lift trucks, car tyres, golf bags, childrens clothing etc. ▶

Hence Scillonian's and islanders alike assisted the authorities in what could best be described as a *'voluntary beach clean up'*, in most cases retaining what they found without fear of prosecution. After the event, when the police sergeant was asked how many ROW/1 forms had been completed he replied, 'Oh, hundreds, but I never knew there were so many people living here named 'Robert Dorrien-Smith'', who of course is the tenant of the island of Tresco! The threat of oil pollution saw Smit Tak appointed salvors who removed 60-tonnes of bunker fuel and 30-tonnes of light diesel using the vessel *Salvage Chief*, and the UK Marine Pollution Control Unit was mobilized who sent to the islands special tracked, all terrain beach cleaning vehicles. With the very real possibility of an ecological and economic disaster on the islands at the beginning of the holiday season, the Isles of Scilly Crisis Management Team, led by the islands Chief Executive and the Maritime Officer, Steve Watt, assisted by Captain Keith Hart of Aquarius International Consultants Ltd, who represented the underwriters, dealt with the many problems as they arose, and a potentially catastrophic situation was averted. Once the threat of oil pollution had been successfully dealt with, floating bulk-gas cylinders, cargo containers and bales of tobacco were dragged up on Porth Mellon beach, which became a common collection point.

Following the wrecking of the *Cita* at 3.35am, when she reported to the Falmouth Maritime Rescue Co-ordination Centre that she was aground at Lat.49 54.7N; Long. 06 16.7W, she remained half awash, her bow on Newfoundland Point, leaning over to starboard, her stern overhanging 45m of water. It had been forecast at an early stage that should the fine weather change she would break in two, which happened overnight on Monday 7 April, her stern lying partially on its port side, with a gap of some 30m between her bow and stern sections, having sheared off just forward of her superstructure. Her location, almost parallel with and close to the remains of the ss. *Lady Charlotte* shipwreck, will attract sport divers for many years to come.

Two small steamships on Admiralty Fleet Messenger Service, HMS *Turquoise*, No.30 and HMS *Nugget*, No.38, thought to have been lost offshore from St Mary's on 31 July 1915, were in fact sunk by U-boat gunfire at roughly 49 05N; 06 58W. The 486-ton *Turquoise* of Glasgow, acting under sealed orders from Glasgow, was 60 miles SW of Bishop Rock when attacked at 4pm without warning. Abandoned immediately, she sank 15 minutes later, her chief-engineer killed by gunfire with two seamen wounded. The smaller, 405-ton *Nugget*, also of Glasgow but from the Dardanelles, was ordered to stop 15 miles further NE, probably by the same U-boat, at 7.30pm. Turning on her attacker, the *Nugget* attempted unsuccessfully to ram her opponent, but after 15 shells had been fired into her hull the crew decided to give up and abandoned ship, being picked up by the Dutch sailing vessel *Annetta*, landing at St Mary's the following day. Pelistry Bay, sheltering behind Tolls Island, saw the wreck of the French chassemaree *Frere et Soeur*, Captain Constant Legien, Swansea to Charlestown in Cornwall with coal, was driven ashore by the same blizzard that

▲ One of two steamships wrecked on Scilly in fog during the same night, the *Lady Charlotte* was lost near Porth Hellick

sent the Padstow smack Porth on to the rocks at St Agnes in March 1891. Of the five Frenchmen aboard only the master and his brother, the mate, were saved.

Further to the north round St Mary's, a 15-ton wooden cutter named *St Christophe* of Camaret, France, was lost on Innisidgen on 16 October 1907, her crew of five landing safely, while on 16 October 1820 the American ship *City of Edinburgh*, from St Johns, New Brunswick, to London, dragged her anchors from the lee of Samson Island and drifted over to Little Crow Rock. Badly damaged by high seas, she fell over on her side and would have been lost but for the local pilots who managed to warp her to the harbour 'pool' three days later. The brig *Rosherville* of London, bound for Jamaica, Captain Brabyn, was at anchor in the Roads discharging some of her cargo of rice, beer, wine and brandy when, at 5pm on 3 March 1855, she caught fire, her anchor hawser burnt through and she drifted ashore at Pendrathen, near Bar Point. Most of her crew were ashore at the time and by the following day the tide had extinguished the flames, leaving only a gutted hulk. Creeb Rock and Carn Moval Point have been the setting for several incidents, usually involving vessels which dragged their anchors in the 'pool' or St Mary's Roads. The French brig *La Maria Clara*, which was carrying timber when captured and taken prize by a Jersey privateer, went ashore on Carn Morval on 30 December 1780, and the *Letitia Tennant* of Stromness, Limerick to London, finished up on the Creeb on 14 April 1829. The following February, a Dutch barque, the *Borodino*, Captain Haines, carrying oil, oak, ivory and gold-dust from Sierra Leone to Milford, dragged onto Carn Morval whilst wind bound in the Roads. An unidentified transport vessel on passage from Boston to Portsmouth with wounded soldiers also dragged and went ashore on Taylor's Island on 4 December 1777, and a French prize-ship followed her in 1793. Taylor's Island also saw the two-funneled Scilly packet steamer *Lyonesse* ashore during thick fog on 22 June 1900, but she was more fortunate than most and was off again that same day.

From here the coastline of St Mary's swings into Porthloo, Sharks Pit, Porth Mellon and finally Hugh Town harbour, a natural anchorage that historically was known as St Mary's Pool. Its use is now restricted almost entirely to movements of the current passenger/cargo ferry RMV *Scillonian* III, which uses the port on a daily basis in the summer season, the cargo ship mv *Gry Maritha*, and local and visiting small craft, but it was once a busy and thriving port. Ships from the far corners of the world lay at anchor out in St Mary's Roads, or else discharged cargo alongside the old quay built by Frances Godolphin in 1601, or the more modern extension started by the Duke of Leeds and completed by Augustus Smith, or 'Emperor' Smith as he was known locally. Four shipyards operated on the towns two beaches having started on Holgates Green with a 12-ton sloop, the *Happy Return* in 1779, until killed off by a lack of orders for wooden vessels and the inability of the islands to build iron ships. At first, locally-built vessels rarely exceeded 40-60 tons, mostly schooners and sloops which were used extensively in the Mediterranean trade, bringing back fruit from the Azores, Spain and Portugal. By 1839 there were 20 sizeable ships registered at St Mary's, all engaged in foreign trade, and the great boom in shipbuilding that followed saw vessels of 300 tons or more on local slipways. Porthcressa also had two yards, owned by the Gluyas and Stediford families, the last vessel to be launched there being the barque *David Auterson* on 12 September 1870, which only the following day went aground in New Grimsby Channel, fortunately with only slight damage to her hull sheathing. The Hugh Town yards managed to survive until the early 1880s and closed only after completing two smacks for the east coast trade, the *Fortuna* and the *Queen of the Isles*.

The beach and sandy shallows of Porthloo are deceptive, and whilst one might imagine any vessel driven ashore here would stand every chance of being saved, in fact several have become total wrecks. A 400-ton West Indiaman, the *Melantho*, Captain Richard Hardie, went ashore here early in February 1801 but was saved, the only casualty being her 23-year-old captain who drowned after falling from a rock. The French barque *Ticina*, with a cargo of oil and nuts, became a total loss on the beach in 1869, and another French barque, the *Express* of Marseilles, on 15 December that same year. Her cargo of pistachio nuts from Rio Congo for Caen was salvaged but the vessel herself was lost. An unusual double-ended paddle-steamer of Liverpool, the *Gem*, owned by John Lander of Birkenhead, was another victim of

Porthloo. Although only a small ship of 118-tons gross, she was on passage from Holyhead for the Brass River, in Africa, with 37-tons of coal as ballast. Her captain was George Gibson, and she carried a crew of 14. A serious leak was discovered on 31 October 1881 and she had to be beached at St Ives on the north coast of Cornwall for examination. By 21 November she was moored to a buoy in St Mary's 'pool' but the cable parted during the night and she drifted ashore to become a total loss.

The closing days of November 1863 saw a sudden deterioration in the weather conditions, which brought some 500 sailing ships into St Mary's Roads for shelter. Amongst them was the 662 tons gross tea clipper *Friar Tuck* of Liverpool, which arrived on the 27th of the month from Foo-Chow-Foo with a full cargo of tea, two of her three masts 'sprung' and the body of the ship's carpenter who had recently died at sea. By the last day of November the elements had erupted into a hurricane from the NW that left a trail of havoc throughout the country, and saw six vessels wrecked or in distress in Scilly alone. These were the *Friar Tuck*; the *Euphemie*, Cardiff to Nantes with coal, sunk by accident in shallow water; the *Adolphe*, also with coal for Nantes, sunk by collision in St Helen's Pool; the Falmouth schooner *Oscar*, ashore on St Helen's; and the brigs *Diana* and *Lavinia*, both ashore on Rat Island, the former being subsequently refloated, whilst the latter, Quebec to Southampton carrying timber, after her mast was cut down was brought alongside the quay on 8 December and repaired. The *Friar Tuck* parted her cables and went ashore on Newford Island

at the height of the storm on 2 December, where Captain Fordyce ordered her masts to be cut away. A rocket line was fired across the wreck by Coastguards from ashore and her crew of 22 were rescued. Salvage work was started as soon as the weather moderated, and three small shiploads of tea, in addition to spars, sails, hawsers and ship's stores, were sent to London. The

◀ Childrens Marks & Spencer clothing from the wreck of the *Cita* was still being washed ashore in Porthcressa in 2004

islanders, however, were not going to miss the heaven sent opportunity of a little something from the sea for themselves and large quantities of the tea found its way into local hands. Launched at Aberdeen in 1857 and owned by J. Beasley, of Red Cross Street, Liverpool, the *Friar Tuck* had been a very profitable ship for her owners, having made a gross profit of £12,389 over her last six voyages.

Many years later during November 1943, a flat-bottomed assault vessel belonging to a different age, Landing Craft Tank No 354, went ashore in exactly the same spot but survived to take an active part in the WW2. D-Day landings in Normandy. Porth Mellon has seen a large number of sailing ships ashore, the majority of which were got off, but some became total losses, including the brig *New York* of London, Captain William Baker, in 1782. On passage from London to Antigua with pork, beef and biscuit, she was wrecked while attempting to leave St Mary's harbour. An Aberyst-wyth schooner, the *Naomi*, parted her cables in the 'pool' and went ashore on 1 November 1859 but, almost incredibly, was successfully warped the 700yds necessary to get her afloat again and so was saved. The brigantine *Skulda* of Sweden put into Scilly on 4 October 1864, discharged cargo and effected repairs, but on leaving on 26 November was driven ashore and lost. In 1885, the cutter *Lurline* of Jersey was put onto the beach on 5 November, and on 18 October 1886 the *Harriet*, a Bristol coasting schooner, broke from her moorings alongside the old quay and drove ashore on Porth Mellon, but was saved. A French lobster ketch, the *Guiding Star*, parted her cables after being fouled by the steam-trawler *St Clyde* whilst at anchor on 1 September 1908. She fetched up on Porth Mellon beach along with the crabbers *Fils De L'Humanite*, *Souf Frances* and *L'Etoile Polaire*, all of which were successfully refloated on 8 September. Carn Thomas, the location of the St Mary's lifeboat station, saw a sloop on the rocks on 23 October 1820; the revenue cutter *Providence* on 11 August 1852; the schooner, *Symmetry*, from Gloucester on 4 February 1840, and the *Mary & Eliza*, a London schooner, Captain Tregarthen, on 9 October 1844. The *Mary & Eliza* was carrying smoked herrings from her home port to Cadiz and Gibraltar and her crew was rescued by the recently introduced Dennett's rocket apparatus, its first recorded use by Coastguards on Scilly. After the wreck had gone to pieces on the rocks, her remains were sold for £9.1s. Yet another wreck in the 'pool' area was the *Janus* of North Shields on 14 February 1825. When the original Hugh Town jetty was extended, it was taken out to and beyond Rat Island, a large outcrop originally named after its rodent population. Leyland's description of Rat Island reads:
' *There is one isles of the Scylles cawled Rat Island, yn which be so many rattes that, yf a horse or any other lyving best be brought thyther, they devore hym.'*

The rats may not have completely disappeared, but are certainly neither as prolific nor hungry! The only total wreck to occur here was the locally-owned *Kitty O'Flanaghan*, a schooner, on 14 February 1838. The *Mary Roberts* also managed to get herself clear after grounding on Bacon Ledges on 19 October 1888, just outside the harbour, but a one-ton wooden cutter, the *Viking*, which went ashore here on 10 March 1905 was wrecked with the loss of one life. The packet-steamer *Scillonian* was very nearly another victim on 5 August 1932, but succeeded in warping herself free with the aid of her kedge anchor after only one and a half hours aground. Offshore from the Star Castle in a NW direction can be found Woodcocks Ledge, where the Fowey brig *Thomas*, Captain Edward Nicholls, after sinking in seven fathoms during a bad SE gale on 23 February 1833, was subsequently weighed and beached on 11 June. Closer inshore, the rocky outcrop known as the Barrel of Butter claimed the *Indipendenza* of Recco, a Genoan barque, in 1881. Steering SSE under plain sail her pilot, William Ouzman, thought his charge was safely SW of Scilly by at least 15 miles. No observations had been possible since leaving Lundy due to the weather, but soundings had been taken regularly, showing an average depth of between 42 and 48 fathoms. Minutes later and still in fog, breakers were sighted ahead and the barque struck heavily four times in quick succession on the Crim Rocks. She was hauled off but struck yet again at 3pm on 24 September, this time remaining fast on the rocks for about five minutes during which time the water level in the hold rose to 6ft. After she had floated clear, Captain Fillipo Caffarena bore up for Scilly through Broad Sound heading towards the Roads, but she was leaking so badly her crew of 14 were soon forced to abandon ship. After rowing around within sight of her for some time then deciding that she was not going to sink after all, the crew re-boarded but were not happy with her condition, so disembarked for the second time and rowed alongside their ship as she slowly drifted down on to the shore and was wrecked. Her cargo of 1,200 tons of hides, horn and guano spilled out, and in a difficult position for salvage, most of it was lost on the tide, leaving St Mary's Pool thick with floating horns at one stage.

Not far from the Barrel of Butter can be found the Steval Rock, notorious for the wreck of the richly-laden *Triumph*, Captain William Cross, which went ashore during a storm on 9 October 1736. From Jamaica to London with rum, sugar and dye-wood, she carried in addition £10,000 in gold coins, which was scattered amongst the rocks of the Garrison shore. Her captain, bo'sun, carpenter and several seamen were drowned after jumping into the sea, while those who remained on board, including the mate and the surgeon were saved. Troutbeck, in his book *'Isles of Scilly'* recorded: *'Some bags of gold were brought ashore, and lives were lost in trying to save the £10,000 on board. A considerable quantity was saved,, and with much rich furniture was divided amongst the salvors. The accident was said to be owing to the ill conduct of the crew intoxicating themselves with rum at coming into the soundings and the thick weather, by account of those who escaped.'*

The wrecking of the 200-ton ship *Mercury* on the Garrison shore on 23 February 1791 began amongst the Western Rocks, then moved to St Agnes and finally St Mary's, as the following account from the *Sherbourne Mercury* newspaper relates:

'On Wednesday the 23rd ultimo about 3 o'clock in the morning, the ship Mercury, *of Boston in America, upwards of 200-tons burthen and about 18 months old, Meally master, from George Town in Maryland to London laden with tobacco and staves, struck on some of the Western Rocks, soon after filled and overset. The master and crew took to the yawl, and all landed safely on St.Agnes island, where the light-house stands. In the morning, soon after daylight, the wind shifting suddenly from south south west to north west, blowing a strong gale with the tide co-operating, the ship was cast on shore on her beam ends, near the town and garrison of St Mary's, but on a very unfavourable spot to save and land the tobacco, which of course, must be extremely damaged. Of the ship there is no hope, she must beat to pieces. Some materials will be saved, and with the property, secured from plunder.'*

A far more fortunate encounter here was that of a mackerel-laden trawler, the 91 ton ss *Lord Haldane* of Lowestoft, owned by the Lowestoft Steam Herring Drifter Co, which went ashore on 20 March 1929 later towed off by the St Mary's lifeboat. Close to Conger Ledge, and well inshore of the wreck symbol shown on Admiralty chart No 883, can be found the remains of a very old 283 ton steam tug HMS. *Blazer* (ex-*Charm*) of Liverpool, built by S.M. Knight of Ayr in 1888. She sank on 10 November 1918 and became notorious locally in 1966 when divers found live ammunition on board. The Garrison shore has seen innumerable wrecks including the *Mecurius*, Captain Esink, a large Dutch East Indiaman, on 19 January 1835, whilst amongst those fortunate enough to be saved were the *Good Intent*, Captain Lefevre, Waterford to Lisbon, aground on the Woolpack Rock on 6 March 1809; the schooner

▲ Although looking like a luxury steam yacht, the *Serica* was a working vessel carrying coal cargo when wrecked on St Mary's in 1893

Vesper also on the Woolpack on 1 May 1844, and the ketch *Charles Francis*, owned by William Mumford of Scilly but registered at Plymouth, which struck but later floated off on 23 February 1898. The final wreck incident in this chapter, although dozens have perforce been omitted, was the ss *Serica*, a particularly fine, steel screw, schooner-rigged steamer of 1,736 tons. Her last voyage began at Cardiff on 16 November 1893, when she left for Port Said with a crew of 25 and a cargo of coal. Bad weather was encountered the following day off Hartland Point, and by dawn on the 18th the *Serica* was in trouble when a storm ripped the tarpaulin covers from off No's 3 and 4 holds, flooded the main cabin and swept away everything that was movable abaft the bridge. Her captain, Sydney Smith, had a remarkable escape in that he was washed clean overboard twice, and twice was flung back aboard by the sea. The *Serica* eventually reached Scilly on the 19th in a distressed condition with pumps choked, serious damage on deck, and a heavy list. To quote the words of the local Receiver of Wreck at the time, *'the only wonder is that the vessel kept afloat'*. On 24 November following repairs, the *Serica* left St Mary's at low water to continue her voyage but struck a rock and had to be run ashore 150yds NNW of the Woolpack beacon, opposite the Woolpack battery. She was abandoned almost immediately and only minor salvage was ever carried out on the wreck, all work ceasing on 3 January 1894. The rock the *Serica* struck was in fact marked as lying in 48ft but was later found to be in less than 24ft. It's doubtful if it was any consolation to her owners, but that rock was given the name of the ship and today is marked on navigational charts as the Serica Rock.

Auction sales of wrecked and stranded ships were frequently held on St Mary's, that of the ship *Sophie* on 8 July 1784 being typical. This was not the first *Sophie* lost on Scilly, since there was a famous barque lost on Tresco in 1896 by the same name. An earlier one was advertised in the *Sherbourne Mercury* newspaper as:

'For sale on Thursday the 8th day of July next, by public auction, at the house of Mr William Edwards, by 2 o'clock in the afternoon, the hull of the ship Sophie, *burthen about 350 tons, lately stranded here in her passage from Wyberg to Liverpool, now lying on St Mary's beach. Immediately after her sale, will be sold her masts and bowsprit, yards, topmasts, windlass and pump, with all her standing and running rigging, sails, cables, anchors and other stores in which she greatly abounds, most of which are very good, particularly her sails and one sheet cable, new. Also a new longboat, burthen about 8 tons and a yawl. The whole may be viewed any time before the date of the sale, and catalogues be had by applying to Captain Alexander Sandland at St Mary's aforesaid. St Mary's, Scilly, June 4, 1784.'*

What is surprising about this particular sale is that William Edwards was already a shipbuilder on the Strand, St Mary's, so begs the question why was he selling this vessel which appears to be intact, but with all its rigging, stores and fittings separate, rather than as a going concern? Shipbuilding started on Scilly in 1774 and by 1784 six ships had been completed. The following year, 1785, an entire cargo was being offered for sale:

'For sale by public auction, for exportation, at the above place on Monday the 10th March next, and on the following days, for cash or bank notes, the cargo of the schooner Phoenix, *Capt, Gilbert L. Chrystie, lately stranded here bound from Amsterdam to Philadelphia and Baltimore in North America, consisting of different merchandise, viz: cordage, mercury, haberdashery, stationery, drapery, hats, steel, looking-glasses, hardware etc. with a variety of other articles too tedious to be inserted here. The same to be viewed 3 days previous to the sale, at the stores of Mr. Thomas Philips, Steward at Scilly, where attendance will be given by Messrs. Levy and Marcus.'*

Other early auctions of wreck cargo include one held on 19 March 1814 at the house of Mr. James John, on St Mary's. which included:

'250 baskets of cheese; 8 bales of damaged paste board; 3 bales of hare-skins, containing 1,500 skins in total; 1 small case containing about 500 pieces of ribbon; 200 silk handkerchiefs; 230 yards of lace, 18 scarves and several dresses.'

Another related to the cargo of the ship *Mary*, stranded within the islands of Scilly on her voyage from Oporto to Liverpool in June 1814:

'For Public Sale, by permission of the Honourable Commissioner's of His Majesty's Customs & Excise, at Edward's Hotel, on Monday 11th day of June next at 11 o'clock. Free of duty, for payment of salvage claims etc. about 800 gallons of Port wine, in full and ullage pipes (casks)'

The *Sherbourne Mercury* newspaper for this period is a fascinating snapshot of life on the islands, recording many incidents that would otherwise pass un-noticed, this being a letter extract from Scilly, dated 11 May 1785:

'Yesterday, William Chown, Joseph Edwards, James Simons and James Oakes, all inhabitants of Old Town in this island, put off in a boat to examine lobster pots placed near the shore; in hauling up one of which near a ledge of rocks, 'tis supposed the sea broke and filled the boat and all perished, each leaving a wife and small children wholly unprovided for. Neither of their bodies are yet cast on shore.'

Smuggling was of course another aspect of island life, one example being:

'The Prince William Henry, *cutter, has taken and carried into Scilly a smuggling cutter (unnamed) laden with 5,000 casks of brandy, 1,500 casks of Geneva (gin) and about 3 tons of tea.'*

Contraband often came at a price, as this account of 1 September 1785 shows:

'This morning arrived in St Mary's the King George, *customs cutter from a cruise, and has brought in with her a large smuggling lugger of near 500 tons burthen, laden with tea, brandy etc and mounting 12 guns. The* King George *took her after an engagement of an hour, in which 6 men were killed on board the lugger and 9 wounded; the cutter had 4 men killed and 8 wounded, two of whom died this morning.'*

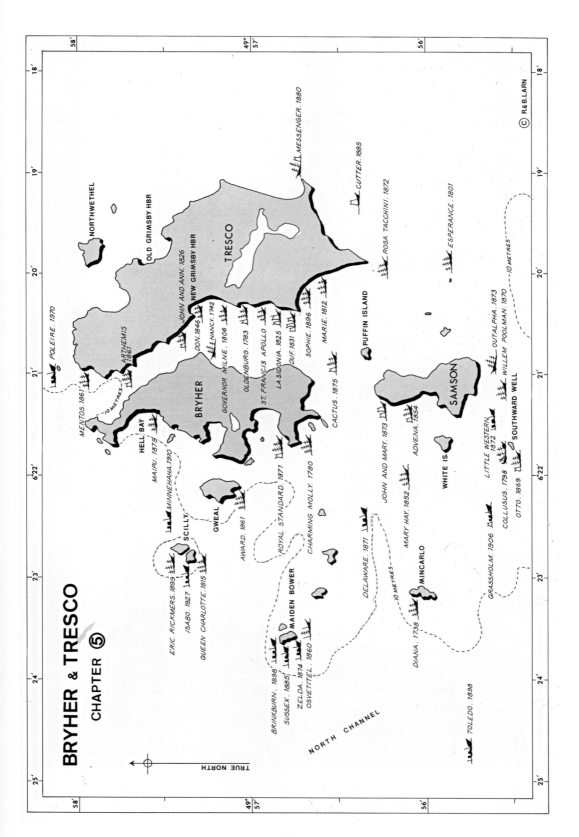

BRYHER & TRESCO
CHAPTER ⑤

TRUE NORTH

© R&B.LARN

NORTHWETHEL

OLD GRIMSBY HBR

TRESCO

NEW GRIMSBY HBR

JOHN AND ANN. 1826

ARTHEMIS 1861

POLEIRE. 1970

MENTOS. 1861

10 METRES

HELL BAY

MAIPU. 1879

MINNEHAHA.1910

SCILLY.

ERIC RICKMERS 1899

ISABO. 1927

QUEEN CHARLOTTE 1815

GWEAL

AWARD. 1861

BRINKBURN. 1898

SUSSEX. 1885

ZELDA. 1874

OSVETITEL. 1860

MAIDEN BOWER

BRYHER

GOVERNOR MILNE. 1806

OLDENBURG. 1783

ST. FRANCIS APOLLO

LA SIDONIA. 1825

DUF.1831

SOPHIE. 1896

CACTUS. 1875

ROYAL STANDARD. 1871

CHARMING MOLLY. 1780

NANCY. 1742

DON. 1846

MARIE. 1812

PUFFIN ISLAND

DELAWARE. 1871

JOHN AND MARY. 1873

ADVENA. 1854

MARY HAY. 1852

WHITE IS.

COLLUSUS. 1798

OTTO. 1869

GRASSHOLM. 1906

DIANA. 1738

MINCARLO

NORTH CHANNEL

TOLEDO. 1898

10 METRES

CUTTER. 1885

MESSENGER. 1880

ROSA TACCHINI. 1872

ESPERANCE. 1801

10 METRES

SAMSON

LITTLE WESTERN. 1872

OUTALPHA. 1873

WILLEM POOLMAN. 1870

SOUTHWARD WELL

10 METRES

5 - Bryher, Samson and Tresco Islands

One mile NW of Hugh Town, across St Mary's Roads lie three islands, Samson, Bryher and Tresco which, with their outlying rock formations, form the most picturesque area in the whole of Scilly. They have an atmosphere and geography peculiar to themselves and 'Fairy Tale Bryher' and 'Tropical Tresco' are but two of the romantic titles which have been bestowed on them. Surrounded by rocks and ledges almost as numerous as those of the Western Rocks, they abound in such descriptive and obscure names as Roaring Ledge, Buccabu, Illiswilgig, Stinking Porth, Hell Bay and Tobaccoman's Ledge. The area has seen its share of sunken ships and drowned seamen, but despite the dangers of the surrounding rocks the number of wrecks is remarkably low in comparison with other areas of Scilly.

Offshore to the south of Samson, now an uninhabited island, a shallow reef known as Southward Well was the site of one of the most famous wrecks on Scilly, that of HMS *Colossus*, which went ashore on 10 December 1798, fortunately with the loss of only one life. Commanded by Captain George Murray, the *Colossus* was a 3rd rate 74-gun man o'war of 1,703 tons, built by Clevely at Gravesend, launched on 4 April 1787. She had been in the Mediterranean for almost two years when ordered home during which time she had seen considerable service, taking part in the Battle of Cape St Vincent, patrolling off Cadiz and Lisbon, and assisting in the blockade of Malta. Long service abroad told heavily on this old 'wooden wall' of England, so that by November 1798 the *Colossus* had rotten sails, worn rigging. soft timbers and little

▲ Working model of the *Colossus* wreck in the Charlestown Shipwreck Centre, Cornwall

18pdr cannon ball and attached brass barrel hoop, artefacts from the man o'war *Colossus* lost on Southward Well, Samson ▶

or no spare gear, most of her stores having been removed to maintain and service other ships that were to remain in the Mediterranean over the winter, some of which were even worse off.

She left Lisbon in charge of a convoy, arriving in St Mary's Roads on Friday 7 December with eight smaller vessels, to shelter from an unfavourable NE wind. Although poorly provisioned and unseaworthy, the *Colossus* carried far more men than her normal complement, having on board sick and wounded sailors from the Battle of the Nile. In addition, she carried private stores, including a unique collection of Etruscan vases and paintings belonging to Sir William Hamilton and a lead coffin holding the body of a deceased admiral. It was said:

'There was scarcely an officer in Lord Nelson's fleet but had put on board the Colossus *some presents for their friends, which had been taken on board the French fleet.'*

It was rumored after the wreck that she carried specie, but although this had been the intention, at the last moment Captain Murray had refused to oblige the Lisbon merchants who had approached him. No doubt he would have been reluctant to decline the offer, since naval officers in those days made a practice of transporting large sums of money for merchant bankers. In return, they received as much as 5 per cent of the gross value, and vast personal fortunes were amassed in this manner, a senior officer receiving as much as £25,000 or more for one bullion shipment on what was after all, normal naval service.

Brass frame of a cannon gun-lock, from the wreck of the man o'war *Colossus* ▶

By the late afternoon of 10 December, the wind had swung to the SE and increased to gale force. At 4pm the main bower cable to which the *Colossus* was riding parted, and although a small bow and sheet anchor were dropped, they failed to take a hold and merely dragged over the sandy bottom. The watch on deck was sent aloft to strike the topmasts in order to reduce windage, but the ship continued to drag and at 8pm struck the rocks. During the night, she lost her rudder and took in water so rapidly that she had to be abandoned at first light. The late afternoon of 11 December saw every man off the ship, including the sick and wounded, with only one casualty, a quartermaster who fell overboard while taking soundings and drowned. That night the warship fell over onto her beam ends and began to break up. A considerable amount of gear was salvaged including 'many useful pieces of masts, spars, copper and iron etc, a 75-cwt anchor and iron cannon'. One unusual item recovered was the embalmed body of Admiral Lord Shuldham in its lead cask which, disguised as a wooden crate, had been shipped as cargo in deference to the seaman's superstition against carrying the dead aboard a ship at sea. On hearing of the wreck and the loss of his priceless art treasures, Sir William Hamilton reacted strongly:

'My philosophy has been put to trial by the loss of the Colossus. *You give me little hope, but I have learnt that the body insolvent of Admiral Shuldham has been saved from the wreck. . . damn his body, it can be of no use but to the worms, but my collection would have given information to the most learned.'*

Some of the guns salvaged from the wreck in 1852 were placed on the Garrison, St Mary's being described as 'fit for service,' but after 54 years underwater and never again fired in anger, their serviceability was never put to the test. The wreck site of the *Colossus* was re-located and identified in 1974 by a team of divers led by Roland Morris of Penzance. Amongst the iron carronade, cannons, shot, buttons, leather shoes, lead gun aprons, broken bottles and personal artefacts the team found, they also raised some 35,000 shards of Hamilton's famous pottery collection. Working closely with the British Museum, who made available a grant of £40,000 to assist excavation and conservation, a condition of the financial support was that all the shards would become the property of the Museum, who were later able to reconstruct at least one complete 'pot' which is on public display in the BM. After nine years as a Protected Wreck under Government legislation, by 1984 there was little left to protect and the Protection Order was revoked. However, on 4 June 2001, Mac Mace, a local commercial diver stumbled across what was obviously an iron gun embedded muzzle down into the seabed in a new area. Initially he thought it was a mortar, not realizing the length of the barrel. In attempting to mark the gun with a buoyed line which was not long enough he was carried away by the tide, but a crewman on his boat *Scavanger* managed to get a GPS position.. Next day, a team from the North Dorset diving club, who had hired Jim Heslin's boat *Moonshadow*, were asked to carry out a search and relocate the 'lost' cannon, achieved by Giles Adams and Gwyneth James. It proved to be not one, but a row of five 18pdr Armstrong iron cannon which had been on the upper deck standing proud of the seabed inside their respective gun ports, their muzzles buried deep in the sand. A sixth lies on the seabed close to the empty gun port from which it came. Three other cannon lie outside of the wreck, two of which are 32pdr Blomfields. There are also two iron cannon embedded in the quay on St Mary's as bollards, which are believed to be 32pdr, and a number of iron cannon, presumably from the *Colossus*, but possibly additional cannon from the wreck of HMS *Venerable*, sunk in Torbay, Devon, in 1804, since two ships were sent from Scilly to raise guns from the wreck, lie within the body of the quay itself, presumably added during building for their sheer weight. The late Roland Morris of Penzance, who financed the recovery of some 35,000 pottery shards, the remains of Sir William Hamiltons 3rd collection, in the 1970's is known to have lifted and taken ashore a number of guns which may have been as many as 22. As the finder of the site, Mac Mace declared himself 'Salvor in Possession' and reported the find to the DCMS (Department of Culture, Media & Sport) as well as the Receiver of Wreck the following day, a Saturday, also the fact he had seen what appeared to be a wooden statue and other carvings at the stern.

The word quickly spread amongst the diving fraternity on Scilly, that a new area of the *Colossus* had been found, and Mac Mace gave permission for local sport divers to visit the site the following day, a Sunday, but only on a 'look but don't touch basis'. Realizing the importance of the find, Mac expressly asked them not to move or lift any artefact material. Unfortunately, the request fell on deaf ears, the temptation of loose copper hull fastening pins, pieces of musket and other items proving too much of a temptation for three of the divers, and there was a 'showdown' with Jim Heslin when they landed their trophies on the quay later that day. It was totally irresponsible to raise artefacts purely as souvenirs from such an historic virgin site, especially when asked not to do

◀ A 3.3 m tall wooden carving of a neo-classical warior figure, found on the wreck of the man o'war *Colossus*

▲ The carving as it looked when first found on the seabed on the wreck of the *Colossus*

so, and the incident clouded the future regarding the *Colossus* wreck thereafter. Exploration of the stern area using a water-lift on the Monday completely uncovered the 'statue', which was one of the port-quarter stern carvings of a 3.4m tall, male neoclassical warrior figure, holding aloft in his left hand a laurel wreath attached to a small flagstaff complete with pennant. This was attached to part of a semi-circular window head, part of the stern window of the captain's 'heads' or toilet, in the port stern gallery. Above the window was a large iron bar attached to the carving, thought to be the remains of a stern lantern bracket. Later the site was re-scheduled as a Protected Wreck for the 2nd time in 18 years! At his own expense Mac Mace, now the nominated Licensee, worked with the authorities for several months, a special lifting cradle being manufactured at Mac's expense by which the carving was raised and placed into a temporary freshwater 'cascade' storage tank on Tresco awaiting developments.

This carving rates as one of the most important relics of the period recovered from the sea in British waters, competing with any found on the Swedish man o'war *Vasa* in Sweden. The carved *Colossus* figure stands with crossed legs, wearing a leather tunic, the head sporting a handlebar moustache and a helmet. The right arm was missing completely when found, eaten away by boring worm, as was the war shield it once held. This relic is now with the Mary Rose Conservation Unit at Portsmouth and by 2009 in its third year of conservation treatment, having taken much longer than originally thought, it is estimated that it could cost as much as £25,000. The final home of the carving has yet to be determined, but it is generally agreed it should be on public display on Scilly, with a strong possibility it will form part of the Tresco Garden's Valhalla collection of ship's figureheads, under the management of the National Maritime Museum. It will of course, require a special environmental display cabinet to prevent further deterioration. Technically the carving is the property of MOD(Navy), previously the Admiralty, but whether they will exercise their right of ownership has yet to be decided.

Southward Well has been the cause of many other wrecks and strandings, including the Swedish brigantine *Otto* laden with Stockholm tar, bound from Jacobstad to Bristol. On bringing up in St Mary's Roads, she parted both cables and after fouling the barque *Dorothy Thompson* drove ashore on 6 December 1869. Her crew were all saved, although several days later there was almost a casualty when they departed for the mainland aboard the Penzance packet. In bidding his crew a fond and no doubt alcoholic farewell, the *Otto's* captain fell off the end of the Hugh Town quay and almost drowned! Only 36 barrels of her cargo were saved before she broke up. On 27 January 1870, the ship *Willem Poolman* of Rotterdam went on the

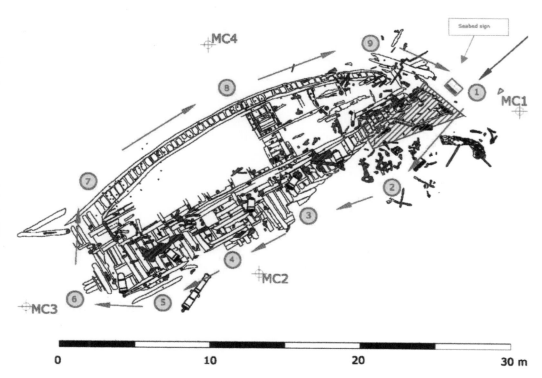

0   10   20   30 m

▲ Site plan of the *Colossus* wreck site, showing the 'diver-trail' markers on the seabed laid out in 2009 by CISMAS

Some of the 35,000 pottery shards found by the late Roland Morris's diving team whilst exploring the wreck of the *Colossus* ▶

rocks here while on passage from Batavia to her home port but, assisted by local boatmen and pilots, plus a steamer, got off and both ship and her cargo of coffee and tin were saved. The full-rigged ship *Outalpha* of London, on entering St Mary's Roads for shelter on 1 February 1873, touched bottom and remained fast in a dangerous position until refloated on the following tide. Bound from Adelaide to London with grain, she was one of 50 or so ships sheltering from a hurricane which swung from SE to N within an hour.

Several incidents have already been mentioned concerning Scilly packet ships in trouble around the islands, and over the years two have become total wrecks, both in the same year, one close to the rocks that claimed the *Colossus*. At 10.30am on 5 October 1872, the West Cornwall Steamship Company's iron screw packet *Little Western*, left Penzance for the Isles of Scilly. She arrived at St Mary's mid-afternoon, but sailed shortly afterwards when news was received that a French brigantine, the *Jane*, laden with ore, had lost both her fore-mast and main topmast and was in distress seven miles SW of the Bishop light. Two cruising pilot-cutters were first on the scene, and when Captain Hicks (not Captain Tregarthen as is so often misquoted) arrived with the *Little Western*, he was much annoyed to find his services were not required. He cruised around for some two hours in the hope that the French master might change his mind, then headed back for port. No specific instructions or course were given to the Mate, the captain merely saying that they would 'keep down for St Mary's Sound'. When abeam of Spanish Ledges, Captain Hicks took the helm and steered the ship close to St Agnes, passing within 60ft of the Bristolman Rock before heading up towards the Roads. At midnight, with the weather fine and clear, the packet doing about four knots across the Roads, all hands were on deck preparing to anchor for the night. No lookout had been posted, and when land was suddenly sighted dead ahead, it was too late to take avoiding action. Mate Tonkin ordered the engine to full astern, while the captain called for port helm, then changed his mind and ordered it to starboard, but all to no effect. The *Little Western* struck a full ship's length north and east of Southward Well and began to settle in four fathoms. At the subsequent enquiry held at Penzance, there was a suggestion that Captain Hicks had

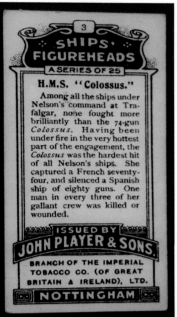

◀ John Player's cigarette card depicting the figurehead carving carried on the bow of the *Colossus*, with its history

been drunk, this allegation being supported by the steward who declared that he had consumed half a tumbler of brandy and water at 8pm, a quantity of ale at about 9.30pm, followed by more brandy. Although drunkenness was never proved, the captain was found guilty of un-seamanlike behaviour and neglect in misjudging the distance of his ship off-shore, and for entering an anchorage without posting lookouts. As a result, his master's certificate was suspended for six months. Captain Hicks had been at sea for 21 of his 55 years, commanding 150 different ships, and had once piloted the royal yacht with Queen Victoria & Prince Albert aboard. As a direct result of the *Little Western* affair Augustus Smith, the 'Lord Proprietor', banished him from the islands, and he never sailed in or out of Scilly again. Launched in 1858 by James Henderson & Sons of Renfrew, the *Little Western* was owned by T.J. Burton of St Mary's. She was a steamer of 115 tons gross, 67 net, and 115ft overall in length. Brought to Penzance in 1859 especially for the Isles of Scilly service, she normally made three crossings a week, on Mondays, Wednesdays and Fridays, plus excursions and salvage jobs in between when the opportunity offered, and was only the second steam vessel to serve between Penzance and St Mary's.

The first had been the *Scotia*, specially chartered for the work in 1858 by the same owners until the *Little Western* had been completed. On 14 November 1872, the wreck of the *Little Western* was sold for £120, and though the purchaser announced his intention of raising the ship intact on the next spring tide, this was never accomplished. Great Minalto, a rock a few hundred yards to the SW of Samson, almost terminated the career of the South Shields steam-trawler *Grassholm* on 21 August 1906.

On passage to Cardiff laden with fish, she encountered fog and in attempting to reach the anchorage went ashore. Although badly damaged in the bow, her crew warped her off and she was lying at anchor filling fast, when the St Mary's lifeboat *Henry Dundas* arrived alongside. The lifeboat coxswain was engaged to save the trawler, and towed her safely into the harbour. Midway between Mincarlo and Samson lie Bream Ledges on which the 225 tons register, wooden barque *Mary Hay* was wrecked on 13 April 1852. From Jamaica to London, commanded by Captain Hogg, she was entering Broad Sound from the NW when she struck the Steeple Rock. There was a Scilly pilot on board at the time, but he was so busy pointing out the dangerous rocks to the master and reassuring him that all was well, that he failed to notice his own position. Two minutes after the pilot had gone below for a meal having declined to eat it on deck, the barque struck heavily and at once began to take in water. With distress signals flying, she was eventually anchored near Samson, but after hours of pumping the *Mary Hay* gave one great belch, lurched, and fell over on her side. There were some 30 men on deck at the time, as well as others in boats moored alongside and though several had lucky escapes, no lives were lost. The following day, 46 puncheons of rum, two casks of lime-juice, 1,170 bags of pimento, ship's stores, gear and clothing were salvaged. Of the remaining cargo, all the sugar was ruined, and only the ebony, logwood, coconuts and fustic were sold with the wreck for £72 on 17 April. When the weather moderated, the barque was refloated and taken to St Mary's quay where she was broken up, her figurehead joining others in the Valhalla collection.

Although not strictly relevant to this chapter, mention should be made of the *Toledo*, a Sunderland steamer of 2,843 tons which on Saturday 20 August 1898, ripped her bottom open on the same pinnacle of Steeple Rock that had claimed the *Mary Hay* 46 years earlier. With a crew of 28 commanded by Captain John Wishart, the steamer carried a general cargo, mostly wheat and oil cake, consigned to Van Stanton & Co of Rotterdam from Galveston. It was late afternoon when the *Toledo* was suddenly engulfed in fog close to the Bishop, and only minutes later she struck the Steeple. Robert Ferrer, the second engineer on watch below when she struck, saw her boilers literally lift off their mountings. With her bottom plates ripped open from bow to engine-room, she filled at the rate of a foot a minute, and the crew barely had time to lower the boats and abandon ship before she rolled over and sank bow-first in 150ft of water. Built by J.L. Thompson of Sunderland in 1882, and owned by J. Tully & Co, the *Toledo*, lying in the fairway with her masts only 18ft below the surface, was considered a hazard to navigation, so divers were engaged to blow her up using explosives.

Mention the name *Delaware* to anyone in Scilly, and they will almost certainly link it with a rescue still considered by some one of the bravest in the history of the islands. It began early on 20 December 1871, when Bryher pilots sighted a large steamer in distress, battling close inshore against a severe NW gale. By noon, the wind strength had increased even more, forcing the vessel between Mincarlo and Seal Rock, towards Tearing Ledges. Watching through their telescopes, the pilots on shore saw her crew hoist a jib only to have it blown away and a staysail following soon after. Beam on to the swell and rolling heavily, the steamer disappeared beneath a huge wave to reappear seconds later stripped of her entire bridge structure. Another huge wave then broke over her decks and she went down within seconds. From a vantage point on Samson's North Hill, five survivors were sighted in the sea; two more in a boat and another three hanging on to wreckage. Realising the men would almost certainly be carried onto White Island, a mile SSW, the Bryher gig *Albion* was prepared for sea. The 30ft boat, weighing almost half a ton, had its six oars lashed across its beam, and 12 men carried it bodily for half a mile from the boathouse at Great Par across to Rushy Bay. Patrick Trevellick, an acknowledged leader in this sort of situation, was chosen as coxswain and the *Albion* set off for Samson manned by William & Stephen Woodcock, Thomas Bickford, John Webber, Richard Ellis, James Jenkins, John Jacob Jenkins, William Jenkins, and Samson Jenkins. After gaining the lee of the island, by which time the men were already soaked and exhausted, some of them landed and got ashore in time to see the boat containing survivors strike White Island and its two occupants scramble to safety. Leaving Richard Ellis on North Hill to signal back to Bryher if more men were needed, the heavy gig was again man-handled overland, this time across the 300ft wide isthmus between East and West Par. Hardly stopping to draw breath after their exertion, they re-launched the gig and in mountainous seas rowed towards White Island. When, utterly exhausted, they at last reached the island and ran the gig up through the foaming surf, it was only to find that the two survivors had collected together a huge pile of stones as ammunition with which to defend themselves! They later told their rescuers that their captain had described the Scillonians as little better than savages, and that they could expect short shrift if they were ever wrecked there. After giving various articles of their own clothing to the two half-naked seamen, the gig's crew made a thorough search of the island before returning to Samson, where survivors and rescuers alike collapsed from exhaustion.

Meanwhile, Richard Ellis had noted their plight and signalled from North Hill for a second gig, the *March*, to come over to Samson. The two men rescued from White Island, the only survivors from the wreck, proved to be chief mate McWinnie and 3rd Mate Jenkins of the 3,423 tons gross Liverpool steamer *Delaware*, of and from Liverpool for Calcutta via Suez, with a general cargo which included cottons, silks, sheet-lead, tin and stationery. Built at Ramsey, Isle of Man, in 1865, the steamer had been lengthened by 60ft after building to 380ft, but left with her original engine, so there had been much controversy as to whether or not she was under-powered. The day following the wreck, after the ship's officers had been cared for on Bryher, every available man on the island set about recovering cargo from the sea. It has been said that the *Albion's* crew received neither public thanks nor reward for their gallant rescue, but this is not so. It is true they received neither testimonials nor certificates, but they certainly received a reward of £15 from the Royal National Lifeboat Institution. Not a great sum even in those days, for a rescue which is still remembered as an outstanding feat of human endurance.

There have been many other minor incidents in this immediate area, such as the *John & Mary*, a Truro schooner abandoned in February 1893 after she had parted her cables and collided with a Greek brig in St Mary's Roads, later found ashore on Samson, towed off and taken to New Grimsby. The *Diana* of Calais, carrying wool, ashore on Mincarlo in November 1738; and the Italian barque *Cactus*, on passage from Tripoli to Cardiff with esparto grass, which struck the northern rocks at 11pm on 11 August 1875 in fog. Boarded by pilots at daybreak, she was anchored off Mincarlo, then run ashore between Bryher and Samson half full of water on the 12th, finally taken to St Mary's quay on the 13th. Another near casualty was the brig *Advena*, Captain Holmes, driven onto Samson by a south-easter on 3 January 1854, and saved only after her masts had been cut down to lighten her sufficiently to float off at highwater. Peaked Rock, at the NE corner of North Channel, brought about the loss of the steamer *Empire* of London, Captain George Woodcock. The 409-ton wooden vessel attempted to get into Scilly without a pilot during a severe gale, struck and sank in 20m on 26 November 1860. The most seaward rock in this sector is the redoubtable Maiden Bower, so that it is not surprising that at least one large barque, three steamers and numerous small craft have come to grief here.

The largest of the sailing ships was Austrian, the *Osvetitel*, Captain Meilicich, carrying barley from Ibrail to Falmouth. Thick fog blanketed the outline of Maiden Bower on 14 July 1860 when she went ashore to become a total wreck, about 1,000 quarters of her cargo being saved before she broke up. The first steamer to be lost here was the *Zelda* and again fog was a contributory cause. It was a little after midnight on 16 April 1874 when the *Zelda's* siren broke the silence of Bryher, and two local gigs were the first to find the 1,300 tons gross, iron vessel hard and fast on the rocks. To say her career had been a short one would be a gross understatement, since she was less than 32 hours into her maiden voyage! Owned by Glynn & Co of Liverpool, bound from Liverpool to Palermo with a crew of 30, two passengers and a general cargo, the *Zelda* was abandoned without loss of life only a short while before she parted amidships, her bow section sinking in 60ft, the stern in 30ft. Her luckless Captain named Peace, was exonerated from any blame for the loss of his ship by the court of enquiry, and almost all the *Zelda's* valuable cargo was salvaged by divers of the Penzance based Western Marine Salvage Company, who worked on the wreck for many weeks. A contemporary newspaper report listed the following goods as having been recovered:

'Numerous cases of cotton goods, 208 cases of lard, 32 firkins of lard, 22 barrels of oil, 12 cakes of copper, 2 cases of copper-bottoms, 4 cases of sheet copper, 3 cases of yellow metal, 10 cases of soda-nitrate, 11 barrels of solder, 29 blocks of tin, frames of felt material, 100 tons of

steel rail, cases of machinery, hogsheads of cotton and other items'.

Some of the spoiled rice was sold off at Scilly and Penzance, but the bulk was shipped to Liverpool. For their services in rescuing the crew and passengers, the crews of the two gigs who had towed ashore the ship's boats holding 30 survivors in all, were each awarded £50.

Sister ship to the ss *Suffolk* and *Surrey*, the *Sussex* was another steamship victim of Maiden Bower in 1885. These three ships maintained a regular service between London and Baltimore during the early 1880s, and although owned by three individual shipping companies, were jointly managed by Hooper, Murrell & Williams Ltd of London. The *Surrey* was extensively damaged in collision off the Bishop Rock with the German ship *Uranus* on 4 January 1884; the *Sussex* totally wrecked at Scilly on 17 December 1885 and the *Suffolk* was lost on the Lizard less than a year later on 28 September 1886. As with the *Zelda*, the deep-throated bellow of the *Sussex's* siren brought the gigs out from Bryher at dawn, although the vessel had, in fact, gone ashore six hours earlier. Fifteen days out from Baltimore with a general cargo which included a great variety of Christmas fare and 250 head of cattle, the *Sussex*, registered at London with a crew of 45 including seven cattlemen, had been navigated on dead reckoning for her last two days. Despite thick fog Captain Robert Robinson, had been pressing on at normal cruising speed without stopping to take soundings, so it is hardly surprising that there was only a matter of seconds between the lookout's cry

▲ Victim of Maiden Bower off Bryher on 15 December 1898, the steamship *Brinkburn* lies a total wreck

◄ Bales of raw cotton being landed on the quay at St.Mary's, from the wreck of the ss. *Brinkburn*, lost on Maiden Bower in 1898

of 'breakers ahead' and the ship crashing on to rocks. The outcrop was Seal Rock; the impact so violent that the watch below was thrown from their bunks, who scrambled up on deck to find her four lifeboats were already being lowered. Within five minutes, the portside plating of the engine-room collapsed, the depth of water inside the ship rose to 18ft and she began to settle down fast. After taking to the boats, the crew suffered considerably from cold and exposure, since most were dressed either for work in the engine-room or for sleeping in their bunks. When finally the Bryher boats arrived, those who had abandoned the steamer returned to collect the others and retrieve papers, instruments and personal effects before landing on Bryher, and eventually St Mary's. With her stern completely submerged and the seas breaking over her bridge, the *Sussex* showed every sign of disintegrating. During the night of 4-5 January, she broke up completely and disappeared, after which timber and sacks of flour began drifting to the surface. Launched by Wigham, Richardson Ltd of Newcastle in March 1883, the 2,795 ton three-masted *Sussex* was fitted with a 2-cylinder, 275 nhp engine made by the same firm.

Twenty-four years after the *Zelda* was lost, her rusting plates were joined by those of another steamship, the 3,229 ton four-year-old *Brinkburn*, which struck and sank in fog on 15 December 1898 in similar circumstances. Bound from Galveston to Le Havre with 8,895 bales of cotton and 6,720 bags of cotton seed, she struck Maiden Bower and was unable to get clear. Her crew, mostly Lascars, took to the boats and remained close to the wreck until daybreak, when once again the Bryher gigs were used to tow the survivors' boats ashore. The Liverpool Salvage Company under-took to recover the cargo valued at £100,000, having been insured by underwriters of that port. When the wrecks of the *Zelda* and *Brinkburn*, which now lie side by side, were examined by Royal Navy divers in 1966, a number of iron cannon were found on the seabed between the two ships, indicating the site of a third and much older wreck. Another cannon site has recently been found on the western side of Maiden Bower, towards Maiden Bower Ledges. Over time the hull of the *Brinkburn* collapsed leaving her huge 3-cylinder steam engine standing upright, a magnet for sport divers who could swim freely between the piston rods and around the three cylinder heads. However, early winter gales in 2008 caused the engine block to collapse, and it now lies at an angle of 25° to the seabed.

Before continuing north to Scilly Rock, another notorious wreck area, some of the lesser-known incidents in the immediate vicinity are worth a mention. These include the Weymouth brig *Charming Molly*, Captain Samuel Marder, stranded and lost on Bryher on 20 November 1780 in what today is called Stone Porth since her cargo was Portland stone destined for Dublin. Nothing of her cargo survives in the shallows or ashore it seems, apart from what it possibly an animal feeding trough hollowed out from a block, now abandoned in a stone wall. The *Royal Standard*, a Kinsale brigantine, bound from her home port to Southampton with oats, drove ashore on the morning of 11 January 1871 but was successfully refloated four days later. There was also the *Award*, a ship of 846 tons, owned in London but registered in Liverpool, which went ashore at Gweal in the early hours of 19 March 1861 whilst on her way to New Orleans in ballast. Her crew saved themselves by scrambling over her foremast which had fallen onto the rocks. Rough seas prevented any salvage work at the time, but she was later got off, only to go to pieces on the beach on Bryher on 28 March. Her fiddle-head and a quarter-board went to the Valhalla collection on Tresco; the other board serving the New Inn on the island as a pub sign for many years. The salvage money awarded for the wreck actually paid for a new gig, the *Golden Eagle*, which served the community well.

Shipman Head, the northernmost point of Bryher, along with outlying Gweal and Scilly Rock, mark the extremities of a large indentation appropriately named Hell Bay. In winter and during severe NW gales, Hell Bay is a fearful place and has an infamous reputation as a graveyard for ships, but in fact not that many have been lost here. A West Indiaman, the *Queen Charlotte*, Jamaica-bound from Greenock under the command of Captain Rayside, struck Scilly Rock on 27 January 1815 and broke up. One seaman and three passengers lost their lives, the remaining 13 clambering over the rocks to safety but were stranded for two days and nights before rescue. Two Bryher pilots, Charles Jackson and James Tregarthen, were drowned during their rescue, the latter having only recently returned home to Scilly after eight and a half years as a prisoner-of-war in French hands. The steamer *Egyptian Monarch* of London, 3,916 tons, New York to London with a general cargo, cattle and passengers, also struck here on 7 May 1888, but got off to reach Falmouth the same day with one compartment full of water. Less fortunate was the German full-rigged ship *Erik Rickmers* of Bremerhaven, which went ashore at 9.0pm on 25 October 1899. This 2,050 ton vessel, built in 1897, was carrying rice from Bangkok for Bremen, and sank in deep water the same day she went ashore.

When the Atlantic Transport Co's liner *Minnehaha* of 13,443 tons went aground on the side of Scilly Rock at 12.50am on 18 April 1910, there were islanders still living who clearly recalled another wreck by the same name on Peninnis Head, St Mary's, 36 years earlier in 1874. On passage from New York to Tilbury with 171 crew, and 66 passengers, all 1st class, the ss *Minnehaha* was also carrying a general cargo which included 243 steers. Captain Sydney Leyland, the company's senior master mariner, had been unable to take an observation since the 14th of the month, and by noon on the 17th could only estimate that he was 170 miles from the Bishop and would pass at least six miles S of the lighthouse without a change of course. Fog dictated a reduction in speed to six knots during the evening, and although a sounding taken at midnight showed 47 fathoms, breakers were seen ahead only minutes later and with scarcely more than a slight bump, the liner slid gently aground. Distress-guns fired by the Bishop light-keepers brought out the St Mary's lifeboat, but by the time it arrived at the wreck all the passengers had been landed on Bryher using the ship's boats. The lifeboat stood by until 3pm, when Captain Leyland ordered everyone except his officers and a few members of the crew to board a waiting tug. The Falmouth tugs *Victor* and *Dragon*, summoned by urgent radio signals, arrived in time

▲ Aground on Scilly Rock on 18 April 1910, the liner *Minnehaha* was later refloated and saved

to see the crew start heaving some of her 8,000-tons of cargo out of No's 2 and 3 holds to lighten the ship by throwing it into the sea. Brand-new Ford motor cars were winched outboard and dropped, followed by grand pianos, crated machinery of every description, sewing machines, carpets, tinned meat, coffee beans, machine oil and other valuable items by the ton. The frightened steers were at first inhumanely dropped overboard to drown, until a Mr Saudry, who was acting locally for the Lloyd's Agent suggested they should be saved, offering £5 per head for every steer landed alive. Using pilot gigs, the cattle were roped by their horns alongside and four at a time landed on Bryher. With a total of 223 animals saved in this way, the Scillonian's put in an invoice for £1,115 as agreed, but with no written agreement Lloyd's declined to pay, a court hearing later awarding them £780 which the judge considered at £3.5 shillings per head was fair recompense for their efforts.

A Lowestoft trawler actually arrived in St Mary's Roads with a crated motor-car on deck, having recovered it floating near the Wolf Rock! When asked what should be done with it, the Receiver of Wreck took the fishermen to the end of Hugh Town jetty and pointed out across the sound where dozens of similar crates could be seen bobbing about in the sea, telling the men, 'As far as I am concerned you can keep it'. By the 20th, a fleet of tugs and salvage vessels were in attendance with the Salvage Association in charge, and the serious business of getting the ship afloat began. One of the three trawlers hired was the *Steinberg*, whose Mate, John Brown, unfortunately got himself into trouble with the Receiver of Wreck. He was charged with having stolen from the wreck, ' - *a clock, six bottles of machine oil, bottles of medicinal tablets and other items'*, and was given the choice of one month in prison or a £5 fine. In his defense Brown insisted *'I saw the things lying about the deck and thought there was no harm in having them.'* At the same court hearing before Justice Chester Jones, a Joshua Davis and Michael Lee were fined 40 shillings or 14 days in prison for *'Unlawful possession of some goods taken from the wreck of the Minnihaha.'*

The first move on the part of the Liverpool Salvage Co and the Swedish firm which was assisting them, was to build a false floor of timber in each hold at low water, caulking every seam so as to make it watertight. Other false decks were built in succession at each hatch level, so that eventually six platforms were in position in each hold. Air compressors were then started but for days there was little apparent result as the increasing pressure under the floors slowly pushed the sea back out through the holes in the hull. Then on 11 May, while a group of British and Dutch divers were discussing some aspect of work on deck, they suddenly saw Bryher Island seemingly start to move across the horizon! Or rather, that was the impression gained as the *Minnehaha* refloated, much earlier than had been anticipated. Under her own power, she came off the ledges so fast that she nearly ran down the waiting tugs, whose assistance was not needed. Later, escorted by the tugs *Dragon*, *Triton* and *Victor*, plus the salvage vessels *Ranger*, *Belas*, *Linnet* and *Herakles*, the liner maintained a steady

10 knots under her own steam all the way to Falmouth, where she was anchored in St Just Pool. Here her remaining cargo was discharged by local labour after London stevedores, specially brought to Cornwall to complete the task, went on strike. Registered and built at Belfast by Harland & Wolff in 1900, the *Minnehaha* belonged to the same company that had owned the *Mohegan*, lost with 103 lives on the Manacles Rocks, near Falmouth, in October 1898.

The last steamship wreck in this chapter and perhaps the most dramatic, was that of the 6,827 ton Italian *Isabo* (ex-*Iris*), which went ashore during thick fog on the afternoon of 27 October 1927. There followed another dramatic rescue, comparable in its way with that of the ss *Delaware*. Ernest Jenkins, a Bryher coastguard, was the first man ashore to be aware of the wreck, having followed the sound of the *Isabo's* siren as she approached the islands. Shortly after, he heard the sound of escaping steam, then human voices. A telephone call at 5pm to Matthew Lethbridge, coxswain of the St Mary's lifeboat *Elsie*, resulted in the boat being launched which headed for the NW corner of Scilly in the record time of eight minutes. When the men of Bryher heard the news, they dropped everything and a mad scramble ensued as they manned the gigs kept at Great Par beach. Of the 19 men who lived on the island, 18 were at the scene of the wreck before the lifeboat! The 19th was missing because he had gone to another island, otherwise it would have been a full muster! No one could say Scillonian men were slow when it came to wrecks!. The gig *Czar* was the first to reach the vicinity of Scilly Rock despite thick fog. This reduced visibility to a few yards and a heavy swell made rowing difficult. Once there the boat encountered a solid wall of floating wreckage: hatch covers, furniture, water tanks, mattresses, broken lifeboats, timber and wheat cargo a foot thick on the surface. Then the heads and shoulders of men were seen above the debris, but so thick was the wreckage that the gig crews had difficulty in handling their oars, its only advantage being that the debris tended to flatten the sea somewhat. Eight men, almost naked, had been picked up by the *Czar* by the time the motor-boat *Ivy* arrived, but the floating grain quickly choked her water circulating pump, and her engine block was near red hot by the time she had rescued just one survivor. Meanwhile the *Czar* had picked up three more survivors and, grossly overloaded with 19 on board, asked the *Ivy* to take 11 of them back to the island. Another motor-boat, the *Sunbeam* from New Grimsby, arrived with a punt in tow, which proved to be the most useful craft available to the rescue fleet. Manned by Charles and Edwin Jenkin, the small boat made three trips amongst the wreckage returning with a survivor on each occasion. With five of the steamer's crew safely on board, the *Sunbeam* then headed to seaward of the rocks where she found the *Isabo* ashore, broken in two just forward of the funnel. Groups of men clung to the stern section which was bumping badly, threatening to break off and sink at any moment. A line was passed across, and so eager were the crew to leave the wreck that there were as many as five men at one moment on the rope. By the time the lifeboat from St Mary's arrived, men could still be seen in the rigging, but darkness, fog and heavily breaking seas around the wreck made it too dangerous for a close approach, and coxswain Lethbridge was obliged to take his boat to New Grimsby and anchor until daylight.

As soon as it was sufficiently light, the lifeboat returned to find huge waves sweeping over the wreck and only three men visible in the foremast rigging, while another, apparently dead, hung out of the crow's nest. Three rocket lines were fired; the first broke, the second fell short, the third fell squarely across its target only to lay untouched as the Italians appeared not to know what to do with it. Eventually, huge seas washed the three men off the wreck enabling the rescuers to pluck them from out of the sea, the *Elsie* making three trips into dangerous water to reach them. Another survivor was sighted on Scilly Rock and a rocket line was fired across to him, but in reaching for the thin rope he was washed off into the sea where fortunately he was picked up. Of the *Isabo's* crew of 38, two thirds were saved, and in view of the appalling conditions under which the rescue was made, it was a feat as meritorious as any in the islands' long history. Before the survivors of the *Isabo* left the islands, they stood bareheaded on the jetty, with right arms extended in the Fascist salute while Captain Alfredo Tarabocchia, said a prayer for the dead, and publicly thanked the men of Scilly who had saved their lives. There was no shortage of recognition or thanks for the rescue, which showered in from all sides. The owners of the *Isaba* sent £70 to be shared amongst the lifeboat crew, and £250 for the people of Bryher who had taken the survivors in and given them clothing, with individual letters of thanks to all concerned. Matthew Lethbridge received two silver medals for his part, one from the Italian government, the other from the Royal National Lifeboat Institution. Charles Jenkins, skipper of the *Sunbeam* also received two silver medals, whilst Ernest Jenkins of the *Ivy* was awarded a silver medal from the Italian government and a bronze from the RNLI, as was W.E. Jenkins of the *Czar*. In addition, the Lifeboat Institution awarded four other bronze medals and 21 vellums, the Italians a further 34 bronze medals. Registered at Lusinpicolo, the *Isabo* had been on passage from Montreal to Hamburg, and was supposedly thirteen miles south of the Bishop when she struck. Launched in January 1914 as the *Iris* by Cont.Nav. Triestino at Montfalcone, she was fitted with an engine of 2,800 nhp built by the Glasgow firm of Rowan & Co.

The largest sailing ship wrecked in Hell Bay was the Liverpool barque *Maipu* of 594 tons. Bound from Iquique to Hamburg with a valuable cargo of saltpetre, she went ashore only a few hours prior to the *River Lune* which was wrecked in Muncoy Neck, St Agnes, both on 27 July 1879. Carrying a crew of 17, the *Maipu* had called at Cork for orders and was attempting to weather the Isles of Scilly in fog, when Captain Thomas Wheeler thought he heard breakers ahead. The 2nd Mate went forward to listen, but could hear nothing for the sound of the wind drumming in the foresail. Unsure of his position, the captain ordered the helm to be put up in order to wear ship but the order was never obeyed, for at that moment land was sighted ahead, under the lee bow. With helm hard down, spanker hauled taut and gaff topsails set, the *Maipu* started to come about, then struck the rocks a terrific blow and began to sink slowly by the bow. The *Maipu*, which had been launched at Birkenhead in 1865, was declared a total loss and on 18 August, 17 days after the wreck had been sold to some Bryher men for £7, she went to pieces where she lay.

NE of Bryher, across Tresco channel and New Grimsby harbour lies the island of Tresco, whose history is inextricably linked with the church, the sea and Augustus Smith in that order. Leyland, in his itinerary concerning the island of Tresco, wrote:
 'Iniscae longid to Tavestoke, and ther was a poore celle of Monkes of Tavestoke. Sum calle this Trescaw or St Nicholas Isle. In it ys a lytle Pyle or fortres and a Paroch Chyrche that a Monke of Tavestoke yn peace doth serve as a membre to Tavestoke Abbey.'
Tresco was the first island in Scilly to become 'civilised' following the establishment of the church, and after its dissolution during the Reformation, it became best known for the haven or anchorage at Old Grimsby. Its potential as a safe haven was reflected in the Government's choice of St.Helen's Pool as the location for the Quarantine Station following an Act of Parliament in 1745, mentioned in some detail in the next chapter.

As trade increased and the size of ships calling at Scilly followed suit, Old Grimsby, despite its defending battery was found wanting and the deeper channel between Bryher and Tresco, known as New Grimsby, became the more popular anchorage. During the 18th-19th centuries, Tresco enjoyed a lively interchange of shipping, and this small harbour and Tresco Channel would be crowded from end to end with sailing vessels. Whilst Augustus Smith was not a Scillonian by birth, his interest and efforts were directed solely towards making something of the islands, to save them from the economic disaster which at the time seemed inevitable, and to bring them some prosperity. It was in 1834 that he took over a 99 year lease of the islands from the Duchy of Cornwall, leaving his family home in Berkhampsted, Hert-fordshire, to live first on St Mary's, and then in a splendid property he had built known as Tresco Abbey, which remains in the family to the present day. It was not without good cause that Augustus Smith, who styled himself as the 'Lord Proprietor' of the Isles of Scilly, earned several nicknames, not all complimentary, including that of 'Emperor' Smith', for he was an autocrat of the old school, a hard, determined man, far-sighted enough to see what the future could hold for Scilly but a fair man. Some of his actions were very unpopular, such as forcing the inhabitants of Samson to abandon their homes and settle on the other islands. Ensuring that no male need be without work by offering anyone employment in the building of the new pier and church on St Mary's, he went on to build his Abbey home, then a school on every island, introducing real full-time education. Appreciating the long-term advantages of schooling, he insisted that every boy be taught navigation, mathematics, geography and a smattering of French which paid off, since by 1860 there were 135 islanders holding master mariner's certificates. The girls were taught English and mathematics, as well as cooking, housekeeping and husbandry, which would serve them well in married life. The religious organization known as the SPCK (Society for the Propagation of Christian Knowledge) had been visiting the islands since the mid 1700's, offering children spasmodic bible classes but little else. On his death in 1872, Augustus was succeeded by his nephew Lieutenant Algernon Smith-Dorrien, to whom the islanders owe the greatest debt, since it was he who introduced horticulture to the islands and built up the flower industry, now a small but essential part of the islands' economy, regrettably in decline. Algernon Smith-Dorrien (he later changed the order of his surname) died in 1918, and was followed by Major Dorrien-Smith who survived until 1955, followed by, Lt.Cdr Dorrien-Smith then Robert Dorrien-Smith who currently has assumed the responsibilities of his forebears.

Hundreds of sailing ships entered and left both New and Old Grimsby every year, and as wrecks and standings' were an all too common occurrence, only a representative few can be mentioned here. Walking around New Grimsby harbour beach today it is difficult to imagine a 256-ton Royal Navy fireship high and dry here for almost three months undergoing repairs. It was such an unusual event that the details

▲ The barque *Maipu* lies a total wreck in Hell Bay, Bryher, on 27 July 1879, sold to local men for £7.00

◀ Figureheads in the Valhalla collection, part of Tresco Abbey gardens. Many are unidentified, having been found at sea ▶

are worth recording in some detail, Captain Sansom having recorded in his log the following:

'*23 October 1707, Islands of Scilly. This 24 hours hard gales and close weather with small showers of rain; about 2 last past we took one reef more in our fore-topsail and handed him and also one main-topsail. At 8 we handed our main-topsail and hauled up E. At 4 Sir William Jumper handed his foresail and we reefed and handed ours and laid a try under our mizzen as the Commander did. Laid up SSE the wind at S&S xW. About 5 the Commander set his foresail and so did I and hauled up ESE.*

About 12 last night lost sight of his light but still steered ESE and at half past one set our mainsail. About half past 2 set our foretopsail with 2 reefs; about 4 it clearing up we saw Sir William Jumper's light again. They bore SSW about fi(sic) mile distant & finding we ran ahead of them hauled up my mainsail and handed the fore-topsail and then saw the light of Scilly, it bearing SSW about five mile.

We were shot so far in that we could not weather the Smith Rock but was forced to ware ship and brought too with out head to the northward and set our mainsail and we laid up NW the wind at WSW. We wore loosing our main-topsail but the wind veered to the WNW so could not weather the NW rocks; we put our ship to stays but would not so that we put our helm a weather and endeavouring to ware her she struck the leeward part of the rock & received a sea which almost filled her, but hove off into 9 fathoms astern; we fired several guns; a boat came from the shore, advising with the pilot finding my ship very leaky & that we could not free her with 2 pumps and having also 8ft of water in the hold; We brought all our stream cable for a spring to cast her & cut our best bower cable away, and ran in between Samson and Bryher islands, and laid her ashore upon the sand, it being about half flood, it was a quarter flood when we struck upon the rock. We unbent all our sails and unrigged our topmasts and got them ashore.'

Smith Rock, or Great Smith as it is known today, lies NNW of St Agnes at the northern entrance to Smith Sound. Although the *Phoenix* had a Scillonian pilot on

board, it is difficult to imagine she was taken through the shallow channel between Samson and Bryher, where Tresco Flats offer no depth of water, especially to a 256-ton vessel with 8ft of water in her hold. It is more likely that she was taken into New Grimsby Sound and Tresco 'channel' from the north, then beached. The captain's log book reveals: *'This morning hove some of our ballast out to lighten the ship; at almost high water we run her into New Grimsby and hove her ashore upon the sand & carried the sheet anchor with the best bower cable ashore. At low water we found some part of our foreground beat away & about 10ft of her false keel. Also five strakes from the keel about 8ft long with several timbers, beaten in on starboard side and about 5 foot of her main keel, so that when the water flood we could not keep her free & she filled full.'*

The following day was a Sunday, 26th October, when no doubt the captain declared an afternoon 'Make & Mend', a naval tradition for a half-day off, free from all duties other than essential security and lookouts, the ship's company ordered to attend Sunday service in the morning. This is confirmed by the masters log: *'This day fair and little wind. This day the Captain, I and all our people went to church to give God thanks for the mercies bestowed on us in so miraculous deliverance.'*

Ashore, damaged and incapacitated, the Navy Board informed of the situation by dispatch, the ship's officers set about repairs. On 1 November the senior Lieutenant sent the ship's carpenter and men out in a boat amongst the Western Rocks: *'Went amongst the wrecks and found timbers to repair our ship.'* The *Phoenix* remained ashore for 106 days, the crew busy landing stores, cannon and ballast, stripping the sheathing from her damaged sections of hull and trying to keep the interior of the ship dry by pumping. They finally got her afloat on 16 January, assisted by carpenters from the men o'war *Southampton, Arundel & Lizard. 'Hove our ship off the shore and moored her afloat with our best bower to seaward and our stream anchor fast upon a rock upon Tresco island & our small bower to westward & our spare cable fast to a rock on Hangman's island. We lay in 10ft at low water and 5 fathom (30ft) at full sea.'*

They left Scilly on 11th February, reaching Plymouth on the 20th where she anchored in the Sound, waiting dry docking. She remained in service for an incredible 50 years, being rebuilt in 1709 as a 6th rate; rebuilt again at Woolwich in 1727, now of 376 tons; was hulked in 1742 and finally sold out of service in 1744.

Another incident concerned the ship *Nancy* which caught fire in New Grimsby on 9 March 1742. Carrying gunpowder, Bristol compound spirits, hemp and iron, she caught fire and blew up, damaging several ships in the vicinity. Another was the brig *Oldenburger*, Captain Hedstrum, with a general cargo for Ostend from St Vincent, which dragged ashore and was wrecked on 24 January 1783. An obscure domestic incident concerning Tresco in 1791 received a short paragraph in a West Country newspaper on 21 February, when two lives were lost:

'*Between the hours of 5 and 6 in the morning, Mr John Badge, here-to-fore master of the Queen, last of his Majesty's ship Atlas, in passing from St Mary's to the island of Tresco where he resided, was overset in a small Norway skiff, with an invalid of this Garrison who attended him, by a squall occasioned by a sudden shift of wind, and were both drowned. Mr Badge was a man very much respected, and will be generall lamented, and his loss most severely felt by his widow and eight children; the soldier also left a widow and 4 children . Both bodies and the boat also were taken up the next day at low water - the mast was found standing and the sheets belayed.*'

The *Governor Milne*, on passage from Grenada to London, parted her cables and went ashore on 10 January 1806, but was later got off and saved. A prize vessel to the Guernsey privateer *Alarm*, the *St Anthony*, Captain Francis Apollo, came in and was run ashore in New Grimsby harbour on 4 November 1806. She was from Havannah, laden with sugar, rum, honey, hides etc, her cargo being landed on orders from the Custom's Officer and warehoused on St Mary's. Also the schooner *La Sidonia* on 10 September 1825, the *Delfon* 27 March 1831, and the brigantine *Don*, of Sunderland, on 7 October 1846. At an unspecified location on Tresco, the *Mentor* of Jersey parted both her cables in a gale, drove athwart the French brig *Arthemise* and was cut down. The crew of the *Mentor* managed to get aboard the Frenchman which was then run ashore on 18 February 1861, and became a total loss. Another brig, the *John & Ann* of London, was wrecked on 29 January 1826, but the French galliot *Maria*, which went ashore on 26 January 1812, was refloated on 14 March after repairs. Elsewhere on Tresco, the Salcombe brig *Messenger*, laden with coal, Captain Skentelbury, dragged from the roadstead at St Mary's and went ashore on Skirt Island, to the SW of Old Grimsby, on 28 October 1880. The St Mary's lifeboat, *Henry Dundas*, took off five men, then stood by the wreck all night until daybreak as her captain and two men insisted on remaining with their ship. She was successfully refloated and saved on 30 October. A 2-ton cutter, locally owned and on its way to work the wreck of the steamer *Sussex*, capsized off Yellow Ledges on 30 December 1885 with the loss of one life. Nut Rock was the scene of the sudden loss on 5 November 1801 of the London brig *Esperance*, carrying a cargo of locally-caught pilchards on passage from Penzance to Venice. The *Esperance*, Captain William Barber, parted her anchor cables during a SW gale, and within five hours of striking the rock the vessel had gone completely to pieces. A little to the north of Nut Rock lie Paper Ledges, and it was here that the Italian barque *Rosa Tacchini* finished up after breaking adrift during a severe SW gale on Friday, 22 November 1872. On passage from Buenos Aires to Antwerp with hides, wool and tallow, she struck twice before settling down on the rocks where she remained to become a total loss.

Exactly where on Tresco the ship *Maria* was lost on 26 January 1812 is not known, but her loss led to the appearance of her master, Thomas Jones, aged 72, at the Cornwall Assizes at Bodmin on 31 July. Mr. Stephen Lemon, Collector of Customs on St Mary's testified to the stranding of the ship and the landing of her cargo, and related that on 25 April he had searched the prisoner's lodgings on Trescow(sic), and found a trunk containing 12 lace handkerchiefs, 20 cotton shawls, 5 dozen silk mitts or sleeves, 7 dozen cotton sleeves, two telescopes, whilst another sea chest held 6 pieces of silk and cotton net. Also, beneath a false bottom of his cot were found 5 pieces of silk net and 15 pieces of cotton lace within his bed, a Mrs Sinclair of Tresco admitted having bought some china from the prisoner. Mr Thomas Robson, the ship's owner, testified he had approved the prisoner taking command of his vessel, and a George Rue, clerk, testified that the ship's manifest included these articles, but only to the numbers of the casks and packages which contained them. With no direct

▲ Wreck of the *Rosa Tacchini* on Tresco, 22 November 1872

evidence that the lace and cotton came from the wreck, the prisoner was found 'not guilty' and discharged.

The last but one shipwreck of any size on the Isles of Scilly, up to 2009, was that of the Cypriot motor-vessel *Poleire* of 1,599 tons gross, which struck the Little Kettle rock, north-west of Tresco at the top end of Tresco Channel on 15 April 1970 in dense fog. Carrying a cargo of zinc ore, she was bound for Gdynia, Poland, from Ireland when she went ashore less than a mile from the Round Island lighthouse, having failed to hear its fog signal. For the best part of a week she sat on the rocks with all the forward part of her hull above water, which gave islanders' an opportunity to strip the wreck of machinery and electronics, even down to the electric food-mixer in the galley! Within a week the vessel broke in two and settled on the sea bed, which is where Peter McBride and the author, both members of the Royal Navy diving team working on the wrecks of the 1707 Sir Clowdisley Shovell disaster, found and recovered the *Poleire's* builders name plate from the front of her bridge structure.

▲ One of the anchors from the wreck of the Norwegian Barque *Sophie*, carrying anthracite, lost on Tresco 14 December 1896

▲ The author with the builders name plate from the Poleire, taken off the front of her bridge superstructure in 1970

◄ A Cypriot motor-vessel of 1,599-tons, the Poleire struck the Kettle Rock off Tresco and sank on 15 April 1970

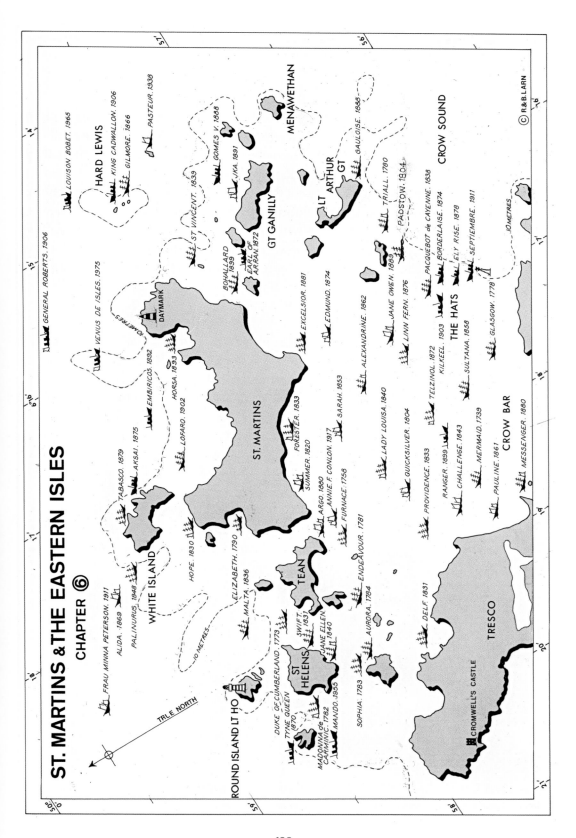

ST. MARTINS &THE EASTERN ISLES
CHAPTER ⑥

© R&B.LARN

TRL E NORTH

ROUND ISLAND LT HO

WHITE ISLAND

ST. MARTINS

ST HELENS

TEAN

TRESCO

CROMWELL'S CASTLE

CROW BAR

THE HATS

CROW SOUND

GT ARTHUR

LT ARTHUR

GT GANILLY

MENAWETHAN

HARD LEWIS

DAYMARK

FRAU MINNA PETERSON. 1911
ALIDA. 1869
PALINURUS. 1848
TABASCO. 1879
AKSAI. 1875
EMBIRICOS. 1892
LOFARO. 1902
HORSA. 1833
HOPE. 1830
ELIZABETH. 1790
MALTA. 1836
DUKE OF CUMBERLAND. 1773
SWIFT. 1831
JANE ELLEN. 1840
SOPHIA. 1783
TYNE QUEEN 1870
MADONNA de CARMINIC. 1782
MANDO. 1955
AURORA. 1784
ENDEAVOUR. 1781
DELF. 1831
PAULINE. 1861
MESSENGER. 1880
GLASGOW. 1778
SEPTIEMBRE. 1911
ELY RISE. 1878
SULTANA. 1858
MERMAID. 1739
CHALLENGE. 1843
RANGER. 1899
PROVIDENCE. 1833
QUICKSILVER. 1804
LADY LOUISA. 1840
ARGO. 1860
ANNIE. F. CONLON. 1917
FURNACE. 1758
SARAH. 1853
SUMMER. 1820
FORESTER. 1833
EXCELSIOR. 1881
EDMUND. 1874
ALEXANDRINE. 1862
JANE OWEN. 1889
LINN FERN. 1876
TELZINOL. 1872
KILKEEL. 1903
BORDERLAISE. 1874
PACQUEBOT de CAYENNE. 1838
TRIALL. 1780
PADSTOW. 1904
GAULOISE. 1888
GOMES V. 1888
JKA. 1891
BOHALLARD. 1899
EARL OF ARRAN. 1872
ST VINCENT. 1839
EMBIRICOS. 1892
VENUS DE ISLES. 1975
GENERAL ROBERTS. 1906
LOUISON BOBET. 1965
KING CADWALLON. 1906
GILMORE. 1866
PASTEUR. 1938

10 METRES
10 METRES
10 METRES

139

6 - St Martin's & the Eastern Isles

There is very little that can be said about St Martins or the Eastern Isles in modern times since their maritime history lies deep in the past. Sprawled across the northern approaches to Scilly from Golden Ball to the easternmost tip of Menawethan, they present an almost continuous barrier of rock four miles long, aptly described as 'fringe' or the 'eastern' islands. Several of these bear the marks of ancient habitation, with ruins and foundation stones of boundary walls reaching down to deserted foreshores. St Helen's holds the remains of what is probably the oldest Christian building in the whole of Scilly; St Martin's has several circular sepulchral barrows of some prehistoric race; whilst on Nornour, foreshore excavation in the 1960's revealed what may be a metal smith's workshop of Roman times complete with jewellery, which is now on permanent display in St Mary's Museum.

St Helen's Pool and its surrounding islands had a maritime connection concerning the Quarantine Station once centered here. Cholera found its way from India into Europe in the 1740's, and the British government sought to keep it out of England by creating a quarantine area for ships in the Isles of Scilly. A Parlimentary Bill of 1752 created a quarantine area in Tresco channel, but the inhabitants of Bryher were far from happy to have possible cholera victims sitting in ships only a few hundred yards from the houses.

A petition was made to government, and the designated area was changed to St Helen's Pool, a safe sheltered anchorage bounded by St Helen's, Tean, Northwethel and Foremans islands. Here an old 1,000-ton ship

◀ Divers from a Royal Navy team explore the wreck of the *Poleire* after it had sunk. The plate in the foreground came from the ship's galley

named *Pandora* was permanently moored which acted as a lazaretto or hospital ship, whose three surgeons could do no more for victims than give them a hammock in which to sleep, attempt to keep the men clean and give them abundant drinking water. The symptoms of this virulent disease were a high temperature, vomiting, severe voiding of the bowel and loss of body fluids. There was no treatment, victims either got better or died, generally from de-hydration, depending on their constitution. There was always a Royal Navy guard-ship in attendance as well, which for much of the period was the gun-brig HMS *Hornet*, whose Royal Marines rowed around the quarantined merchant ships at anchor from dusk to dawn, prepared to shoot any seamen who attempted to swim ashore. It must have been hard on the merchant crews and passengers, who were obliged to stay at anchor there for 30 days if they had cholera on board. It could be financially crippling for owners, since cargoes were also tied up for that period, unable to be sold, and if perishables, such as fruit or vegetables, could deteriorate to the point they had to be thrown overboard. The station continued for 75 years, until after the end of the Napoleonic War, when cholera disappeared and the station closed, bringing to an end the profitable business open to the off-islands of Scilly of providing the many ships at anchor with meat, vegetables, fish, water and beer, with more than a little smuggled rum, brandy, gin, wine and tobacco thrown in.

In support of the quarantine station a small building consisting of just two rooms, a kitchen and probably a living room with a double fireplace between, was erected on St Helen's in 1754, which has been variously called the Pest House, Plague hospital or isolation hospital, but it was far too small to have been any of these. It is more likely to have been erected for the convenience of a St Mary's doctor accompanied by his boatman or assistant, who would help the quarantine station medical staff from time to time, the building acting as an overnight shelter for them to have their meals and sleep.

Apart from the *Torrey Canyon* which was wrecked on the Seven Stones reef, the largest shipwreck of any size to occur in this area was that of the Panamanian steamship *Mando*, which went aground in fog on Golden Ball Bar at 8.30 pm on 21 January 1955. Captain Syras Svoronoss first contacted Lands End Radio that his 7,176 ton steamship, Hampton Roads for Rotterdam with 9,000 tons of coal was in distress, 120 miles W of the Isles of Scilly. Several large vessels went to her assistance, including the mv *Cyprian Prince*, and the steamships *Greece Victory*, *Artillero* and *Vestfoss*, the latter already in the immediate vicinity but was unable to locate the *Mando* in the dark. Lighthouse-keepers manning the Round Island light first saw the Panamanian ship ashore, less than half a mile to the west, near Men-a-Vaur rocks, and summoned the St Mary's lifeboat. With Coxswain Matt Lethbridge at the helm of the lifeboat *Cunard*, despite bad visibility and low water tidal conditions she made the long journey around Samson, Bryher and Shipman Head in order to reach the

▲ The Panamanian ss *Mando*, a total wreck on the Golden Ball Bar, off Tresco, on 21 January 1955 in fog

distressed vessel. They had no difficulty in locating the wreck of the *Mando* since her crew had made a bonfire of tar barrels on deck, which could be seen a long way off. Two of the vessel's lifeboats had been lowered which were being filled with personal baggage by the time the lifeboat arrived on scene, but it was 11pm before her somewhat reluctant captain could be persuaded to leave his ship. Only then could the *Cunard* head back with all 24 crew aboard and two of the ship's boats in tow. The 70 year old gig *Sussex* also arrived on scene to assist in the rescue, managing to get within 100 yards of the wreck before its crew realised the *Mando* had already been abandoned. It would appear from records that the *Mando* was only the second vessel ever to be wrecked on Golden Ball Bar, the previous wreck occurring 173 years earlier. This was the Venetian ship *Madonna de Carmine*, whose captain had the splendid name of Basselle Vuclossaniach. Bound from Rotterdam to Smyrna with cloth, she was wrecked on 14 July 1782, her crew having to sell part of her cargo in order to pay their passage to Falmouth. Half-a-mile NE of the bar, the lighthouse on Round Island nightly flashes out its 10 second white warning light. This lighthouse was built by W.T. Douglass, concurrent with the strengthening and raising of the Bishop light, and whereas, prior to its construction, Round Island had been a puffin colony, not a single puffin inhabited the island whilst the lighthouse remained manned.

A Milford Haven-owned, Hull-registered steam trawler, the *General Roberts*, sank some distance offshore here on 5 June 1906. Almost ideal conditions prevailed when the trawler reached the fishing grounds some 12 miles N of St Martins at 8pm that day, but before the trawl could be put out the engineer reported to Captain John Pettit that they were making water. Pumps were started, but coal dust blocked the bilge-pump strainer boxes and in less than two minutes the vessel had settled low in the water. Her crew took to the punt, riding to 45 fathoms of log-line attached to the ship's rail, until a freshening wind forced them to cast off and row for Round Island. For half an hour the masthead light of the *General Roberts* continued to burn, taunting her crew that she was still afloat, but was then extinguished as she foundered in 240ft. Due to their proximity to Old Grimsby harbour, Tresco, St Helen's Island, St Helen's Pool and St Helen's Gap have all been the site of several strandings. A snow from Boston, Mass, the *Duke of Cumberland*, carrying oil, lumber, deals and other timber for London, went ashore and was wrecked 25 September 1773. The following year, on 1 February, the *Royd* of London, bound from Barcelona to Roscoff with brandy and wine, parted her cables in a gale and was deliberately run onto a shoal to save her. Captain John London of the Teignmouth brig *Endeavour*, on passage from Liverpool to Portsmouth, also had to beach his ship on 3 March 1781 in order to save life, but lost both ship and her cargo of rum, brandy, coal and herrings.

Ashore on 27 March 1831, the same day that the *Delf* went onto the rocks in Old Grimsby harbour, the *Swift*, Captain Bond, Liverpool to Rotterdam, grounded on St Helen's while proceeding to sea but got off on the next tide, a happier fate than that of the Beaumaris brig *Jane Ellen*, Bangor to London with slate, wrecked on St Helen's on 17 March 1840. Other minor incidents concerned the *Sophia* of London, Viborg to Liverpool with deals, which stranded and sank 25 November 1783, and the *Aurora*, Captain Robert Dixon, which struck a rock off Land's End but managed to reach St Helen's Gap before sinking on 31 December 1784. She was later salvaged and returned to service. There was also the *Malta*, Cardiff to Malta with coal, wrecked on Black Rock, seaward of St Helen's Gap, on 29 December 1835; and the small steamship *Tyne Queen* of Liverpool, Cardiff to Marseilles, which struck Men-a-Vaur in fog at 8am on 21 July 1870 and was on the rocks in St Helen's Pool for an hour before reaching New Grimsby and discharging her cargo. Between St Helen's and St Martin's lies the islet of Tean where, in 1852, a wooden box marked 'Agnes Ewing' was washed ashore. It was later identified as having come from an East Indiaman of that name on passage from Liverpool to Calcutta, but nothing more was ever heard of either ship or crew. In 1880, the 61-ton wooden schooner *Argo* went ashore on Tean Island, and was so badly damaged that she became a total wreck. Owned by John Small of Bridgwater but registered at Dublin, the *Argo* had left Newport on 22 October with 105 tons of anthracite for Polruan, in Cornwall. At midnight, when about 20 miles W of Lundy, she shipped a heavy sea which split her mainsail, carried away both gangways and broke her boat gripes. It was only by chance that her captain, going below to collect a towel, found two feet of water in the cabin. Her pumps were promptly manned, and the *Argo* bore away for Scilly with frequent seas breaking clean over her. At 7pm lights were sighted ahead but in making towards them the *Argo* struck a ledge, and, despite having both anchors down, dragged ashore on 23 October. Her crew of eight took to the rigging, awaiting low tide and daybreak, when they were able to gain the shore without incident. Only four days later, on 28 October, the 194 ton wooden brig *Messenger* of Salcombe dragged onto Skirt Island but refused to refloat even after the St Mary's lifeboat had saved all her crew and put a line aboard the wreck in an attempt to refloat her. Carrying steam coal from Cardiff to Portsmouth, owned by Abraham Skentelberry of Looe, the brig, which had been launched in 1866 by Gough of Bridgwater, was so badly damaged that she had to be broken up where she lay, her cargo sold by auction on St Mary's.

Of the many wrecks on St Martin's, the largest of the 'fringe islands', the earliest authenticated occurred on 20 April 1790. This was the *Elizabeth* of London, laden with salt from Alicante, which was sighted coming up on the evening tide, her mainmast overboard, decks smashed and a tangle of rigging trailing astern. Every effort was made to get her ashore, but she drifted right round the islands three times before finally beaching itself on St Martin's. Some forty years later the brig *Hope* was homeward bound from Africa to London with a valuable cargo when, on 19 January 1830, her captain, Alfred Noble, mistook St Martin's Daymark for the St Agnes lighthouse during fog, got too close inshore and struck a rock on the north side of the island. Of the two boats which got away from the wreck, one contained a Dutch naval officer and his wife, their negro servant and another passenger, all of whom were killed or drowned when the vessel's mainmast collapsed across their boat, smashing it to pieces; the other boat holding Captain Noble, the mate and four of the crew reached shore safely. One hundred casks of palm oil, 300 elephant tusks, a box of silver dollars and two small boxes of gold dust valued at £400 each were salvaged. St Martin's Daymark, a prominent, 20ft high conical tower erected in the 1680s by Thomas Ekins, steward of the islands, had until then been plastered white, but after the tragic loss of the *Hope* it was repainted red, and later given the red and white distinctive horizontal bands it bears today.

On 13 February 1833, the naval brig-sloop *Forester*, a 'Cherokee' class vessel of 10 guns and 229 tons, launched at Chatham dockyard on 28 August 1832, was at anchor near Crow Bar close to the East Indiaman *Providence* in a WSW gale when she parted from her small bower anchor. Having lost her best bower in Scilly the day previous, she let go both sheet and stream anchors, firing guns in distress for a pilot. Both hawser cables then parted and she went ashore on the Bar. From here she drifted on to Cruther's Point, St Martin's where the crew cut down her foremast, which in falling brought down her mainmast as well. All the ship's stores were landed on St Martin's and on the 15th her guns were dropped into the sea where she lay to lighten the ship.

According to her log book, ' - on the 16th she was hauled off using her kedge anchor, and taken round the point into the bay'. On the 21st HM steamer *Rhadamano* and the dockyard lighter *Tavy* arrived to take away her stores, shot and any guns they could raise. Originally on passage from Plymouth to Africa, the *Forester* was towed back to Devonport Dockyard on the 30th, where she was dry docked. There are a number of iron cannon underwater just S of Menawethan, and for years were thought to have come from the *Forester*, but are in the wrong place completely and probably came from a merchant ship wreck.

A French chasse maree, the *St Vincent*, commanded by Captain Rio, struck and sank on 6 December 1839 near the Chimney Rocks, towards the eastern end of St Martin's, but all her crew were saved. Three-quarters of her cargo of barley from Marans in France for Penzance, was salvaged before she was sold by public auction where she lay. Sunday morning, 27 November 1881, saw the 640 ton iron barque *Excelsior* of Hamburg laying at anchor in St Mary's Roads in bad weather. Despite 100 fathoms of cable out on the port anchor, eighty on the starboard and stoppers to ease the strain on the windlass, both cables parted, and at 3pm she drove towards Crow Bar. The St Mary's lifeboat and two gigs put out in answer to her distress signals, but despite her crew frantically trying to cut down her topmasts and slipping the broken cables, they were unable to prevent the five-year old, German-built ship from striking the bar, and finally Cruthers Point at the SW corner of Higher Town Bay. There she lay on the rocks for the best part of two months until 22 January 1882 when, on the top of a high tide, with the 64-ton ss *Queen of the Bay* lashed alongside and the ss *Lady of the Isles* ahead, the tow towards St Mary's began. Despite two steam auxiliary pumps working full bore on deck, it was obvious within 15 minutes of the tow commencing that the salvors were fighting a losing battle. Half an hour later the barque heeled over to port and sank in 30ft of water, taking the valuable steam pumps with her, as well as breaking the *Queen of the Bay's* mainmast and damaging her bridge, railings and paddle-boxes. The *Excelsior* had left Rangoon on 7 June under Captain Rudolf Loose with a crew of 15 and a cargo of 915 tons of rice, rattan and teak, the vessel bound for Scilly for orders. A contract to break her up was given to the Western Marine Salvage Company of Penzance, who worked on her for months.

Whilst no steamers have been lost on St Martin's itself, several have hit outlying rocks such as White Island, Hard Lewis or the Hats, the Greek ship *Embiricos* being a typical example. Heavy rain, which seriously reduced visibility during the early hours of Saturday, 6 February 1892, caused the steamer to strike a rock at the back of St Martin's, probably either John Thomas or Deep Ledge. So thick was the weather that her lookouts caught only a brief glimpse of Round Island light seconds before breakers were seen and she struck. Captain J. Lukisias ordered the her crew of 25 to abandoned ship and her starboard life boat, manned by 12 crew plus three Maltese seamen who were passengers on board, was successfully launched. Fifteen minutes later, before the port-side boat could be manned, the *Embiricos* of Andros, a ship of 1,256 tons, went down by the stern foundering in 240ft of water. She took with her the captain, mate, bo'sun and three others who were attempting to launch the other boat. The following day four of her crew, three engineers and a seaman, were rescued from a boat found drifting off the Lizard by the British ss *Rutland* and landed at Le Havre, the other 11 men in the starboard boat having presumably been washed overboard and drowned. The *Embiricos*, built in 1889 by McIlwaine & McCall of Belfast, owned by A. Embiricos of Andros and valued at £20,000, had left Cardiff with coal for Malta and Odessa only the previous afternoon.

Although the full-rigged sailing ship *Horsa* of Liverpool finally sank 21 miles SW of Bishop Rock on Tuesday, 4 April 1893, it was rocks in Bread and Cheese Cove, St Martin's which tore holes in her plating. Homeward bound under Captain Rolson from Bluff Harbour, New Zealand, with tinned meat, wool and grain, this 1,163 ton iron ship came too close inshore while weathering St Martin's during a full easterly gale, missed stays and went hard aground. The St Mary's lifeboat was called out and arrived to find the *Horsa* settling down on the ebb tide. That same afternoon on the flood, after the captain's wife, her child and nanny had been landed, the packet steamer *Lyonesse* went alongside, passed a tow rope and pulled the *Horsa* off. During the tow, which went on well into the evening, three hawsers parted and eventually Captain Rolson decided to sail his ship the rest of the way to St Mary's Roads, but requested the steamer remain in attendance. It was fortunate that he did, for she was able to rescue the entire crew when the *Horsa* rolled over and sank at 1.30am that morning. Owned by the Star Navigation Co. of Liverpool, the *Horsa* had been launched by Scotts of Greenock in 1860. During a full SW gale on 16 February 1869, the Dutch schooner *Alida* of Veendam, Swansea to Taragonna with patent fuel, was lost off White Island while attempting to reach St Mary's with a bad leak. Her crew were rescued by the pilot-gig *Linnet* just as she was about to sink. Another steamship lost in the same area was the Russian *Aksai*, early in the morning of 2 November 1875. She was on passage from Cardiff to Odessa with coal, and when fog blurred the outline of the Scillies Captain Boltine took her too close in on the N side of St Martins, where she struck White Island and remained fast. Again, it was the ss *Lady of the Isles* which went to the rescue of her captain and crew of 39, leaving the steamer to go to pieces where she lay.

A 215-ton Bordeaux barquentine, the *Tabasco*, with 300 tons of coal and bottled beer from Greenock valued at £150, also struck and sank on White Island on 24 March 1879. Her loss was attributed to a language barrier between the English and French members of the crew, and her master having mistaken the Seven Stones lightship for Trevose Head. The *Tabasco* was, in fact only two weeks off the stocks and on her maiden voyage. Distress rockets and flares normally heralded a shipwreck, but it was the bellowing of frightened cattle on shore that first gave the alarm to the islanders of St Martin's on 27 December 1848, when the ship *Palinurus*, Captain Gorl, Demerera to London, went ashore on Lion Rock during a NE gale. It was the noise created by the wind in her torn and thrashing sails that alarmed the grazing animals. All 17of her crew drowned, 12 bodies going ashore on St Martin's on 5 January, and two more on the 19th. Nine quarter casks of rum, plus 71 puncheons and14 hogsheads of spirit were saved by the islanders, which were immediately seized by the Customs Officer on St Mary's and placed in the bonded warehouse. Another large sailing ship in trouble nearby was the Neapolitan barque *Lofaro*, Hamburg to Cardiff in ballast, which struck Merrick Rock, close to White Island on 2 February 1902. A St Martin's coastguard was the first to see the vessel, but not noticing anything amiss left the watch-house to have his tea at home. By the time he had finished and returned to his post the ship was too close inshore to be saved. Lighthouse-keepers on Round Island fired the distress rockets which summoned the St Mary's lifeboat, while 14 local men manned the gig *Emperor*, only to be beaten back by high seas as they attempted to round St Martin's Head. From the shore, anxious watchers saw men swimming away from the wreck, but by the time night fell none of them had come ashore. When the lifeboat arrived it was pitch black, so dark in fact the coxswain had to call to those ashore in order to establish his position from time to time. They searched around the Devil's Table with lanterns but found only wreckage, and were then forced to make the perilous return journey along the north side of St Martin's, past Round Island and through Tean Sound. Next morning the wrecked vessel's keel, complete with stem and stern post, was found ashore, along with three bodies and a wooden chest. Ship's papers and a captain's gold watch in the chest identified her as the 664-ton *Lofaro*, launched at Savona in 1876, which had left Hamburg on 14 January.

Half-a-mile off-shore from St Martins Head, the Hard Lewis Rocks thrust up from 200ft of water, rocks that have taken the bottom out of at least two ships, and probably several more. It has been claimed and generally accepted that a barque called the *Chieftain* was wrecked on Hard Lewis back in 1856, and a figurehead of a Highland chieftain in full-dress in the Valhalla Collection, plus a piece of ship's timbers in the Admiral Benbow restaurant, Penzance, are offered as evidence, but in fact there was no such wreck. No doubt the figurehead washed ashore from some wreck out at sea, perhaps a ship with a Scottish name or connection, but the records of Lloyd's, the Board of Trade, Royal National Lifeboat Institution and Customs & Excise show no *Chieftain* as being afloat at or about that time. Another wreck on the Hard Lewis which can be substantiated was that of the 535 tons barque *Gilmore* of Southampton, Captain Duff, on 12 April 1866. She was en route to Quebec from Southampton in ballast when she struck, and her crew got away in their own boats just as she foundered. Fog, the prime cause of so many wrecks around Scilly caused the 2,126 ton King Line ss *King Cadwallon* of Glasgow to go ashore on the same rocks at 5am on 22 July 1906. After loading 5,032 tons of coal at Barry, shipped by the Tredeager Coal & Iron Co of Cardiff, Captain George Mowat and his crew of 26 sailed at 8am on 21 July, bound for Naples. The *King Cadwallon* left harbour in dense fog which continued until they were off Lundy, when it thinned for half-an-hour, long enough for the captain to obtain an accurate sextant position fix. From Lundy, the steamer set a course of S56°W until the log showed a distance of 77 miles had been covered, when her heading was altered to S34°W. Dense fog prevailed throughout the passage, but frequent soundings showed no sign of shoaling water. At 4.57am a sounding showed 27 fathoms (162 ft), yet three minutes later she struck the rocks, listed to starboard, and within ten minutes her forehold was completely flooded. Later, she slipped back into deep water and foundered, to lie close to a wreck which has been claimed to be the *Chieftain* but is almost certainly that of the *Gilmore*. Close at hand, Hanjaque Rock made a backdrop for the spectacular stranding of the French crabber *Pasteur* of Cameret, on 12 September 1938. She was leaving Scilly when the wind dropped and she drifted ashore, and as the tide fell she was left completely out of the water with her mast leaning on the rock. Fortunately, she refloated herself on the next high tide without any damage..

In 1872 communication between the islands and Penzance suffered a double catastrophe with the loss of both packet steamers, the ss *Little Western* being wrecked on Southward Well, Samson, on 6 October, and the auxiliary packet paddle-steamer *Earl of Arran*, a Clyde-built vessel which grounded on Irishman's Ledge on 16 July. The *Earl of Arran* left Penzance about 10am bound for St Mary's with a crew of eight

▲ Carrying 5,032-tons of coal cargo, the ss *King Cadwallon* got lost in dense fog and was wrecked on hard Lewis in 1906

▲ The loss of the packet vessel *Earl of Arran* in 1872, shown here ashore on Nornour, was a severe blow to the islands communication, especially since the *Little Western* packet was wrecked the same year

hands, 100 passengers, mail, general cargo and supplies. On reaching the islands Captain Richard Deason gave his excursion passengers the opportunity to see something of the Eastern Isles by allowing Stephen Woodcock, a Scillonian hobbler, to take the vessel between St Martin's Head and Hanjaque, thereby it seems, saving 20 minutes. Woodcock steered the steamer too close to the rocks and she struck heavily on Irishman's Ledge. Her engine was put full-astern but she struck again, and again. Her boats were then lowered, and all the ladies taken off first; the vessel being run ashore on Nornour. By 3pm all the passengers, luggage, fittings and some stores had been saved, but by now her engine-room and lower areas were flooded. Two days later she broke in two, the owners receiving only £1,000 in compensation, despite the fact she had cost them three times that much. Her engine block was recovered by the Western Marine Salvage Co, but her boiler continued to show intact at low water until the 1980's, when it collapsed and by 2009 only rusty plating is obvious at low water. The passengers and the whole of the cargo were saved, but nothing could be done for the paddle-steamer and she was broken up for scrap. At the Board of Trade inquiry Captain Deason was found guilty of a grave error of judgment in allowing a passenger, of whose competency he had no knowledge whatsoever, to take charge of his ship, and his certificate was suspended for four months.

Built at Paisley in 1860 for the passenger run between Ardrossan and the Isle of Arran, the little *Earl of Arran* served on the Clyde from 1860 until 1868, when she then worked excursions between Ayr and Troon before going south to Scilly in 1869 under new owners.

The Padstow schooner *J.K.A.*, Captain Escott, Ballinacurra to Poole with 86 tons of oats, was wrecked on the Shag Rocks, on 11 November 1891. Owned by William Escott of Watchet, the 60-ton schooner's passage had been uneventful until 5am on the day she was wrecked. When close to Scilly, she encountered a moderate SSE gale, which quickly swung round to the NNW and increased in force, throwing the vessel on her beam ends. After righting all her canvas was taken in and when the vessel was brought before the wind it was discovered that her port bulwarks and everything movable on deck had been washed away. Her main-boom then fell down over the starboard quarter, carrying away the rail and bulwarks, preventing the wheel from being turned. She drifted helpless until 6.45am when land was sighted, which at first was not identifiable. When close inshore two anchors were dropped but both cables soon parted and she drove ashore. Her crew abandoned ship and reached Great Innisvouls, from where they were rescued by a St Martin's gig, by which time the schooner had drifted clear and sunk. Another of the smaller wrecks in the same area was the 76-ton, wooden brigantine *Bohallard* of Nantes, lost near English Island on 12 February 1899. Bound from Newport to Audierne with coal, the *Bohallard* parted her cables in St Mary's Roads during a WNW hurricane and went ashore at Pendrathen. Later, she floated clear, only to be lost in Higher Town Bay, St Martin's, near the Carn, when she broke up on the 14th.

When St Martin's pilots found 19 members of a steamer's crew and one passenger drifting seaward in two ship's lifeboats past Hanjague on 9 August 1888, it was the first that anyone knew of the foundering of the Portuguese steamer *Gomes V*. Under Captain Antonio de Azevedo, the vessel had sailed from Cardiff the previous day, loaded with 629 tons of steam coal consigned to a Henry Kendall of Oporto. At 1.30am on the 9th, dense fog had been encountered and, despite her speed having been reduced to dead slow, she struck the Shag Rock before the lookouts even saw land ahead. Distress rockets were fired and the crew took to the boats, but fortunately they were sighted before they had time to drift out to sea. At high water the wreck lay completely submerged, and it took until 18 October for divers to recover all that was required, mostly steam winches, anchor cables and deck fittings. A comparatively new ship, the 736 tons *Gomes V*, of Lisbon, owned by Alonco Gomes, had been launched as the *Strathcarron* in 1883, by Bursell & Sons of Dumbarton. That same year, Great Arthur Island on the northern edge of Crow Sound, claimed the 332-ton barque *Gauloise* of Bordeaux, Captain Raul Herand, at 3am on 15 January. With a crew of 11, she was carrying 437 tons of pit-props to Porthcawl and was under plain sail heading NNE, with St Agnes light visible about 14 miles ahead, when fog came down. Despite a good lookout, nothing was seen until 2.10am when the mate went aloft to the fore-yard and saw rocks all round them. He ordered the helmsman to luff-up, but when the captain countermanded the order, the vessel missed stays and fell away. Despite her main and fore-yards being backed, she drove onto Great Arthur. Her crew took to the boats, but later re-embarked to find that the ship's hull had been pierced by a large rock. Her cargo was worked out at intervals during the following six months, after which what little remained and the hulk itself were sold for £14.10s to Joseph Delley of Penzance, who burnt her to the waterline to get at the remaining timber and copper fastenings.

Approaching the Isles of Scilly from the east, unless one is familiar with the islands, the wide expanse of Crow Sound can be deceptive. At first glance it would appear to be a wide, deep sound, flanked only by St Mary's to the south and Great Arthur and the Gannicks to the north, whereas, in fact, it is the most dangerous of the main approaches to St Mary's Roads, as many a ship's master has found to his cost. Untold numbers of incidents have occurred in the Sound, or else on the Hats Ledges and Crow Bar which straddle the channel, though fortunately most have been cases of vessels going aground and being subsequently refloated. On 31 August 1780, the brig *Tryal* of Bristol, laden with sugar and cotton from St Christopher, was wrecked in Crow Sound, and a French barque bound from Rio de Janeiro to Havre, the *Pacquebot de Cayenne*, Captain C. Muny, drove onto the Hats during a full SSE gale on 27 November 1838 and was lost. Although her crew were saved, when the vessel bilged and broke up most of her cargo of hides, wool and coffee was washed out. It was said that she also carried a large sum of money in silver dollars which was never reported as having been recovered.

Interesting wreck remains were found in 2005 near Little Ganinick Island, part of the Eastern Isles, by two local divers. It consisted of a large mound of cargo, made up of iron pipes, clack-valves, cast iron spooked wheels and boiler tubes, and hence the site became known as the 'Wheel Wreck'. Wessex Archaeology was commissioned by English Heritage to survey and evaluate the site in July 2006, to establish whether or not it should be classified a Protected Wreck. The location is in Crow Sound, 300m S of the island and lies at 49° 56.445N; 06° 16.381W, at a depth of between 14-18m. Following a formal diving investigation and survey, it was noted that no ship structure or fittings were obvious, any loose artefact material having been prematurely and unwisely lifted by the finders. Wessex Archaeology identified the cargo as consisting of components supposedly of 'mining equipment, representing a consignment from a Cornish foundry, likely to date from 1850 onwards.' The site was subsequently designated a Protected Wreck in April 2007. Artifacts raised by the finders included four lead scupper pipes, a copper kettle, parts a small brass fireplace, door lock, rigging sheaves, a large earthenware pot, pottery shards and two muskets, some of which are on display in St Mary's Museum.

WILLIAMS' PERRAN FOUNDRY CO. 29

WEARING PARTS OF ENGINES, &c.

PLUNGER POLE, STUFFING BOX and GLAND, with BOLTS COMPLETE, as used in the CORNISH MINES.

These parts are required to be renewed oftener than some portions of the work, because, being working parts they are more subjected to wear. In

ordering these, the dimensions of the top flange of the Pole case should be given.

NOTE.—These are parts of the Plunger Lift.

WROUGHT IRON RISING MAIN PIPES, FOR PUMPS.

These Pipes are placed between the head of the Pump and the working barrels, to permit the Pump to be worked to a greater depth than 28-ft. below the surface or point of delivery; they are usually made in 10-ft. lengths, and are only about one-fifth of the weight of cast iron Pipes.

Diameter.						£ s. d.	Diameter.						£ s. d.
8½-in. to clear	8-in. Buckets	..	..	..			16-in. to clear	15-in. Buckets	..	..	..		
9¼-in.	„	9-in.	„	..	..	..	19-in.	„	18-in.	„	..	..	..
10¼-in.	„	10-in.	„	..	..	..	26-in.	„	24-in.	„	..	..	..
13-in.	„	12-in.	„	..	..	..							

WORKING BARREL, CLACK DOOR PIECE, DOOR, AND WIND BORE.

METALLIC PISTONS,

With Single or Double Rings, with or without Piston Rods. Piston Rods of best Faggotted Iron or Steel, turned and fitted by Machinery of the best modern construction.

▲ A 19th century catalogue of iron water pipes and 'clack' valves, which match closely those lying in the 'Wheel-wreck' which is probably the *Padstow* of 1804

Neither Wessex Archaeology nor the finders were able to identify or date the wreck, so why the former picked on the date c1850 and why anyone thought the cargo was a consignment from a Cornish foundry and not a Welsh one was a somewhat premature assumption. The author of this book, an authority on shipwreck research accepted identification as a professional challenge, and extensively researched this 'mystery' wreck. The list of wrecks around Scilly at the end of this volume does not claim to be definitive for the early years (ie.prior to1740), but from the end of the 18th century to the present day is definitive, therefore the name of the ship had to be already recorded. There was no procedure to formally report wreck to HM Customs & Excise or any other authority prior to 1846 and then purely for the purposes of dividing the proceeds between salvors, nor was there a Receiver of Wreck on Scilly until 1856. However, there is a section in Customs & Excise records in the National Archive (NA/PRO) which specifically deals with wreck for the outports of Penzance, St Ives and Scilly dating from 1722 up to 1938, with wreck letter books relating to vessels and goods lost on Scilly starting in 1821. Therefore the 'Wheel Wreck' had to have sunk before 1856 when a Receiver of Wreck was appointed on Scilly, otherwise its name and details would be well documented. Likewise, if it had taken place between 1821 and 1856 it would appear in the letter books, therefore was pre 1821. The only remaining sources for research are the *Royal Cornwall Gazette*, the earliest Cornish newspaper dating from 7 March 1801, the *West Briton* from 1810 and *Lloyd's List*, going back to 1741. Having previously extracted details of every single wreck incident for Scilly, mainland Cornwall and Devon mentioned in all of these sources, only one vessel fitted the evidence lying on the seabed, suggesting that the wreck was much earlier than previously thought.

The most likely candidate is the *Padstow*, Captain Stephens, registered at Padstow, Cornwall, lost on Christmas Eve 1804. whilst carrying a cargo of iron from Cardiff to London. She had been built in Spain in 1789 and the Lloyd's Underwriters 'Red Book' states her last port of survey was London in 1802, although the rival 'Green Book' states Chester. The two Registers also disagree where she was mostly trading, one quoting London to St Petersburg, the other London to Cork! *The Royal Cornwall Gazette* report of the incident reads:

'Scilly, 24th December 1804. East wind; we have not experienced such a gale as this in a number of years. The Active, *Morgan master, from Portsmouth in ballast for Chepstow, of about 300-tons burthen, is totally lost; the crew saved by the exertions of our pilots. Another brig driven from her anchorage, in a very dangerous situation, has also been saved, and her crew from death by the exertions of the* Hope *packet, Captain Tregarthen, he being prevented from sailing (to Penzance) by the gale. I am sorry to add, that one of the pilots from the packet is drowned. The* Stag *of St Ives, Thompson, from Liverpool to Falmouth and Plymouth, has cut away her main and mizzen masts. The* Padstow *of Padstow, Stephens, from Cardiff with iron for London is totally lost. The crew were saved in their own boat, and perhaps some of the cargo will be saved. Two vessels, a brig and a sloop, were driven out of Broad Sound; we hope they are safe, but they have not been seen since.'*

Four vessels named *Padstow* were built at that port, the one wrecked on Scilly being a 91-ton brig first registered in 1799, owned by Rawlins, the most prominent Padstow merchant in the town at the time. Her three captains up until she was lost were W. Cundy, P. Billing and J. Stephens. She traded regularly with Bristol, London, St Petersburg, Chester and Cork. Lloyd's List No.4178 of 28 December,1804, recorded the incident on Scilly simply as: *'The Brig Padstow, from Cardiff to London, is wrecked at Scilly.'* What is particularly interesting and relevant is that she was trading regularly with London, always from Cardiff, and is likely to have carried iron before.
Lloyd's List entry, No.4418 of 13 January 1804 reads: *'The* Padstow, *from Cardiff to London, has been on shore on some rocks near Falmouth, since got off with considerable damage, and put into Falmouth.'*

Following her stranding, the *Padstow* was put up for sale by auction at the Hamburgh Arms, St Mawes, on 8 February 1804, the auction notice reading: *'The good*

Brig Padstow, *Length aloft - 60ft 1ins; Extreme breadth - 19ft.6ins; depth in hold 10ft.1ins. Measures 91 and 49/94 tons. A remarkably strong, firm-built vessel and well found in all her principal Materials and Stores. For a view of the said vessel, and for further particulars, apply to Captain John Stephens, on board at St.Mawes. January 26th 1804'*

We know that the vessel, if it is the *Padstow*, which is most likely, was carrying a mixture of cast iron wheels, boiler tubes and flanged cast iron pipes, some with clack valves, from Cardiff to London, and that it was not the first trading voyage she had made to the capital that year. From the middle of the 17th century Cardiff was the leading exporter of cast iron from the large ironworks at Merthyr Tydfil, which were respectively Dowlais, Penydarren, Plymouth and Cyfarthfa. In 1804-5 the spread of population in London led to the setting up of nine private water companies to supply fresh drinking water, many of which were still using pipes made of wood or lead. The Lambeth Waterworks for example, expanded in 1802 to supply Kennington and set about *'replacing its wooden pipes with iron ones.'* The many London waterworks used boilers to drive steam engines for pumping, and concentric iron tube boilers such as that invented by Trevithick were producing pressures of 50-60psi, whose tubes would require frequent replacement as they corroded. Pumps and pumping gear all used spooked cast wheels - all of which sits well with the cargo carried by

▲ Having lost her rudder, the Spanish steamer *Septiembre* entered Crow Sound in March 1911 but ran aground on the Hats and became a total wreck in March 1911

the 'Wheel Wreck', which can be tentatively identified as the *Padstow*. Her loss in 1804 would explain why no remnant of her wooden hull remains showing, since worm would long ago have demolished her timbers. If timber remains, then the cargo is probably sitting on top of her lower frames, keel and keelson.

Four steamers have fallen victim to the rocks known as the Hats, two of which left their rusting plates scattered over the sand, the first of the quartet being the 379 tons net *Bordelaise* of Liverpool, bound from Newport to Oporto with coal and railway iron. On 4 April 1874, Captain O'Keefe attempted to bring his vessel in at half-tide without a pilot on board, and was about to anchor when she struck heavily. Anxious to save their vessel which had been built at Whiteinch, Paisley, only the previous year her owners, the Boscawen Steamship Co of Liverpool, sent out lighters to remove the cargo and had special salvage pumps brought down from Glasgow. But shortly after the pumps had been installed on deck the *Bordelaise* sank, and divers had to be employed to salvage the equipment. After most of the cargo had been saved, the hull and engine were sold to Francis Banfield & Sons of Scilly, Shipping Agents, for £455. The *Ely Rise* of Cardiff was the next steamship incident on the Hats. While attempting to gain the shelter of St Mary's Roads during a westerly gale on 23 October 1878, Captain William Vickerman took his ship into Crow Sound at 5.30pm with the tide at half-ebb, and struck the rocks. Within an hour her engine-room was flooded and boiler fires extinguished. Hand-pumps were rigged, and with the ss *Lady of the Isles* alongside, the *Ely Rise* was kedged off and beached for repairs, later going alongside St Mary's quay. Bad weather brought the Spanish steamer *Setiembre* into the Sound on 26 March 1911. Registered at Bilbao and on passage from Porman to Maryport with iron-ore, this 2,171-ton vessel lost her rudder and badly holed her hull when she hit the Hats. By midnight she had flooded from bow to stern and although her entire cargo of ore was dumped overboard in an attempt to lighten ship, she was eventually abandoned to the sea. Her boiler still shows above the surface at low water, a point of interest to holiday-makers visiting the eastern isles in local launches. The fourth and last victim was the *Kilkeel*, Glasgow to Nova Scotia with a general cargo, which struck the Hats on entering Crow Sound with choked pumps on 17 October 1903, but was later successfully refloated.

The wide expanse of shallow water north of the Hats, known as St Martin's Flats, saw the 95-ton Brixham schooner *Sarah* sink at anchor on 27 January 1853. Bound from Cardiff to Tenerife and Santa Cruz with a crew of six and a cargo of coal, she sprang a serious leak on the 25th and had to be brought into the Sound. Her hull and cargo were sold three weeks later for £38. A Cardiff brig, the *Alexandrina*, laden with coal, was abandoned in the roadstead on 24 February 1862 during a gale, but pilots saved her by running the vessel on to the flats, a service for which they received £97 from a grateful owner. The schooner *Edmund* was involved in a similar incident on 13 April 1874. At low tide, the worst obstacle in the Sound is Crow Bar and the ledges around Guthers Island, which have been the cause of several stranding incidents over the centuries. On 30 December 1739, the *Mermaid* of Plymouth was wrecked on the bar, and on 20 January 1758 the *Furnace* of London on Broad Ledge, after striking Guthers. Bound for Gosport, Captain William Park, the *Furnace* was carrying brandy, pewter, oil, rosin and prunes, but despite having sunk, Customs officers and local inhabitants saved most of her cargo. HMS *Glasgow*, a 20-gun 6th rate struck the Crow in 1778 and exchanged part of her forefoot for a huge rock which she carried back to Plymouth embedded in her hull, which was exhibited in Devonport Dockyard. Launched by Blaydes of Hull on 31 August 1757, the *Glasgow* was later lost by fire in Montego Bay, Jamaica, the following year. Other incidents locally involved the *Quicksilver*, carrying a cargo of salt for Newfoundland, totally wrecked on 30 May 1804; the schooner *Summer*, run on shore on 28 November 1808; the *Providence*, bound for Bombay, which struck on 13 February 1833, was scuttled two days later, then raised and floated off on 6 May; and the less fortunate *Lady Louisa*. This was a brig owned in London, Captain Henley, which arrived at Scilly in distress whilst bound from Rio de Janeiro to Cowes and London with coffee on 2 February 1840. Unfavourable weather and tidal conditions made it impossible to get her into the Roads, and she drove on to Guthers Bar. Hundreds of bags of cargo were thrown overboard, but she remained fast and eventually went to pieces. On 21 November 1843, the London schooner *Challenger*, Surinam to her home port, struck the Nundeeps and sank near Bryher Island, and a German ship, the *Sultana* of Hamburg, was totally wrecked there on 24 March 1853. Her crew all drowned, and a name-board from the wreck washed ashore as far afield as Padstow a month later. Other casualties on Crow Bar have included the *Pauline*, a French schooner bound from Ardrossan to Rouen with railway iron, which drove ashore on 18 February 1861 and went to pieces; *Telxinoi*, a Greek brig, on 17 February 1872; a full-rigged ship from Glasgow, the *Linn Fern*, totally wrecked on 9 March 1876, and the *Jane Owen*, another total loss on 3 March 1889. The Liverpool Salvage Association's steamer *Ranger* also struck the bar on 7 June 1899, but was refloated the same day.

Navigational charts of the Isles of Scilly show a wreck situated 30m NW of Broad Ledge, at the entrance to Tean Sound. This is the American schooner *Annie F. Conlon*, which was badly damaged by gunfire from a German submarine, and was towed into Crow Sound on 5 October 1917. She began to break up immediately on arrival, and her cargo, consisting of casks of oil, washed clear. By 1 December she was a complete wreck, masts and deck gone, her hull lying on its beam ends and empty of cargo. A total of 455 casks of oil were salvaged and realized £1,406 9s for the owners, the Marine Transport Co of Mobile, Alabama.

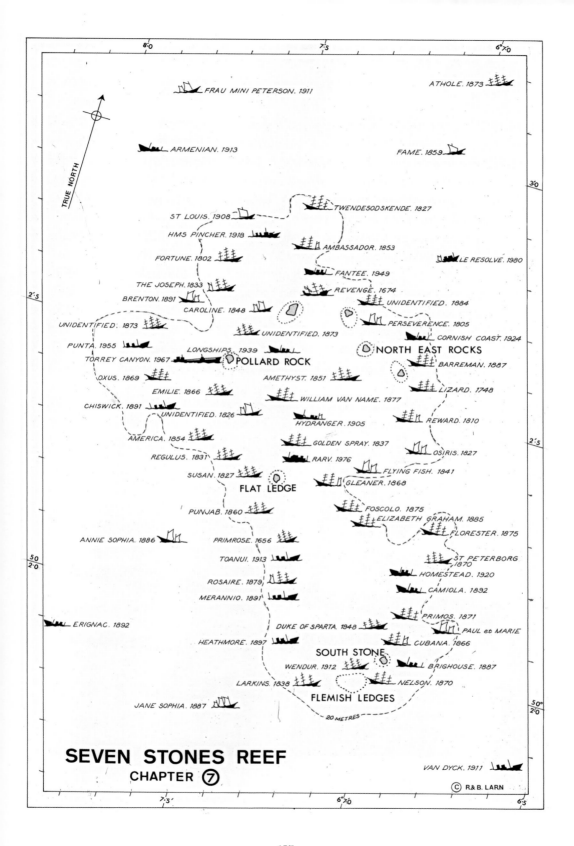

SEVEN STONES REEF
CHAPTER ⑦

FRAU MINI PETERSON. 1911

ATHOLE. 1873

ARMENIAN. 1913

FAME. 1859

TRUE NORTH

ST LOUIS. 1908

TWENDESODSKENDE. 1827

HMS PINCHER. 1918

AMBASSADOR. 1853

FORTUNE. 1802

LE RESOLVE. 1980

FANTEE. 1949

THE JOSEPH. 1833

REVENGE. 1674

BRENTON. 1891

UNIDENTIFIED. 1884

CAROLINE. 1848

PERSEVERENCE. 1805

UNIDENTIFIED. 1873

UNIDENTIFIED. 1873

CORNISH COAST. 1924

PUNTA. 1955

NORTH EAST ROCKS

TORREY CANYON. 1967

LONGSHIPS. 1939

POLLARD ROCK

BARREMAN. 1887

OXUS. 1869

AMETHYST. 1851

LIZARD. 1748

EMILIE. 1866

CHISWICK. 1891

WILLIAM VAN NAME. 1877

UNIDENTIFIED. 1826

REWARD. 1810

HYDRANGER. 1905

AMERICA. 1854

GOLDEN SPRAY. 1837

OSIRIS. 1827

REGULUS. 1831

RARV. 1976

FLYING FISH. 1841

SUSAN. 1827

GLEANER. 1868

FLAT LEDGE

FOSCOLO. 1875

PUNJAB. 1860

ELIZABETH GRAHAM. 1885

ANNIE SOPHIA. 1886

FLORESTER. 1875

PRIMROSE. 1656

TOANUI. 1913

ST PETERBORG. 1870

HOMESTEAD. 1920

ROSAIRE. 1879

CAMIOLA. 1892

MERANNIO. 1891

PRIMOS. 1871

ERIGNAC. 1892

PAUL et MARIE

DUKE OF SPARTA. 1948

CUBANA. 1866

HEATHMORE. 1897

SOUTH STONE

WENDUR. 1912

BRIGHOUSE. 1887

LARKINS. 1838

NELSON. 1870

FLEMISH LEDGES

JANE SOPHIA. 1887

20 METRES

VAN DYCK. 1911

© R & B. LARN

7 - The infamous Seven Stones

Until 1967 the Seven Stones Reef enjoyed a quiet notoriety for shipwrecks, most of which happened long in the past and had almost been forgotten. Then, on Saturday 18 March that year, a ship whose name was to become familiar to half the world went ashore on the reef to give the British government and the West Country a serious problem of unprecedented magnitude. Besides being the largest ship ever lost by stranding on the coast of the United Kingdom, the *Torrey Canyon* was at the time, one of the largest tankers in the world, carrying a prodigious 119,328 tons of crude oil when she hit the Pollard Rock, tearing a 610ft long hole in her starboard side, creating the first of a spate of oil spills which stretched from France to Alaska. Since 1967 there have been at least 85 vessels larger than the *Torrey Canyon* lost at sea, several of which were tankers, resulting in massive oil spills. The nearest of these to the United Kingdom was the Liberian registered *Amoco Cadiz*, 109,700 tons, which was wrecked on 16 March 1978 near Ushant. She broke in two the following day, depositing 223,000 tons of crude oil on the French coast, giving the authorities no time to contain the spill.

A radio message from the *Torrey Canyon*, sent at 8.45am to the agent in Milford Haven, stated simply: '*Aground on Seven Stones. Require immediate assistance.*' It was a

▲ Aground on the Seven Stones in March 1967, the super-tanker *Torrey Canyon* was already leaking oil by the time Royal Navy helicopters carried out an aerial survey

nearby fishing trawler, probably the French *Mater Christi*, that informed the world on an international distress frequency of the stranding, and so the rescue organisation swung into action. The St Mary's lifeboat was launched, two Search & Rescue Wessex helicopters lifted off from the Royal Naval Air Station at Culdrose, and several ships reported they were closing on the wreck at full speed. These included the Fleet Auxiliary *Brambleleaf* which was the nearest ship, reported 13 miles S of the 'Stones', the Dutch motor-vessel *Bierum*, the British tanker *Tillerman*, the steamship *Helenus*, and the tugs *Atlantic*, *Albatross* and *Utrecht*. The latter, a huge, Dutch ocean-going salvage vessel, was on her regular station in Mount's Bay and reached the Seven Stones shortly after the Scillies lifeboat. The deck watch aboard Trinity House lightship No.19, the Seven Stones lightship, first saw the huge vessel at 9.05am, three or four miles S of their position, thus putting the tanker between three-quarters and a mile and three-quarters S of the Pollard Rock. Warning rockets were fired, followed by the international flag hoist 'JD,' meaning, *'You are standing into danger'*, the same signal being flashed repeatedly on a signal lamp. Assuming that the time of the stranding given by the captain of the tanker was correct, the crew of the Seven Stones lightship were still attempting to warn the *Torrey Canyon* of danger when in fact she was already ashore. The time factor is still in dispute, but is irrelevant since the lightship had no operational responsibility to warn individual ships, its mere presence being considered sufficient. That such a disaster could happen in broad daylight, with near perfect visibility and a relatively calm sea, within easy visual range of the Wolf Rock lighthouse, Round Island light, the Longships and the Seven Stones lightship itself is almost inconceivable. But happen it did, and the monstrous vessel impaled itself at 17 knots on the largest and most westerly rock on the reef. By 11am, a small fleet had gathered around the wreck, maintaining a respectful distance between themselves and the broken water which marked the rocks. Situated 15 miles W of Lands End and seven miles from the Isles of Scilly, the reef is supposedly named after seven rocks, whereas in fact there are eight which protrude above the surface at low water, the whole occupying an area of some three-quarters of a square mile.

As the tide fell and more broken water appeared around the stranded vessel, only the lifeboat was able to go alongside her, to transfer salvage officers and other experts. After one such trip, coxswain Matt Lethbridge of the St Mary's *Guy & Clare Hunter*, expressed a fear that the wreck would soon break its back. Eight and a half days later his prophecy came true, but only after the *Torrey Canyon* had survived three attempts to refloat her, two gales, and an internal explosion. By the afternoon of her first day ashore, an estimated 5,000 tons of dark brown heavy fuel oil had spilled from her ruptured tanks, and already pollution was on a scale never previously experienced. Devonport dockyard despatched the minesweeper HMS *Clarbeston* with 1,000 gallons of detergent to emulsify and sink the oil, followed by the tug *Sea Giant* with a further 3,500 gallons, almost the entire stock held by the Royal Navy. The tug *Utrecht* made the first attempt to refloat the tanker alone that evening at high water, but failed to

▲ The government took the decision to bomb the *Torrey Canyon* wreck, setting it on fire, to burn off as much oil as possible

move her, after which the weather deteriorated so that by morning a full gale was blowing from the NW. Aircraft were already reporting an oil slick covering an area of 18 miles by two, spreading into the English Channel and towards Cornwall. HMS *Barrosa*, already in attendance off the Seven Stones, joined the *Clarbeston* in spraying detergent, but it was already painfully obvious that their efforts were totally inadequate being unable to keep pace with the flood of oil pouring out of the tanker. During the early hours of Sunday afternoon the *Torrey Canyon* was abandoned by all except her captain, her principal officers, four seamen and two salvage experts. The St Mary's lifeboat, relieved by the one from Penlee, retired to Hugh Town with nine of the tanker's crew aboard, all Italians, having been on station for 31 hours, possibly the longest continuous service performed by an Isles of Scilly lifeboat since its installation in 1837.

By Monday 20 March, the slick had increased until it measured 30 miles by eight, its stench quite plain at Truro, 48 miles away, and later as far afield as Newton Abbot, in Devon. Captain Pastrengo Rugiati expressed an opinion that same day that his ship still had a 50/50 chance of survival, but fears had been expressed at government level that the *Torrey Canyon* might never be re-floated. Consequently, the Under Secretary for Defence (Navy), Mr Maurice Foley, flew to Plymouth and set up a co-ordinating headquarters at Mount Wise. It had been suggested that the ship and her remaining oil should be burnt, but even governments cannot legally set fire to private property without the owners' consent, and in this case the owners were still making strenuous efforts to save their ship. On the Tuesday, the tugs *Utrecht, Titan, Stentur* and *Praia de Adrago* stood by ready to pull their hardest, and compressors poured high-pressure air into the damaged starboard tanks. Then came a violent explosion in the engine-room, seven men were injured, another two blown off the ship into the sea, and a hole 18ft square was blasted clean up through three decks just forward of the funnel. It was a terrifying experience for those on board and in nearby ships, for the wreck still contained at least 95,000 tons of oil and could remotely have exploded, destroying everything within a large radius. The tanker was immediately abandoned, the injured being transferred to the West Cornwall Hospital at Penzance, where Captain Hans Stahl, the chief salvage officer, one of the two men blown overboard, was found to be dead. At least 30,000 tons of oil was promptly added to that already floating on the surface, covering an area now 35 miles by 22 miles, and worse was to follow. At sea, 19 ships sprayed the surface continuously, the oil being now less than 12 miles from the beaches of Cornwall.

That Easter holiday was ruined for thousands of families. Meetings between salvage officials and the government went on throughout the night, troops were sent to the West Country, factories turned out detergent in quantities never seen before, and in a plastics factory near Liverpool men worked on the construction of 130 blocks of plastic foam, each measuring 30ft long by 3ft square, designed to support a boom to encircle the wreck and contain the oil. Meanwhile, in Devonport dockyard riggers worked on a special canvas skirt to hang beneath the boom, whilst on the cliffs at Land's End, look-out posts were established, reminiscent of the days in 1939-40 when the country awaited the arrival of a different sort of seaborne enemy. On Good Friday the first of the oil came ashore at Sennen Cove, and every available boat that could hold a 45-gallon drum of detergent converged on the area. Easter Saturday and Sunday offered the salvage men two days in which to prepare for an all-out effort on Monday, the highest tide of the season. A second attempt to pull the *Torrey Canyon* clear of the rocks on Saturday succeeded in moving the vessel slightly, but nothing more, whilst Sunday's efforts ended in complete disaster. At 7.45pm on Easter Sunday, half supported on compressed air, half on rock, battered by two severe gales during the previous week, weakened by the internal explosion and four tugs almost pulling her apart, the *Torrey Canyon* broke in half abaft the bridge and oil simply gushed out. 24 hours later the wreck lay in three pieces, with her bridge section awash. At least 80,000 tons of oil had by now been released, threatening hundreds of miles of the loveliest coastline and beaches in the country, immediately prior to its holiday season.

It was a situation no country in the world had ever had to face, there was no experience and very few answers, and people found out as they went along how best to treat the 'black tide'. At sea 53 major vessels were spraying night and day, whilst on land thousands of troops, sailors, airmen, firemen, cadet forces and volunteers used anything that would hold detergent, even down to watering cans! Well over half a million gallons of detergent were poured over the oil, but even this was insufficient. Meanwhile, on the Seven Stones Reef, the three broken sections of the wreck still held nearly a third of the original cargo, and the decision was taken to set it alight. The Trinity House tender *Stella* moved the lightship off station, and an area within a 20-mile radius of the wreck was declared closed to all shipping. At 4pm on Tuesday 28 March, 'Buccaneer' strike aircraft of the Royal Navy delivered the first thirty 1,000-lb bombs, followed by 'Hunter' aircraft of the Royal Air Force, which dumped 5,400 gallons of kerosene from wing drop-tanks, and flames were soon reaching a height of 500ft, and smoke 8,000ft. The following day more high explosive bombs were dropped, then napalm, and by Thursday morning it was all over. What had once been a ship was now only a burnt-out tangle of steel, the sea finally demolishing the wreck so that no part now shows above water. It had taken 200,000 lb of explosive, 11,000 gallons of kerosene and 3,000 gallons of napalm to destroy her - the most dramatic, spectacular and publicised wreck in the long history of Cornwall. Built by the Newport News Shipbuilding & Dry Dock Company in 1959, the *Torrey Canyon* had a gross tonnage of 38,562, 65,920 tons deadweight. During 1965 she had been 'jumboised' by the Sasebo Heavy Industries Co of Japan, who had cut her in half and added an extra 164ft to her length, almost doubling her carrying capacity and increasing her deadweight tonnage to 118,285. With a draught of 51ft, she was only a matter of 50ft shorter than the old liner *Queen Elizabeth*. The *Torrey Canyon* has been in the news three times since the last visible part of her super-structure disappeared underwater. In 1982 her entire forepart, still intact, was refloated and converted into an oil storage barge, and shortly after two of the four blades of her huge phosphor-bronze propeller were removed by divers. One was lost overboard accidentally in 120m depth whilst being carried to Padstow, the other was impounded by Customs and Excise, the salvor appearing in Bodmin Court on a charge of theft from wreck.

Exactly how many ships have been lost on the Seven Stones Reef over the centuries will never be known. One author suggests *'only fourteen wrecks have been recorded on the reef'*, another *'257 for Scilly and the Seven Stones together between 1679 and 1923'* but this chapter alone will mention the details of at least 76 and there have been many more which went unrecorded. The earliest recorded wreck is that of the 6th rate, 22 gun English man o'war *Primrose*, which put to sea with the *Mayflower* in search of two Spanish frigates which were cruising the area. In early March 1656 the *Mayflower* lost her main topmast in heavy weather off the Longships, and whilst Captain Sherwin of the *Primrose* was away from his ship arranging with Captain Brown to supply him with a spare, the *Primrose* drifted on to the Seven Stones. Although they managed to get her off, badly damaged she sank in 60 fathoms, 16 men, two women and a child going down with the ship. When Trinity House were requested by the Admiralty to investigate the obstruction, they pronounced there had been no neglect either in the officers or company, the place where the *Primrose* miscarried being a rock not visible nor described in any chart they could find. Another early wreck was the *Revenge* on 30 November 1674, from which only two of her 17 crew were saved, followed by the 14-gun sloop HMS *Lizard*, Captain Siffon, wrecked with the loss of over 100 men on 27 February 1748. The *Lizard* was a small vessel of 272 tons, 92ft long and 26ft in the beam, and had been built by Ewer at Bursledon on the River Hamble on 22 December 1744. During the next 100 years

◄ The *Seven Stones* light-vessel, whose crew tried desperately to warn the *Torrey Canyon* they were heading for the rocks

there must have been innumerable other wrecks here and as early at 1826 the government was being petitioned to place a light on the reef.

Unfortunately, history has not recorded many of the names of ships lost here in the early 1800s, but we do know about the *Fortune*, lost while carrying a general cargo from London to Dublin. She struck the reef on 12 February 1802, her crew being picked up by a Yarmouth brig. Four pilots from Scilly attempted to save the derelict, but it sank beneath them, drowning two of the men. The British brig *Perseverence* was another of the early wrecks. Bound from Dublin to London, she struck during fog at 7am on 14 November 1805, her crew rowing themselves to St Mary's. She was followed by an Exeter brig, *Reward*, on 6 November 1810, laden with oats and butter from Limerick, and by the *Hope* of Fowey on 5 May 1814. An unidentified schooner was seen to hit the 'Stones' on 16 January 1826, and on 29 October of the following year, the American ship *Susan* of Boston, Matanzas to Hamburg with logwood and cotton, struck in rough seas. Her crew was rescued by the Tresco pilot cutter *Hope*, except for a Negro who drowned. The Dutch galliot *Twende Sodskende*, Bilbao to Copenhagen, also hit the reef late in 1827, sinking two miles off Bryher on 9 September. A brig, the *Joseph* of Sunderland, carrying pig-iron from Cardiff to London, was wrecked here on 18 November 1833, and in 1837 the barque *Golden Spring*, of and from London for Liverpool with general cargo, found the reef in fog on 16 May but was refloated at high water, a similar but less dramatic experience to that which befell the East Indiaman *Larkins* the following year. It was 8am on Sunday, 18 November 1838, when the *Larkins* hove-to between Scilly and Lands End to take on a pilot named Hicks. The pilot had no sooner gained the main deck than the vessel struck heavily three times, then floated clear, leaking badly. With the pumps unable to hold their own, Captain Ingram, the passengers, mail and pilot transferred to the pilot-cutter, the crew remaining aboard. Upon arrival at Penzance, Captain Ingram hired 50 men, and they set off in boats to find the Indiaman. After a fruitless search lasting all one day and night, the men returned, and Captain Ingram departed for Falmouth to consult Captain Plumridge RN, who ordered HMS *Meteor*, a wooden paddle vessel, to find the *Larkins*. She was located between Falmouth and the Lizard, having already been taken in hand by a pilot named James of Coverack, who had recruited 26 local men to work the pumps. The *Larkins* reached Falmouth with 8 ft of water in her hold, and after going alongside Boyes cellars, discharged cases of indigo, silk and saltpetre from the lower hold.

The first petition for a light on the Seven Stones met with no success, but a second, supported by the Chamber of Commerce of Waterford, merchants from Liverpool and the British Channel ports in 1839, carried more weight. At a meeting held in Falmouth on 21 February 1840, it was declared that a light positioned on or near the reef would shorten the passage around Scilly by as much as 36 hours. As a result, a lightship appeared at St Mary's on 31 July 1841, and was moored in position after considerable difficulties by the 20th August and exhibited its first light on 1 September 1841, Regrettably it was too late by nearly a year to have prevented a wreck on 4 October 1840, that of a Scilly-registered schooner, the *Flying Fish*. Bound from Liverpool to Constantinople with general cargo, the schooner struck the rocks and nearly became a total loss, her crew being picked up by St Martin's fishermen. At first, the new lightship was in constant trouble, breaking her moorings and dragging out of position. On 25 November 1842 she was almost wrecked when the cable again parted and she drove over the reef, fortunately at high water. Her crew had evidently had enough, for they slipped the broken cable and set sail for New Grimsby, remaining there until 6 January the following year. Back in position again, she broke adrift within a matter of days, and in the March went clean over the reef for the second time. In 1848, on 29 September, one of the light-ship's two longboats was used to rescue the mate of the Barnstaple schooner *Caroline*; the sole survivor, his ship carrying a coal cargo from Newport to Tarragona, having struck the reef in fog and foundered. The same longboat capsized in a squall and drowned two of the lightship's crew on 15 October 1851, whilst returning from Scilly with stores.

Earlier that same year, on 23 April, the timely appearance of the barque *Mary Laing* had saved the crew of the Exeter brig *Amethyst*, carrying china clay from Teignmouth to Quebec, when she slipped off the rocks and sank six hours after striking in bad visibility. As well as displaying a warning light, the Seven Stones Reef lightship also offered sanctuary to the crews of shipwrecked vessels, and the first arrival of these 'temporary guests' was in 1853, following the loss of the Maltese brig *Ambassador* on 12 June. Deep laden with Cardiff coal bound for her Mediterranean home port, she struck and sank within half an hour. Thick fog also put the full-rigged Cape Horner *America* on the reef on 2 February 1854. Registered at St Johns, New Brunswick, this 16 month-old ship was carrying guano from Callao to Queenstown and London when she struck. Within the hour she had sunk, her crew being rescued by the Scilly boat *New Prosperous* and landed at St Ives. One of the many fishing-boat incidents on the reef occurred on 27 April 1859, when the Newlyn-owned *Fame* was caught in a severe ESE gale whilst attempting to reach Scilly for shelter. She capsized and sank in heavy seas just off the lightship with no survivors. In 1860, the Seven Stones claimed the Sunderland barque *Punjab*. Commanded by Captain Dale, the *Punjab* was carrying 300 tons of wool and hides from Algoa Bay to Amsterdam, when she hit the reef at 3.15am on 14 September. With her bow shattered and filling fast, she drifted clear to leeward, and it was whilst she was being abandoned that the wife of one of the passengers, the Reverend Arbouset, was drowned as she clung to the rigging, too terrified to let go. Although a schooner passed close by the waterlogged long-boat containing the rest of the passengers and crew, the lookout failed to see them and it was not until dawn that they were sighted and rescued by the *Joshua & Mary* and landed at Falmouth.

More 'temporary guests' appeared alongside the lightship in a boat on 18 September 1866, when the crew of five from the Glasgow schooner *Emilie* escaped after she was wrecked in fog. Bound from Poole to Runcorn, the vessel had heeled over and sunk within five minutes of striking the reef. When another Sunderland barque, the *Cubana*, struck bows-on to the rocks on 25 April 1866, both her master, who should have been on watch at the time, and the mate, were below asleep in their bunks. Under the influence of a strong SE wind, the barque had been beating down Channel, having recently left Swansea for St Jago, Cuba, with 16 crew, one passenger and a cargo of coal, iron, and mining gear. Her master rushed on deck after the impact but, apparently paralysed by fright, was quite unable to take command of the situation or himself. Taking matters into their own hands, the mate, nine of the crew and the passenger took to one of the boats leaving the captain and six shipmates to perish. After a hard row, the lightship loomed up out of the haze and they were taken aboard. Next morning, when they were transferred to St Mary's by pilot cutter, they found they were not the only survivors to reach Scilly that day, the pilot cutter *Agnes* having previously landed Captain McKeller and his crew from the *Ebgante* of Quebec. Bound from New York to Liverpool with oak, the *Ebgante* had been abandoned in a sinking condition on the 4th, when some 100 miles W of Scilly, her crew having been taken off by the ship *Ferdinand* of Bremen before meeting up with the pilot cutter.

Following 1867, there was at least one wreck a year on the 'Stones', often more right through until 1890. On 8 May 1868, the 135-ton brig *Gleaner* of Newport, Captain William Prance, on passage from Bilbao with iron ore, went missing off Land's End and was later found to have sunk some 30 miles NW by W of Land's End, presumably having hit the reef. An East Coast fishing lugger found her captain's writing desk, a meat safe, and other identifiable wreckage in the vicinity. More visitors to the lightship, 14 in all – this time must have strained the resources of the lightship to its limits – appeared on 1 September 1869 after the captain of the *Oxus*, John Dixon Wilson, mistook the 'Stones' light for the Longships and passed too close, a not uncommon occurrence. Loaded with 720 tons of rice from Akyab, Burma, this Dundee-registered ship of 536 tons had left Queenstown with orders for London on 29 August. Between 8 and 10.30pm on 31 August, following some confusion over identification of the three lights in sight, she struck the reef, then foundered on for a short distance before going down. By morning, only her main royal and sky-sail could be seen above the surface. Her crew had something of a struggle to reach the lightship, taking from 10.30pm until 3.30am to row the short distance between it and the wreck against the tide. Launched at Dundee in 1857, the *Oxus* was valued at £6,000. In 1870, on 4 April, the *St Peterborg*, Glasgow to Rotterdam, struck part of a submerged wreck on the edge of the Seven Stones and immediately foundered, to be joined on 7 October by the timbers of the barque *Nelson* of Shields. After discharging coal and coke at Cartagena, the 549-ton *Nelson*, registered at Fleetwood but technically owned in Shields, sailed from Aquias for the Tyne on 16 August with a cargo of pig-iron and esparto grass. All went well until 6 October, when she was running under foresail and reefed topsails before a strong SSW gale, accompanied by thick drizzle and rain. At 3 o'clock that afternoon, just as Captain Henderson took over the deck watch, the barque hit either the South Stone or Flemish Ledge and lurched heavily, throwing everyone to the deck. Her gig was lowered but was caught by a breaking sea and drifted away with five men aboard but with neither oars nor tholepins. Both her lifeboat and jolly-boat were found to be jammed solid in their chocks, and with the sea lapping over the main deck, the remaining crew grasped what they could in the way of oars, casks and ladders and jumped overboard. Two minutes later, the 10 year-old *Nelson* went down by the bow, drowning her 50 year-old captain, his nephew and able seaman Moon. The occupants of the gig and five other survivors managed to reach the lightship.

In 1871, a seaman named Vincenzo Defelice was landed at St Martin's by a pilot-gig after a remarkable escape from the wreck of the Spanish barque *Primos* on 24 June. This 600-ton vessel from Bilbao was carrying sugar from Havana to Falmouth for orders when she hit the rocks at 5am. The first boat to be launched drifted away, a second manned by her captain and four crew capsized, after which the barque foundered, drowning all the remaining 11 crew except for Defelice who found himself alone in a stormy sea. He swam about for two hours before finding a floating hen-coop onto which scrambled, remaining there for about an hour until he spotted the ship's figurehead. This life-sized female figure, now in the Valhalla collection at Tresco, kept him afloat for several more hours and when one of the ship's boats drifted close to him, he managed to get aboard and row to English Island Neck, from where he was rescued by pilots. Although not a wreck incident, the barque *Athole* of London, Swansea to Cape Verde Islands with coal, has the doubtful honour of being the one and only ship to hit the Seven Stones lightship. This occurred on 30 January 1873, during a fine, clear afternoon, when the *Athole* ran alongside and caught her rigging on the lightship's bumpkin, carrying away her main and mizzen halyards and starboard light. On 3 February that same year an unidentified brigantine foundered nearby in heavy seas. A French schooner was near enough to have rescued her crew but the master decided it was too dangerous to go close in, and all were left to drown.

Another unidentified wreck, that of a full-rigged ship, occurred in December 1873, and during the following year, the 1,780 tons register *Rydall Hall* was fortunate in being taken in tow by the *Queen of the Bay* when dangerously close to the reef on 20 April, for which service the crew of the packet received £150 despite their tow sinking. Registered at Liverpool and outward bound on her maiden voyage for San Francisco with a general cargo, the *Rydall Hall* had lost almost all her head gear in a gale. During 1875, two barques went on the rocks, the *Floresta* of Sunderland and the *Foscolo* of Naples. The 299-ton *Floresta* went ashore in fog at 4am on 14 February and sank very quickly, her crew of 10 being rescued by a St Malo lugger named *Josephine*, and landed at Falmouth. The 452-ton Italian vessel was more fortunate. After striking the rocks at 2pm on 23 November, she managed to reach Crow Bar at Scilly, only to sink in the shallows where she was later raised and saved. The *Floresta*, inward bound from Taganrog to Falmouth for orders, was loaded with wheat, while the *Foscolo* was carrying the odd mixture of bones and scrap iron from Montevideo to Dundee.

A year later, on 13 November, the French schooner *Paul et Marie*, carrying a cargo of wheat, was dismasted after going ashore, and eventually brought into Scilly as a derelict. The victim for 1877 was the *William Van Name*, an American barque of 700 tons net, which had left New York with a choice of calling at either Queenstown or Falmouth for orders. Captain Cogniss chose the former but struck the reef at 3.45am on 16 October. He and his crew of 11 were picked up and landed at Penzance by the schooner *Caroline* of Looe. Then there was the brig *Rosaire* of Nantes in 1879, with coal from Newport for Brest, which struck and went down on 26 February, four of her crew being picked up by the famous St Mary's pilot-cutter *Queen*. In relatively quick succession there followed an unidentified brig on 13 September 1884, the barque *Elizabeth Graham* of London, ashore but refloated and saved, 29 September 1885; and the 89-ton Plymouth schooner *Jane Sophia*, which was lost on 20 August 1887 after colliding with the steamer *Zenobia* close to the Seven Stones although her crew of five were saved. Next to fall victim to the reef was the iron full-rigged ship *Barreman* of Glasgow, which hit on 9 July 1887 in rough foggy weather and sank without a single survivor from her crew of 27. She quickly went to pieces and next day hatch covers, a deckhouse and some loose wreckage ashore on St Martin's were all that was found. Owned by Robert Thomas of Glasgow, the *Barreman*, 1,399 tons net, had left South Shields for San Francisco loaded with coke, bricks, cement and pig-iron, under the command of Captain Law. At the subsequent enquiry following her loss held at Glasgow in September, a charge of culpable negligence was made against Mate Hayhar of the Seven Stones lightship for not going to their rescue.

Belonging to the Clyde Shipping Co, the ss. *Longships* struck the Seven Stones and broke her back on 22 December 1939 ▶

The following decade saw a prodigious number of ships lost on the 'Stones', including three steamers. The first of these was the *Brighouse*, which had been launched by Palmer & Co at Newcastle in 1864. A three-masted iron steamer of 604 tons net, her dimensions were an overall length of 236 ft, beam 28.1 ft and depth 17.4 ft, and she was fitted with a 99-hp engine. On passage from Bordeaux to Cardiff with pit wood, the *Brighouse* loomed out of the fog near the lightship on 12 December 1887, only to seemingly disappear. An hour later, two lifeboats pulled alongside the lightship, the two crews identifying themselves as having come from the Cardiff steamer. They were obliged to remain on the lightship for two whole weeks before being taken off, by which time the authorities had presumed the *Brighouse* lost with all hands, since one of her lifeboats and other wreckage had by then been washed ashore at Porthmeor, St Ives, three days after the wreck had occurred. At the enquiry which followed, the certificate of Captain Tregurtha of St Ives, was suspended for three months for his failure to observe proper precautions in fog. Two more steamers went on the rocks in 1891, and the 77-ton schooner *Brenton* in the intervening years. The latter, carrying china clay, washed clear after hitting the Pollard Rock on 28 October 1890, and reached Falmouth full of water. Of the two steamers, the first was the 1,261-tons gross *Chiswick* of London, Cardiff to St Nazaire with coal, which went ashore in perfectly calm weather at 4.45am on 5 February. When her engines were put full-astern, she lunged off into deep water and began to fill by the head, going down so quickly that only her port lifeboat floated clear. Her captain, mate and nine men were drowned, but eight survivors were able to clamber onto the upturned boat and remained there for 10 hours before being rescued by the lightship's own longboat. Later that year, on 5 December, the *Merannio* of Leith, with 1,300 tons of iron ore on board bound from Bilbao to Newport, also hit the Seven Stones but managed to reach St Ives, where she was beached in the harbour with a 10ft hole in her bow.

Owned by the Elder Dempster Line, the motor-vessel *Fantee* was lost on the Seven Stones on 6 October 1949, her crew being rescued by motor launches from Scilly ▶

Although not directly attributable to the Seven Stones, a French steamer was lost on 19 February 1891 midway between Scilly and the reef. This was the *Trignac*, Newport to St Nazaire with coals, whose hull was so badly strained in rough seas that she sprang a leak and sank within five minutes after her boiler blew up. Despite warning rockets fired from the light-ship on 1 October 1892, the 2,226 tons gross steamer *Camiola* of Newcastle continued on her course and went ashore at full speed, shaking violently from stem to stern with the impact. In the ensuing confusion, the engineer on watch drove her even further on the rocks when he put the engines to emergency 'full-ahead' instead of 'full-astern' after which she commenced to fill. Her lifeboat lowering gear was in such a deplorable state, with fastenings and pins rusted and blocks seized, that it was impossible to get them clear at first. Eventually, using hammers and chisels, they were freed and pushed over the side. Owned by Chapman & Mills, the *Camiola* had sailed from Barry Docks and was bound for Malta with 3,400 tons of coal. A further sidelight on the character of her master was that, after reaching Penzance in the Trinity House tender *Alert*, Captain Story and his officers made for the Union Hotel, leaving the crew to fend for themselves. At midnight, the disgruntled crew demanded to see the captain, who reluctantly advanced them two shillings each out of his own pocket. It was the second ship that Captain Story had lost, the other one being off Nova Scotia two years earlier. During the early hours of 5 July 1897, the steamer *Heathmore* of Liverpool ran full tilt into the Seven Stones, and at first there was every hope that she could be saved. Laden with 2,400 tons of iron-ore from Santander for Glasgow, she floated clear at 8am and was brought to anchor two miles clear of the reef with her crew pumping furiously. An offer of assistance from a passing steamer was declined, and only after the *Alert* arrived did Captain A.F. Hird decide to go to St Mary's and telegraph Penzance for tugs. The steamer's crew pumped all that day but by evening, when it was obvious that they were fighting a losing battle, they took to their boats. Ten minutes later, the *Lady of the Isles* packet steamer arrived, just in time to see the waterlogged steamer sink bows first into 40 fathoms. Launched in 1883 by J. Key & Sons of Kinghorn, the *Heathmore* had only recently been sold to W. Johnston & Co of Liverpool by her former owners, the Heathmore Steamship Co.

Following the turn of the century, the Milford Haven steam trawler *Hydrangea* set out from her home port for fishing grounds off Scilly, but got off course and hit the reef at 10.30pm on 15 June 1905. Filling fast, she was abandoned, but her crew were able to reach the lightship in their own punt. In 1908, the French crabber *St Louis* of Douarnenez, struck and foundered on 20 June; a 180-ton. Norwegian schooner, *Frau Mini Peterson*, was lost some distance off after collision on 3 August 1911, and later that year there was a tragic loss of life in the wreck of the steamer *Van Dyck*. It was pitch dark and mountainous seas were running when the 1,132 tons gross *Van Dyck* of Antwerp, Valencia to Liverpool with oranges, onions and nuts, smashed into the Seven Stones at midnight on 6 December. Within minutes her engine-room was

flooded to a depth of several feet and her boiler fires swamped. The port boat was got away with 18 men aboard but capsized, drowning the captain and 13 of the crew, leaving only four men alive who scrambled back aboard. During the night the steamer floated off the rocks by itself and had drifted several miles up-Channel when the four men still aboard were able to attract the attention of the steam collier *Ashtree*, which attempted a tow but found conditions too rough. The *Van Dyck* survivors then hastily assembled and launched a raft, reaching the *Ashtree* not long before the *Lyonesse* and *Greencastle* arrived and towed the derelict to Penzance, where she was beached.

When the reef claimed the Glasgow full-rigged ship *Wendur* on 12 March 1912, the world lost one of its fastest sailing vessels. She held the record for the fastest passage between Newcastle and Valparaiso, and had been a regular visitor to West Country ports, sailing from Plymouth with 2,900 tons of grain on her last voyage. She struck the Seven Stones 23 minutes after midnight, throwing the deck watch off their feet, and the apprentice at the helm clean over the top of the wheel. Five minutes later her main and mizzen masts broke off and collapsed, followed by the fore topmast, leaving the *Wendur* a crippled hulk. In the process of launching her two boats, the starboard one with 10 men aboard was smashed to pieces against the side of the ship, but its occupants were picked up by those in the port boat. Of the *Wendur's* total crew of 21, three men were lost in the wreck. Built in 1884 by Connell & Co of Glasgow, the *Wendur*, of 2,046 tons gross, foundered on the southernmost rock of the Stones.

Another steamer, the *Toanui* of Glasgow, was lost on the reef with no survivors between 6-14 June 1913. A Penberth fisherman found a wooden box drifting off Tolpedn containing female clothing and jewellery, and next day a lifebelt marked 'Toanui-Glasgow' was found below Land's End, together with broken boats and wreckage. A destroyer of 975 tons, HMS *Pincher*, was totally wrecked after striking the Seven Stones on 24 July 1918, sinking a short distance away to the E. The steamer *Cornish Coast* stranded there on 28 November 1924 but survived to run down and sink the steamer *Fagerness* off Trevose Head on 17 March 1926; and a Clyde Shipping Co steamer, the *Longships*, Belfast to Plymouth with general cargo, stranded and broke her back on the rocks on 22 December 1939. Nine years later the steamer *Duke of Sparta* became one of the few modern steamers to have escaped after stranding on the reef, when she was successfully refloated on 19 April 1948. Dense fog on 6 October 1949 put the motor-vessel *Fantee* of Liverpool, belonging to the Elder Dempster Line, on the rocks, her crew of 58 officers and men all being rescued by the Scilly motor launches *Kittern* and *Golden Spray*. She, too, broke her back and settled down with her cargo floating out, covering the surface with palm kernels, palm oil, cocoa, rubber, hardwoods, cotton, coffee beans and copra. Some 43 years after the loss of the *Fantee*, hardwood tree logs were salvaged from the wreck, landed on St Mary's and after being cut into planks were used for building decoration and furniture.

Prior to the *Torrey Canyon*, the last wrecks of any size on the Seven Stones Reef included the Panamanian steamer *Punta*, Captain Mathiasso. Carrying phosphate rock from Spain to Portishead and Bristol, she struck two miles from the lightship on 22 July 1955 where she was abandoned by her crew of 24. The St Mary's lifeboat

▲ A Romanian fish-factory ship carrying a crew of 84, the *Rarau* became a total wreck on the Seven Stones in March 1980

was again in constant attention, returning only after completing a 14-hour vigil. Before tugs could begin to pull the *Punta* clear, she had filled and sunk in 15 fathoms, damaged beyond all hopes of salvage. A newspaper report at the time stated that tugs pulled her off but, in fact, she came off the reef and sank of her own accord. The other victims include the Constanza registered Romanian fish-factory trawler *Rarau*, wrecked on 29 September 1976, and the French trawler *Le Resolu*, lost on 17 March 1980. All 84 Romanian crew on board the *Rarau* were saved before she broke in two. When boats from Scilly arrived alongside, and their occupants commenced to 'rescue' items of value from the bridge, the captain ordered them to leave immediately. Knowing that the ship would never be saved, and would be partly submerged at high water, the Scillonian's produced copies of *'Playboy'* magazine and gave them to the captain, who promptly lost all interest in anything else, and with a wave of his hand agreed they could help themselves – a very good bargain indeed!

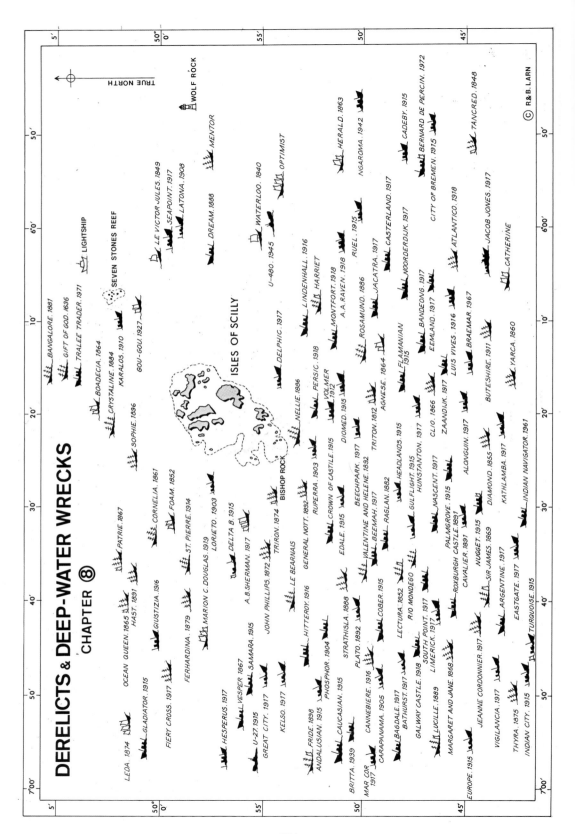

DERELICTS & DEEP-WATER WRECKS
CHAPTER ⑧

TRUE NORTH

WOLF ROCK

SEVEN STONES REEF

LIGHTSHIP

ISLES OF SCILLY

BISHOP ROCK

© R&B. LARN

LEDA. 1874
OCEAN QUEEN. 1865
GLADIATOR. 1915
HAST. 1891
GIUSTIZIA. 1916
PATRIE. 1867
CORNELIA. 1861
FOAM. 1852
FERHARDINA. 1879
FIERY CROSS. 1917
ST. PIERRE. 1914
MARION G. DOUGLAS. 1915
LORIETO. 1903
DELTA B. 1915
A.B.SHERMAN. 1917
JOHN PHILLIPS. 1872
TRIRON. 1874
LE BEARNAIS

BANGALORE. 1881
GIFT OF GOD. 1636
TRALEE TRADER. 1971
BOADECIA. 1864
CRYSTALINE. 1884
KARALOS. 1910
SOPHIE. 1696
GOU-GOU. 1927
LE VICTOR JULES. 1849
SEAPOINT. 1917
LATONA. 1908
MENTOR
DREAM. 1888
WATERLOO. 1840
U-480. 1945
OPTIMIST
HERALD. 1863
LINDENHALL. 1916
PERSIC. 1918
HARRIET
VOLMER. 1912
MONTFORT. 1918
A. A. RAVEN. 1918
NGAROMA. 1942
DIOMED. 1915
TRITON. 1812
AGNESE. 1864
RUEL. 1915
ROSAMUND. 1886
JACATRA. 1917
CASTERLAND. 1917
CADEBY. 1915
BERNARD DE PERCIN. 1972
TANCRED. 1848
DELPHIC. 1917
NELLIE. 1886

HESPERUS. 1917
VESPER. 1867
SAMARA. 1915
GREAT CITY. 1917
KELSO. 1917
PHOSPHOR. 1904
HITTEROY. 1916
GENERAL NOTT. 1892
RUPERRA. 1903
CROWN OF CASTILE. 1915
EDALE. 1915
BEECHPARK. 1917
VALENTINE AND HELENE. 1892
BEEMAH. 1917
RAGLAN. 1882
GULFLIGHT. 1915
HEADLANDS. 1915
HUNSTANTON. 1917
CLIO. 1866
ELAMANIAN. 1915
BANDEONG. 1917
NOORDERDIJK. 1917
EEMLAND. 1917
CITY OF BREMEN. 1915

FRIDE. 1898
ANDALUSIAN. 1915
CAUCASIAN. 1915
PLATO. 1892
STRATHISLA. 1888
LECTURA. 1852
RIO MONDEGO
SOUTH POINT. 1917
NASCENT. 1917
PALMGROVE. 1915
ROXBURGH CASTLE. 1891
ZAANDIJK. 1917
LUIS VIVES. 1916
ATLANTICO. 1918
CATHERINE

BRITTA. 1939
MAR COR. 1917
CARAPANAMA. 1905
CANNEBIERE. 1916
BAGDALE. 1917
BATHURST. 1917
GALWAY CASTLE. 1918
LIMERICK. 1917
CAVALIER. 1891
NUGGET. 1915
ALONGUIN. 1917
DIAMOND. 1855
BUTESHIRE. 1911
BRAEMAR. 1967
JACOB JONES. 1917
YARCA. 1860

EUROPE. 1915
JEANNE CORDONNIER. 1917
MARGARET AND JANE. 1868
LUCILLE. 1889
ARGENTINE. 1917
SIR JAMES. 1869
KATHLAMBA. 1917
INDIAN NAVIGATOR. 1961
VIGILANCIA. 1917
THYRA. 1875
EASTGATE. 1917
INDIAN CITY. 1915
TURQUOISE. 1915

8 - Deep water wrecks and derelicts

There are many wreck incidents connected with the Isles of Scilly which have no place in the preceding chapters, simply because they occurred some distance from land. These distances vary considerably, and the vessels concerned have been lost by fire or collision, by foundering due to stress of weather, been torpedoed, bombed, scuttled, leaked, capsized, struck by lightning or simply fallen to pieces. All, however, had some connection with the islands, indirect though it may have been, usually because their crews landed there, wreckage was washed ashore, or ships were found derelict by island pilots or fishermen and towed in. Many such derelicts have been found off the Isles of Scilly, some burnt to the waterline, others with several feet of water in their holds, some with only a few inches and virtually undamaged. Such vessels, successfully towed to safety in St Mary's Roads, represented considerable sums of money to the salvors, and local pilots would make superhuman efforts to save a derelict when others had failed. On 6 August 1849, *Victor Jules*, a Nantes lugger, Captain Ridal, France to Mumbles for orders, was towed into the roads, waterlogged and derelict. She was thought to have struck the Runnelstone or Seven Stones Reef, and it was not until her crew had been landed at Gloucester that their story became known. Her cargo of flour was auctioned off locally on 13 August, and the vessel sold. A similar incident concerned the Bridgwater schooner *Boadicea*, picked up on 27 November 1864 by a St Agnes pilot cutter. With the pilot boat tied astern to assist in steering, the derelict having lost her rudder, she reached St Mary's safely. It was eventually established from her owners that she had sailed from Newfoundland, and the pilots involved received a total of £530 salvage money in return for saving a vessel and cargo worth £ 1,763. Instances of a master being found guilty of needless abandonment must be rare, but such was the case with the *Margaret & Jane*, a 324-ton barque registered at Scilly since 1856. She sailed from Cardiff on 18 November 1868 with 520 tons of coal for Alicante, but although her papers showed John Stephens as captain, it was in name only, the owner's son, David Hughes, actually being in charge. He had no certificate and was quite unqualified to act as captain, having signed on as bo'sun and purser. Moreover, the barque put to sea inadequately caulked and leaked from the moment of sailing, carried an unseaworthy quarter boat and had no spare washers for her bilge pumps. When 120 miles from the Isles of Scilly, she met bad weather and turned back with one pump choked and out of commission. When the *Inez* of Sunderland hove in sight, the officers of the *Margaret & Jane* tried to lower the longboat but stove in some planks, where-upon the *Inez* sent over her own boat and took off the captain, the owner's son and two other men. The rest of the crew, quite unaware that a distress signal had been flying from their own masthead, at first refused to leave their ship and were confident that with only 27inches of water in the hold, there was every chance of saving her. Eventually, however, they obeyed the captain's orders to abandon her, but assured him that she would probably be in Scilly before the *Inez* reached Swansea. That same day, the Scilly pilot-cutter *Ezra* found the derelict, took her in tow, and reached Crow Sound without even touching the pumps. At the enquiry held at Caernarvon, the captain had his certificate suspended for 12 months, the court expressing their regret that they had no power to punish Hughes who had virtually dominated proceedings on board. Some months later, on 8 April 1869, the sailing-ship *Sir James* was abandoned to the SW of the islands after a sudden squall had carried away her masts. She was then on her way to Madras from Hartlepool with a cargo of iron and coal. Her distress signals were sighted simultaneously by a French schooner and the steamer *Atlantic*, the former taking off the crew and landing them at Scilly, while the latter took the derelict in tow and reached Falmouth. A Danish ship, the *Thyra*, was found abandoned some distance W of Scilly by the Liverpool-owned *Hoang Ho* on 30 January 1875. On passage from Philadelphia to Copenhagen with petroleum, the *Thyra* had apparently encountered a severe gale since her main and foremasts, jib-boom and boats had all gone overboard. Four seamen and the chief mate of the *Hoang Ho* boarded her, rigged jury sail and made Falmouth seven days later. A year earlier, on 14 February 1874, a German brig had also sailed into Falmouth to land the crew of the abandoned 326-ton three-masted schooner *Leda* of Stettin. Five days later, the steamer *Flandre*, Troon to Bayonne, came into the harbour with storm damage and reported that she at one time had the *Leda* in tow, but rough seas had parted the hawsers. The derelict was located again on 20 February by Falmouth pilots, but they were unable to do anything with her and it was not until three Scilly pilot cutters got lines aboard that she was worked into St Mary's and saved. It was not at all unusual for steamships to pick up derelicts whilst on passage; the *Gladiator*, for example, found the German brigantine *Gerhardina* in this condition with 5ft of water in her hold on 13 January 1879. She eventually succeeded in getting the vessel to Scilly, but the fate of the missing crew was never determined. By an odd coincidence, a steamer named *Gladiator* was sent to the bottom by a German submarine on 19 August 1915 when 50 miles NW of the Bishop, but was not the same vessel that had saved the *Gerhardina*.

In 1884, it took the combined efforts of four Scillies pilot boats and the tenant of Tresco's private yacht, the *Surprise*, to get the barque *Crystaline* to New Grimsby harbour. She was first sighted apparently in distress three miles N of St Martins by Douglas Skinner, a Trinity pilot, on 16 November. The *Crystaline* of Liverpool, an iron-hulled vessel, was found to have been abandoned, her forward compartments flooded and water still pouring in through holes in her bow, the obvious result of a collision. When close to Scilly and under tow, her bow went under water and she would have foundered but for the timely assistance of local boats. Such derelicts adrift on the high seas were a serious navigational hazard, and when the 273-ton brig *Lucille*, carrying casks and tallow to Falmouth for orders, was in collision with a steamer on 27 November 1889 60 miles SW of the Bishop, four tugs were sent out to locate her. For three days the Falmouth tugs, *Emperor, Eagle, Armine,* and *Triton* searched the area assisted by the Royal Navy gunboat *Pelican* and another warship, and it was only when wreckage which included casks and tallow was sighted that the *Lucille* was presumed to have sunk, and the search called off. Owned by W. Williams of Newport, the 117ft long *Lucille* had been built and launched by Yeo, of Prince Edward Island in 1874. Although the steamer *Cavalier* of Newcastle was sighted and reported as derelict 16 miles WSW of the Western Rocks in 1891, a long and tedious search proved fruitless, the vessel apparently having sunk in the meantime. The *Indian Prince* reported sighting her, with a heavy list to starboard, on 20 December after arrival at Rotterdam, and her owners, Walter Scott & Co of Newcastle, confirmed that she was homeward bound from Odessa to Falmouth for orders. The same day that the *Indian Prince* reported the derelict, a bunk head-board was washed ashore at Scilly from the wreck, and a glass and decanter rack marked ss *Cavalier* found near Land's End was identified as having come from the Chief Officer's cabin. Nothing more of the ship or her crew was ever found, and the 1,197 tons vessel, built in 1878 by Doxfords of Sunderland, was declared a total loss.

As the 1800s came to a close and steamships became predominant on the world's shipping routes, so the numbers of derelicts fell sharply, but they still occurred, and two such instances off the Scillies were the barque *Sophie* in 1896, and the *Marion C. Douglas* in 1919. At first, the case of the *Sophie* appeared to offer a mystery equal to that of the *Mary Celeste* of 1872, at least until her crew turned up at Gibraltar on 20 December aboard the British steamer *Glenmore*. A Norwegian barque, the *Sophie* of Frederikstad, carrying anthracite from Swansea to Christiania, which had been sold out of British registration in 1888, was sighted on 15 December wallowing dismasted in heavy seas, four miles N of Shipman Head. Ten local men put out in a Bryher gig and found her derelict apart from a well-fed dog. The cabin table was laid as for a meal, there was half-prepared food in the galley, still warm, and the ship's clock was wound up and ticking. Assisted by Tresco and St Martin's gigs, the ss *Lady of the Isles* and the St Mary's lifeboat, *Henry Dundas*, the barque was towed the four and a half miles to New Grimsby and anchored. It later transpired that Captain Bjorgeand his crew of 18 had been picked up from their boat by the ss *Glenmore* shortly after the *Sophie* was abandoned when the vessel commenced to disintigrate, and been landed at Gibraltar. The owners claimed the derelict through the dog, since technically with 'life' aboard she was not abandoned, then sold her and the cargo to T. Dorrien-Smith, the proprietor of Tresco for £250. The wreck was broken up on the beach at New Grimsby, her timbers used for building and fence posts, the anthracite as fuel to heat the Tresco Garden's greenhouses. One of her anchors now adorns an end wall of the Tresco Store, opposite the Estate Office (see p138).

The *Marion G. Douglas,* a wooden, three-masted schooner from Fox River, Nova Scotia, was also found derelict in less dramatic circumstances in December 1919 and successfully towed to Scilly. This 491-ton schooner, which had been launched by Hatfield in 1917, was close to her destination of Le Havre, when she was abandoned. Amongst the hundreds of vessels which come under the heading of 'deep-water wrecks' off the Isles of Scilly, it is possible to mention but a small percentage. The American brig *Triton*, Boston to Liverpool foundered a few miles offshore on 13 May 1802, when her master and four crew drowned; a pilot cutter, the 25-ton *Waterloo*, built on Holgates Green, St Mary's by Thomas Edwards in 1830, shipped a heavy sea whilst off the islands with a Captain Richard Nance in charge and sank on Christmas Day 1840; 4 April 1848 saw the 16 year-old Sunderland brig *Tanered* of 350 tons sink in deep water after developing a leak, Captain Oliver, the sole survivor, being rescued by the schooner *Merlin* and landed at St Mary's. In 1852, the schooner *Foam* went down on 16 April, and the 40-ton sloop-rigged *Lectura* of Salcombe on 10 January 1852, lost with her cargo of oranges after a collision in which one of her five crew was drowned.

An Irish schooner, the *Catherine* of Cork, with oats from Kinsale for London, filled and sank when her pumps were unable to cope with a leak on 8 February 1854; the *Diamond* of Swansea was lost on 30 October 1855; a brigantine, the *Mentor*, laden with copper ore, sank after hitting the Wolf Rock during fog on 18 May 1856; and the American cotton ship *Yarea* was destroyed by fire in 1869. News of the loss of the *Yarea* reached Falmouth on 3 April via the Neopolitan brigantine *W.E. Routh*. Her master reported that, whilst off the Scillies the previous afternoon, they had met up with the *Yarea* ablaze from stem to stern, and had kept watch on her until 4am when three masts collapsed and a schooner appeared on the scene. This was the *Express* of Shoreham, which already had the *Yarea's* 36 crew on board. A wooden ship of 1,262 tons, the *Yarea*, under the command of Captain Taylor, had left Liverpool for Bombay with steam coal for the Indian Station bunkers, but leaked so badly in the Irish Sea that the crew asked to be allowed to take to the boats. The captain refused, saying he intended to investigate the leak first, also a peculiar sulphurous smell which had been apparent in the cabin for some time. No sooner had the tarpaulins been rolled back and the wooden hatch covers removed than flames shot skyward, setting fire to the sails and rigging. The *W.E. Routh* reported that shortly after she left, the *Yarea*, valued at £15,000, she rapidly sunk. Somewhere north of the islands, two railway locomotives lie on the seabed amongst the wreckage of the *Cornelia* of Portland USA, lost along with a part-cargo of railway sleepers and coal from Greenock to Santos. She was striving desperately to reach Scilly with a serious leak when she sank on 4 April 1861.

In 1863, the British schooner *Herald*, dismasted and damaged by storm 15 miles W of the Bishop, would almost certainly have foundered but for the intervention of the wooden screw frigate HMS *Highflyer*, which towed her to the safety of St Mary's Roads. As the years passed, so ships continued to be lost in deep water in apparently ever increasing numbers, although they peaked during the late 1860s. In 1864, the French schooner *Agnese* was sent to the bottom after collision with the *Circassian* of London on 5 January. The master of the badly damaged *Circassian*, Captain Smith, died of a heart attack two days after the incident. A British barque, the *Ocean Queen* of Bristol went down on 17 May 1865, 14 miles NNW of Scilly; a unidentified brig on 23 March 1866, the *Harriet* of Ardrossan; the *Clio*, a full-rigged ship, on 1 July 1866, and the paddle steamer *Vesper*, on 19 January 1867.

The latter has rather an unusual story, since she was on passage from the Clyde to Bahia, in Brazil, where the 80-ton vessel was to serve as a passenger river boat under the name *Leito Cunha*. Commanded by Captain Samuel Lindsay, the *Vesper* left Glasgow on 3 January, but 15 days later had only five or six days bunkers left, having encountered severe gales most of the way. However, this was of no real consequence since it was the intention to steam down to warmer latitudes, then sail the rest of the way to South America. When off Scilly at noon on 19 January there was a sickening crash and without warning, the vessel broke clean in two. The drifting sections were flung against each other time after time, but watertight bulkheads fortunately kept them afloat. Soon after the accident, the Danish steamer *Vigilant*, Dublin to Bayonne, hove in sight and rescued the crew, though three had already drowned in the wreck. A Norwegian brig, the *Patrie*, carrying linseed from Odessa to Falmouth, was running before the wind with a heavy list after her cargo had shifted, when she collided with the Norwegian barque *Vulcan* of Riisder on 17 March 1867, the *Patrie* sinking only a few miles NW of the Bishop Rock. The *John Philips*, a Glasgow full-rigger, sprang a leak and sank offshore on 9 June 1872; and the coal-laden brig *Triron* of Cardigan foundered near the Western Rocks on 16 April 1874. In 1882 a steamer, the *Raglan* of Cardiff, owned by J. Cory & Sons, sank in three minutes after a collision, her boilers exploding and tearing up half the deck as she went under. The vessel with which she collided was the ss *P.A.Vagliano*, sister-ship to the Greek owned ss *Spyridion Vagliano* lost on the Manacles reef off Falmouth on 8 February 1890. Other losses in the area included the 40-year old wooden barque *Bangalore*, which capsized and sank 25 miles N of Scilly on 4 March 1881; the Swansea brigantine *Rosamund*, carrying phosphate from Sombrero to Gloucester, on 7 January 1886; the *Nellie*, another brigantine, on 26 March 1886 after striking a rock near the Bishop which caused her to go to pieces in ten minute. Also the Penzance steamer *Dream*, after springing a bad leak between the Wolf Rock and Scilly on 5 March 1888; and the *Roxburgh Castle*, a Newcastle-registered steamer, after colliding SW of Scilly on 13 March 1891 with the ss *British Peer*.

Another steamer lost the following year was the *Plato*, which suffered a broken propeller shaft on 29 February, water leaking back up the stern tube past the packing glands until she foundered, despite attempts by her sister-ship, the *J W. Taylor*, to take her in tow. Launched at Newcastle by A. Leslie in 1878, the *Plato* was owned by a subsidiary of the Lamport & Holt Line. The Norwegian brigantine *Hast* of Arendal,

Cardiff to Newhaven with coal, sprang a leak and sank 15 miles NW of the islands on 22 April 1891, her crew being rescued by the Porthleven lugger *Harbinger*, while *Le Bearnais*, a French barque in ballast, was run down and sunk six miles W of the Bishop by the steamer *Llanberis* on 10 March 1893. Collision, which accounted for so many of these losses, also terminated the career of two barques on 2 March 1892, when the *General Nott*, bound from Chile with nitrates, almost cut the French barque *Valentine & Helene* clean in half 20 miles from land. The Frenchman sank so quickly that her master, Captain Jonajean, leapt overboard wearing only his night-shirt. Her crew was picked up by the badly damaged *General Nott*, and for 16 hours the two crews managed to keep her afloat, pumping furiously until, when some 15 miles WSW of the Bishop, a steamer, the *Barden Tower* of Glasgow, came alongside and took them off. She then took the barque in tow but late that same evening she rolled over and sank.

So the long list of casualties continued, the brig *Pride* of Gottenburg foundered at sea in August 1898; the new river gunboat *Loretio*, on delivery to the Peruvian government, sank on 25 May 1903 when close to Scilly; the *Ruperra* of Cardiff, Barry to Port Said with coal, was cut completely in half and sunk at midnight on 29 July 1903, after being run down by the 3,400-ton British cruiser HMS *Melampus*. Another British steamer, the *Phosphor*, was found capsized W of Scilly and taken in tow by the *Birkhall*, only to sink on 13 July 1904; the *Carapanama* was lost on New Years Day 1905; the transatlantic liner *Latona*, of Dundee, on 20 May 1908, and the *Buteshire* in 1911. The *Latona* sank near the Wolf Rock after being rammed by the Sunderland steamer *Japanic*. Carrying 45 crew, four passengers, 12 cattlemen, steers and a general cargo, the *Latona* kept stopping due to fog, and was not under way when the *Japanic* loomed out of the murk and struck her amidships. When the crew and passengers were mustered after rescue, there were four more than could be accounted for, the additions being stowaways who appeared only as the ship was sinking. Although there was no loss of human life in this incident, all 310 steers were drowned, their carcasses coming ashore along the south coast of Cornwall and Scilly.

On 29 March 1911, the master of the steamer *Duva* wrote in his log, *'I saw the four-masted barque* Buteshire *of Glasgow take her departure from the list of ships this day, at about 3.00am, abandoned, on fire and full of water. We stopped and boarded her but had to get off pretty quickly. About 10 minutes later she foundered, but I took a snapshot of her before she left, position about 28 miles SW of the Longships'*. So ended the career of the famous 1,910-ton ship *Buteshire*, which had begun in July 1888 when she was launched by Birrells' for the Shire Line, the first of two four-masted barques commissioned by Law & Co. She had loaded coal at Newcastle for Valparaiso, arriving after a passage of 61 days. From there she proceeded to Pisagua and loaded nitrates, leaving for home on 18 November. A serious leak developed on 19 March and for the next eight days the crew, including the captain's wife, toiled continuously at the pumps. On the

▲ A four-masted barque *Buteshire* of Glasgow, caught fire and was abandoned 28 miles W of the Longships to sink

morning of 27 March, when some 100 miles west of Brest and, convinced that his ship would sink any minute, Captain Purdie signalled the steamer *Ardeola*, the first ship they had sighted, and all hands were taken off the barque. But the *Buteshire* remained afloat, was reported by the steamer *Milton* in position 48°47'N, 07° 19'W, waterlogged and abandoned, but with lights still burning in the cabin and galley. She had been a very fast sailor in her day, reaching Hamburg from Iquique in 110 days in 1897, and Sydney from Hamburg in 96 days during 1898.

Of the many wrecks lying in deep water around the islands, the majority occurred during World War 1. Merchant ships sailed alone and unarmed in the years prior to 1917, making the busy shipping lanes in the Bristol Channel along the north coast of Cornwall, and Bishop Rock, a submarine commander's paradise. Exactly how many were lost here due to enemy action is speculation, for even the official records are hopelessly incomplete. On the very first day of WW1 Scillonians' had the excitement of seeing the British cruisers HMS *Doris* and *Isis* capture and bring in two prize ships, the three-masted schooner *Bolivar* carrying hides and tallow, and the *Roland*, of Bremen, laden with tobacco and coffee from New Orleans. Both ships were deprived of their sails to prevent escape, but four of the *Bolivar's* crew commandeered a small open boat and put to sea. Some weeks later it was learnt that the steamer *New Pioneer*, owned by the Co-operative Wholesale Society, had arrived in the Mersey with the four men aboard, having picked them up in St Georges Channel, exhausted and without food or water. As the war progressed, so the number of sinkings increased ten-fold. Between 27 January and 18 February 1915, nine vessels were torpedoed or sunk by scuttling charges, and in March the submarine *U-29* sank three steamers, the *Headlands* of Liverpool, 2,988 tons gross, the *Indian City* of Bideford, 4,645 tons gross, and the *Andalusian* of Liverpool, 2,349 tons gross. The submarine commander was Otto Weddigan who, in *U-9*, had previously sunk tbe armoured cruisers HMS *Cressey*, *Aboukir* and *Hogue* on 22 September 1914. The *Headlands*, in ballast, ordered to stop and her crew to take to their boats, was so close inshore when the submarine torpedoed her that school children, watching from the heights of St Mary's, cheered and clapped, thrilled by the explosion and smoke. She floated for some hours but sank less than a mile SE of the Bishop after a drifter, a motor-boat and the packet vessel *Lyonesse* had all attempted a tow. Less than two months old, the *Indian City* of Bideford, bound from Galveston to the UK with cotton and spelter, had a Chinese crew who tried the patience of the submarine commander, making him wait whilst they put on their best clothes and packed their bags before manning the boats! No sooner had they got clear than a single torpedo ripped open her engine-room, and she caught fire.

The *Andalusian* was 35 miles from the Bishop Rock when ordered to stop, but her captain headed for Scilly in an attempt to outrun the U-Boat. However, she was soon overhauled and forced to be abandoned, the Germans boarding her and taking all her instruments, cutlery, and charts before scuttling her with an explosive charge. The *U-29* did not enjoy her victories for long, being depth-charged and lost with all hands on 26 March 1915 in the North Sea. The 3,500-ton steamer *Plaminian* was sunk by gunfire on 29 March 1915, the 4,505-ton *Crown of Castille* the following day, and on 1 May a submarine attacked the steamers *Edale*, *Europe* and *Gulflight*. The *Edale*, of 3,110 tons, took two torpedoes and nine shells, proving difficult to sink, as did the *Europe*, a French vessel of 2,026 tons gross carrying a cargo of coal. She was stopped three miles NW of the Bishop and absorbed 20 high-explosive shells without showing any sign of sinking. In sheer desperation, having spent over an hour on the surface dealing with one merchantman, the submarine's commander fired a precious torpedo at her, whereupon the *Europe* folded in the middle and sank. The torpedoing of the *Gulflight* proved to be a bad mistake on the part of the Germans and caused them considerable embarrassment as she was American owned, and the USA at that time was still neutral. Carrying naphtha from Port Arthur, Texas, her home port, for Rouen, the *Gulflight* was stopped west of the Bishop and hit by one torpedo, whereupon her crew abandoned ship by jumping overboard, three of whom drowned. Her captain, a naturalised German named Gunther, died of heart failure on the bridge of the naval patrol vessel HMS *Lago*. Her survivors were picked up by naval patrol vessels, but was found to still be afloat next day, with her bow under water. The armed Lowestoft drifters HMS. *Premier*, *Difldem*, *Primrose*, *Dusty Miller* and *All's Well* took her in tow taking two days to cover eight miles, eventually getting her into St Mary's Roads. While she was at anchor in the shallows, barrels of naphtha drifted out of the huge hole in her bow, and the government offered a reward of 10 shillings for every barrel recovered. Built at Camden, New Jersey, in 1914, this 5,189-ton ship, owned by the Gulf Refining Co, was eventually towed to Le Havre with a 'scratch crew' from amongst the islanders, each of whom received £25 for the trip.

Other war losses included the Belgian steam fishing-vessel *Delta B* of 220 tons, sunk on 2 June 1915; the steamer *Cober*, 3,060 tons, on 21 August 1915; the steamer *Ruel*, 4,029 tons, and the *Palmgrove*, 3,100 tons on the same day, and the *Diomed*, 4,672 tons, only 24 hours later. The *Cober*, Captain Peterfield, made a dash for it when his ship was ordered to heave-to, and successfully eluded the submarine's gunfire for an hour before several direct hits brought her to a standstill and forced her crew to abandon ship. One torpedo was then fired into her port side, and she sank very quickly. A similar fate befell the *Ruel*, Captain Henry Storey, which was chased for an hour before one shell hit her stern, passing clean through her hull, but another exploded on the bridge. After the crew had taken to the boats, the submarine closed the range and when within 150yds its crew opened fire on the survivors with small arms, wounding many of the defenceless men. As the submarine departed it was

▲ On exercise with six other K-Class Royal Navy submarines, the *K-5* failed to surface after a dive on 20 January 1921 with the loss of 57 crew off Scilly

noticed she had *U-23* painted on one side of he conning tower, and *U-26* on the other, so that her true identity was never established.

One of the largest vessels lost off Scilly during World War 1 was the British ss *Armenian*, an 8,825-ton Liverpool registered ship belonging to the Leyland Line which was carrying 1,300 mules from Newport News to Avonmouth, for use on the Western Front. Under Captain Trickery, she carried a crew of 162, which included dozens of mule stockmen. When a surfaced submarine was sighted some three miles off the port bow, the ship altered course to put it astern and increased speed but was soon overhauled at which point *U-24* opened fire with her deck gun. For 30 minutes shell after shell hit the *Armenian* and exploded, after which she stopped her engine and her crew took to the boats. The enemy then fired two torpedoes into her, causing her to sink, along with all the animals that were tethered in stalls. One boat capsized whilst being lowered, survivors in the other boats remaining adrift for 12 hours before being picked up by the Belgian trawler *President Stevens*, transferred to torpedo boat destroyers and landed at Avonmouth. The *Armenian* sank exactly 42 miles N of Hugh Town in 300ft of water, with the loss of nine crew and 20 cattlemen. The wreck was finally located and identified by divers in 2008, who brought up a piece of china bearing the Leyland Line company crest, and one animal rib bone, which was identified as having come from a mule. The *Armenian* had narrowly escaped being lost on the Seven Stones Reef on 26 May 1913 when, on passage from Rotterdam to Cardiff in ballast, she hit the rocks but got off, putting back to Falmouth for repairs, being only slightly damaged.

The West Hartlepool Steam Navigation Co's *Lindenhall*, 4,003 tons, built by the Irving Ship Building Co in 1900, was attacked seven miles offshore on 1 November 1916 but survived. On 22 February 1917 a convoy of eight Dutch steamers, which had left Falmouth in company only the previous day, were attacked by the submarine *U-3*, which sent six of the eight ships to the bottom. It was a beautiful sunny day with no wind, the sea like a millpond, when three of the ships were hit by torpedoes in a matter of minutes, the others being stopped and sunk by scuttling charges. Remarkably, not a single life was lost, and the combined crews of all six ships, now in 28 lifeboats, accompanied by the St Agnes RNLI lifeboat, made quite a spectacle as they entered St Mary's harbour. For this particular service, each member of the lifeboat crew was awarded a special medal, struck by the Netherland section of the League of Neutral Countries. The six vessels lost were the *Jacatra*, 5,373 tons; the *Gaasterland*, 3,917 tons; the *Noorderdijk*, 7,166 tons; the *Eemland*, 3,700 tons, and the *Zaandijk*, 4,189 tons. The *Medado*, 5,874 tons, reached Falmouth, and the *Ambon* of Amsterdam, 3,598 tons, put into Plymouth with only slight damage. By 1917, the majority of merchantmen were armed with a either a 12pdr or 3inch 'stern-chaser' gun, and although these were often ineffectual due to their vintage or small calibre, they did at least give the merchant ship something with which to hit back. At the same time, they unfortunately brought to an end the merciful practice of submarines stopping vessels and allowing the crews to escape unharmed. Ships were now sent to the bottom without warning, submarine commanders unwilling to risk being shelled whilst surfaced, and the monthly tonnage lost in the Western Approaches reached immense proportions. The entire crew from a Portuguese steamer landed on the islands on 12 March 1917, to be followed next day by two boatloads of men from the American steamer *Algonquin*. The crew of another American ship, the *Vigilancia* of Wilmington, 4,115 tons, came ashore on 1 April, and later a total of 18 survivors from the steamers *Argentine* and *Hunstanton*. The latter, ex-*Werdenfels*, 4,505 tons, had been requisitioned by the Admiralty earlier in the war and re-registered at London. A Yarmouth trawlers crew reached St Mary's Roads on 25 April 1917 in their own lifeboat, an unidentified steamer's crew numbering 40 on 27 April, another steamer's crew on 8 May, and men from the Australian ss *Limerick*, ex-*Rippington Grange*, 6,827 tons, built by Workham Clark & Co of Belfast in 1898, soon afterwards.

On 2 June, crews from the torpedoed steamers *Bagdale* of Whitby, 3,045 tons, and *Bathurst* of Liverpool, 2,821 tons, reached the Isles of Scilly in their own lifeboats; as did Frenchmen from the *Jeanne Cordonnie* sunk on 31 May, and an Italian crew on 3 June. Two ships were towed into the roads on 18 June with gaping holes in their sides made by torpedoes, the steamers *Kathlamba* of North Shields, 6,382 tons, and the *Great City* of Bideford, 6,999 tons gross, a Ropner-built ship launched in 1914. Two days later, the Wilson Line steamer *Kelso*, 1,292 tons, was towed in with her decks almost awash, to be followed on 27 June by the three-masted schooner *A.B. Sherman*, escorted by the armed trawler HMS. *Nancy Lee*. This American sailing ship of 510 tons had been caught supplying a U-Boat with oil at sea. She was towed to Devonport, stripped down and laid up at Fowey, where a local shipyard later rebuilt her as a four-masted ship. With so many losses, there were endless incidents worth recalling, but since all of them cannot possibly be recounted here four random incidents have been chosen, concerning a cross-section of shipping, a famous sailing ship, a warship, liner and a tramp steamer. The sailing ship was the *Fiery Cross*, a barque from Larvik, Norway, built in September 1878 by Connell & Co of Glasgow. This 1,448-ton Cape Horner was carrying oil from the United States when she was stopped by a German submarine and her crew ordered to abandon ship. Her master rowed a dinghy across to the German vessel and demanded a receipt from her commander for the *Fiery Cross*, whose sinking was delayed for half an hour while this was being prepared. The document read:

'I hereby certify that I have sunk the Fiery Cross, *Capt. John Geddie, on 3 July 1915 at 3.0 pm as she had contraband aboard, i.e. lubricating oil for France. Signed, Forstman, H. Lieut. Cdr, Imperial German Navy'.*

The seal on the document bore the words, 'Imperial Marine, His Majesty's Submarine U-' followed by a blank, the identification number having been erased.

Fresh water cask from the wreck of the *Lojaro*, an Italian barque, lost off St Martin's on 2 February 1902. The spelling on the brass plate of the ship's name is incorrect. It was sold at auction in Penzance in 1999 for £1,200 ▶

Among the American escort destroyers based on Queenstown, southern Ireland, in 1917 was the USS *Jacob Jones*, commanded by Lt-Cdr David Bagley USN, brother of the first naval officer killed in the Spanish-American war. A Conyngham class, four-funneled vessel built by the New York Steamboat Co in 1915, the *Jacob Jones* was in company with six other destroyers returning from convoy duty off Brest when she was hit in the stern by a torpedo at 4.25pm on 6 December. She settled down very quickly and as the quarterdeck went underwater, depth-charges, already primed and fused for action, rolled overboard and sank. Those of her 108 crew who could reach the upper deck promptly leapt overboard, unfortunately taking the full stomach-tearing impact of the explosive charges as the depth-charges, each containing 500lbs of explosive detonated, killing them outright and blowing a whaleboat and its occupants to smithereens. She sank in less than eight minutes, in a position roughly 25 miles SE of the Bishop, taking 64 men with her. The German submarine responsible, the U-53, then surfaced nearby, and obligingly radioed Land's End, asking them to send help to pick up the remaining survivors. Two of these were in such a bad way that Captain Hans Rose had them taken aboard, and eventually landed them at Heligoland for medical attention.

The same submarine was responsible for the sinking of the ex-German vessel *Housatonic*, south of the Bishop on 3 February that same year, but only after the survivors were well clear of their ship. The day before the *Housatonic* was sent to the bottom, Captain Hans Rose had stopped a French sailing ship and ordered her crew to abandon the vessel, but on being told the lifeboats were so rotten that the men would never reach land in them, he allowed them to proceed unharmed. The White

Star liner *Persic*, of Liverpool, was torpedoed on 8 September 1918, almost a year after a sister-ship, the *Delphic*, a twin-screw vessel of 8,273 tons, built by Harland & Wolff in 1897, had been sunk 135 miles SW of Scilly on 10 August 1917. The *Persic* was more fortunate in that she survived her attack. She carried a crew of 56 and 2,108 troops when hit by a torpedo, but was abandoned without the loss of a single life, a remarkable feat which owed much to Captain Harvey's insistence on regular lifeboat drill from the moment they left New York in convoy. The first torpedo fired at her missed, but a second struck her port side and tore a hole 72 x 22 ft, completely flooding No's 3 and 4 holds. The troops were later transferred from the ship's boats and life rafts to destroyer escorts and landed at Plymouth, the *Persic* herself being towed into Crow Sound, in the Scillies, and saved.

A Pomeranian dog was the saving of an entire crew on 1 July 1915, after the 4,656-ton steamer *Caucasian* had been attacked. Seventeen shells were fired into the vessel by a German submarine when the steamship turned and fled after being challenged, until finally, with her bridge, wheelhouse and steering gear shot away, she hove-to and her crew began to abandon ship. The dog, named Betty, the pet of Captain Robinson of South Shields, was accidentally dropped into the sea as the boats were being manned, and struck out for the surfaced submarine, to be quickly followed by its master. When the captain caught up with his pet and put it on his shoulders, he found the submarine now close alongside and was told by her commander that he had intended to machine-gun the crew for not stopping when ordered, but had changed his mind having witnessed the captain's willingness to rescue his dog. Before the war, the *Caucasian* had been stranded on the N coast of Cornwall, at Cape Cornwall, during fog on 30 May 1906, but had been towed off by the tug *Dragon* and

Evidence of early Mediterranean ships visiting Scilly, this fragment of a pottery jug is dated as 13th century, found in Tresco Channel by David McBride ▶

the ss *Lady of the Isles*, which got the steamer to Cardiff for repairs. After the ss *Great City* was brought into St Mary's Roads in 1917, the stench of rotting grain was appalling. Four men died from the fumes whilst clearing choked pumps on board, and after she left for Liverpool on 25 September to have her torpedo damage repaired, she had to put into Holyhead en route to land the bodies of another four men killed in the same manner. Unbelievably yet another three died whilst the ship was in Liverpool docks from the same cause!

With German submarines sinking so many merchant vessels around the Isles of Scilly, it was almost completely one-sided but not quite, since at least one U-Boat met its end in these waters between 1914-18. *UC-19*, a mine-laying submarine, under the command of Alfred Nitzsche, left Zeebrugge on 27 November 1916 to operate in the Western Channel, carrying a crew of 25. The destroyer HMS. *Ariel* spotted her conning tower above the surface on 28 November, ran over the area where she had dived then streamed a paravane carrying an explosive charge which detonated at 30ft bringing to the surface much oil and air bubbles, which was claimed as a 'kill' since the *UC-19* never returned to base. WW2 saw five U-Boats sunk off the islands. *U-247* was lost on 1 September 1944. A Class VIIC boat she was unfortunate enough to have been detected on 31 August 1944 by the 9th Escort Group made up of six Canadian frigates who were sweeping the convoy routes off Land's End for submarines. On only her 2nd war patrol, *U-247* under Gerhard Matschulat and carrying a crew of 52, all of whom were to be lost, she was picked up by HMCS *Swansea*, who dropped a single depth-charge, which brought oil bubbling to the surface. At that point *U-247* seems to have made a temporary escape, since it took surface vessels until 1 September to relocate her. She was then heavily depth-charged and presumably destroyed, since a paper certificate, a door panel, clothing and German documentation floating up from 223ft.

◀ Part of a very large pottery storage jar, found by diver Andy Williams at the entrance to St. Mary's harbour

U-1209 was another victim in 1944, which collided with the Wolf Rock on 18 December 1944 whilst on her first patrol. She surfaced so close to the Wolf Rock lighthouse in a sinking condition that one of the astonished keepers saw her and radioed Land's End for warships. Two Canadian corvettes and a British vessel plucked 44 survivors from the sea. However, Captain Hulsenbeck and Chief Engineer Claussen died of exposure and were both buried at sea. 1945 was a bad year for German submarines in the Western Approaches, since they lost *U-1208* with all 49 crew on 24 February, *U-327* and all her 40 crew on 27 February and *U-681* on 10 March, already mentioned in Chapter 2.

In marked contrast was the steamer *Eastgate* of London, brought in to St Mary's Roads by tugs after being torpedoed off the Bishop on 16 August 1917. Of 4,277 tons, the *Eastgate* was outward bound for the United States with a 'goodwill' cargo of luxury items, consisting of cosmetics, medical requisites, perfume, Paris fashions, fur coats and lingerie. Bundles of silk stockings, lace by the mile, hair dye, cough mixture, tooth-paste and scent by the gallon washed out of her, and was much sought after by the women of the islands. Eau-de-Cologne in quart bottles, skin creams, Houbigant and Dior perfumes worth hundreds of pounds, all washed about amongst the rocks between Samson and Tresco, scenting the islands in another and much more pleasant manner than the grain cargo of the *Great City*.

The last of the World War I casualties in the vicinity of Scilly were the *Rio Mondego*, the *Galway Castle*, the *Atlantico* and the *Montfort*. Damaged by submarine gunfire and abandoned on 1 September 1918, the *Rio Mondego*, a Portuguese sailing vessel, was later towed to St Mary's and beached on the eastern side of Stoney Island. She was carrying a cargo of port wine valued at a quarter million pounds, some of which leaked out through the shell holes and into the sea, possibly an even more acceptable smell to some than that from either the *Great City* or the *Eastgate*! After being torpedoed on 13 September, the Union Castle steamer *Galway Castle* broke in half and sank, and the *Atlantico*, another Portuguese sailing ship, was shelled and sunk at 2.00pm on 30 September. Two of her boats were towed in by the St Agnes lifeboat, with one dead seaman and a badly injured boy aboard. The ss *Montfort*, a Canadian Pacific Steamship vessel, was also sunk by a submarine some distance off Scilly to the west on 3 October, the last before the armistice was signed on 11 November.

Between the two world wars, offshore wrecks continued to occur, the majority of which have been mentioned in previous chapters. Those which have not include the wooden, three- masted schooner *Optimist*, lost off Scilly in March 1922. Built at New-foundland in 1919 for A.E. Hickman of St Johns, she was of 130-tons gross and 100 ft overall in length. In 1927 another schooner, the 198-tons gross *Gougou* of Vannes, was in distress after being dismasted during a gale on 22 December. She drifted helpless for 20 hours, until sighted by the *Westphalia*, a German steamer, during the evening of the 23rd. Alerted by radio, the St Mary's lifeboat was launched and found the vessel only 300 yards SSE of the Seven Stones, waterlogged and in complete darkness. Her crew were taken off and landed back at the islands, after which the Trinity House steamer *Mermaid* set out from Penzance to find the derelict. When located 10 miles further E, the *Gougou* already had a Dutch tug standing by her, which had attempted a tow but failed. Two men from the Trinity House vessel went aboard the schooner, passed a hawser across and both ships reached Penzance without further incident.

There are less than ten Royal Navy capital ships lying on the seabed around the British Isles, one of which sank 55 miles due S of Hugh Town, in 400ft(122m) with the top of the wreck at 341ft(104m).The exact location is Lat.49 07.241N;Long. 06 20.953W, and as far as is known has never been visited by divers to date, although the salvage company Risdon Beazley put a manned observation chamber down in 1972 to see if her bronze propellers had actually been removed before she left Portsmouth Dockyard.. She was the battleship HMS *Monarch*, 22,500-tons, armed with ten 13.5inch and sixteen 4inch guns, as well as smaller armament and torpedo tubes. Built by Armstrong's in 1910 as a Dreadnought of the Orion Class she was massive, 545ft (166m) long, with a crew of over 800 men. Unlike other wrecks around Scilly which were lost either by accident or enemy action, the *Monarch* was deliberately sunk by friendly fire. Having survived WW1, by 1922 she was considered redundant and selected for special gunnery trials, to test the alleged weakness of deck armour and other shortcomings of Royal Navy ships. Stripped of her four bronze propellers and 'A' frames, searchlights, range-finders and other equipment, she was towed out of Plymouth on 20 January 1925, to face the guns of the entire Atlantic Fleet. Six inch guns on cruisers battered her, then she was bombed by aircraft from the carrier *Argus*, then shelled by battleship guns ranging from 12 to 15inch.

▲ The battleship HMS. *Monarch*, 22,500-tons, sunk off Scilly on 21 January 1925 as part of a series of gunnery trials

▲ The bow of HMS. *Monarch* showing above the surface before she sank in 104m of water, 55 miles due south of Hugh Town

Stationary, she was not exactly difficult to hit, and between bouts of shelling officers from the Royal Navy gunnery school at Whale Island went on board to assess the damage, take photographs and measurements and prepare reports. A simulated aircraft bomb holding 2,000lbs of explosive was detonated 40ft beneath the surface just yards from her hull, and although now a total wreck from bow to stern, still she would not sink! In the end the battleship HMS *Revenge* was ordered to finish her off, and at night, with searchlights illuminating the target at one mile range, it took 30 minutes for all eight 15inch guns to put her under, which was a tribute to British shipbuilding. Sonar traces of the wreck later suggested she now lies upside down, her gun turrets scattered on the seabed having fallen out of their mountings as she turned turtle.

During WW2, all merchant ships of any size were armed and sailed in convoys from the outset, escorted by naval ships and aircraft when close to land, hence the 'deep-water' wrecks were well outside the Isles of Scilly, and beyond the coverage of this book. New Years Eve of 1961 saw the 7,660 tons gross *Indian Navigator* of Calcutta rocked by a violent explosion in No 4 hold when 60 miles S & W of the Scillies. A fire immediately followed and a distress call went out, to be answered by the Blue Funnel ss *Menesthems*, the Hamburg-Amerika liner ss *Dalerdyck* and the Indian ss *Success*, a sister-ship of the distressed vessel. Although the *Indian Navigator* was abandoned by her crew in appalling conditions of high seas and wind, only one life was lost. Later, 13 of the crew of the *Indian Success* went aboard the *Indian Navigator* to fight the fire. During the night of 2 January, there was a second violent explosion deep inside the ship and half a minute later she rolled over and sank, taking the entire salvage party to their death. Owned by the India Steamship Co of Calcutta, the *Indian Navigator* had been launched in 1944 by the Californian Shipbuilding Co of Los Angeles as the USSR *Victory*, one of the 'Standard' class of vessel built during WW2, commonly known as 'Victory' ships. Of all-welded construction, the *Indian Navigator* was a single-screw, steam-turbine vessel with an overall length of 455ft.

Incidents concerning the sea and ships continue to the present day, and a RNLI lifeboat at Scilly is still as much a necessity as it has ever been. At 6.48am on 22 May 1967, the *Guy & Clare Hunter* was launched to go to the aid of the motor-yacht *Braemar*. The wind was WSW force seven, gusting to force nine with a rough sea and bad visibility, when Coxswain Lethbridge set a course to intercept the *Braemar*, some 28 miles from the Bishop Rock. By the time the lifeboat arrived on the scene, the mv *Trader* had already attempted a tow but abandoned the attempt, and eventually asked the St Mary's boat to pass a second line for them, but this too was abandoned. The lifeboat then took the *Braemar* in tow and managed to shorten the distance to Newlyn before the leaking motor-yacht settled lower in the sea and took a dangerous list to starboard. Slipping the tow, the coxswain of the *Guy & Clare Hunter* placed the lifeboat alongside the sinking vessel and in a brilliant display of seamanship took off 15 men and one woman, leaving the yacht's master and two crew still aboard. The tow was then resumed in almost impossible conditions since the wind was now gusting force 10, but eventually both vessels reached Mount's Bay and the safety of Newlyn harbour. For this gallant service, a silver medal was awarded to the coxswain and two bronze medals to members of the lifeboat crew.

Grim reminders of shipwreck continue to come ashore on the islands' beaches, one example being the sternboard of the *Venus*, a French trawler sunk on 8 September 1969. A more tragic reminder was the body of a man wearing only a life-jacket, washed up on Tresco on 25 February 1970. The number on the life-jacket, D11714, and other evidence proved beyond doubt that the unfortunate man came from the French trawler *Jean Gougy*. This 246 tons gross vessel had put into Newlyn on 20 February to land the mate who had a suspected fracture of the arm. She sailed again to carry on fishing over the weekend, returned for the mate three days later, but nothing more was ever heard of her again. Bunks, a ladder, timber and insulating material of the type used in a trawler's fish-hold, drifted down through Broad Sound that week, which suggested that the trawler had struck the Western Rocks and sunk with the loss of her 14 crew. Another French trawler with an almost identical name, the *Jeanne Gougy*, also met a tragic end in Cornish waters. This was on 3 November 1962, when she struck Land's End and sank with the loss of 12 lives. Many items of cargo have washed ashore on the islands beaches, cut and rough timber, chemical drums, children's 'Pamper' nappies, bags of hospital saline solution and other chemical drips, all from containers washed off the deck of ships.

An old island prayer, attributed to the Reverend Troutbeck, chaplain of St Mary's in the 1780's says:

'We pray thee, O Lord, not that wrecks should happen, but that if they should happen, that thou wilt guide them into the Scillies for the benefit of the poore inhabitants'.

This book bears witness that his prayer has been answered in full measure. Happily in recent years, entries in this grim record have become few and far between, and though it will never be closed so long as the elements endure and man continues to be his own worst enemy, the time may come one day when it will be remembered only as a part of the islands' history, but still a mere fraction of the toll the sea has taken in coastal waters of the British Isles.

Acknowledgments

Apart from *The Island News* which was printed locally on Scilly from 10 June to 12 September 1939 (No's. 1-14) which was more of a newsletter than a broadsheet, the Isles of Scilly has never had its own newspaper, relying on the Cornish and national press to record local news and world affairs. Hence the record of events on the islands, and any in-depth research into a subject as old and varied as shipwreck has of necessity to be conducted predominantly on the mainland in public repositories. An important source of local information is of course the *Scillonian* magazine, which has been printed twice a year since 1925. West Country newspapers dating back to Trewman's *Exeter Flying Post* cover from 1763, the *Royal Cornwall Gazette* (1811), Lake's *Falmouth Packet* (1829) the *Cornishman* (1878), and the *West Britain* (1811) have all been the prime recorders of shipwreck information. Some or all of these are available in the Morab Library, Penzance; the Cornwall Studies Library, Redruth, the Royal Institute of Cornwall, Truro, and the British Library - Colindale Newspaper Collection in London, whose Librarians and staff I wish to acknowledge and thank for their patience and assistance.

I also extend my thanks and acknowledgment to Declan Barriskill, Lloyd's Collection, London's Guildhall Library; Barbara Jones, Senior Corporate Information Officer and her assistant, Anne Cowan, both at Lloyd's Register; the Historic Manuscript Commission; National Archive, Kew (PRO); and the British Library (Burney Collection, State Papers & East India Company Records in particular). Also the National Maritime Museum Library at both Greenwich and Falmouth; HM Customs & Excise Library and the Salvage Association.

On a more personal note I extend my thanks for the assistance and friendship of John Davies and Tony Pawlyn, both of Chacewater; John Behenna of Slapton; Amanda Martin, Curator of the Isles of Scilly Museum; Innis McCartney, Kevin Camidge and the late Clive Carter, all of Penzance, all of whom have helped with information. CISMAS supplied the front and back cover photographs, and David McBride numerous artefact photographs, and to both I extend my gratitude. Also to Kyne Gibson for permission to use their photographs.

To Pat & Padriac Keady, my in-laws, who gave my wife and I a bed on so many research visits during their time in Palmers Green, London; also Tony & Francis Taylor for their kind hospitality on the Isle of Dogs; and John & Jane Selby, of Watford, London for their hospitality and support.

Finally, to Bridget, my wife and constant companion, with whom I have been privileged to share so many adventures, who actually enjoys shipwreck research; who has a much better memory than I, and has played a major role in our writing, publishing and diving activities.

Richard Larn OBE, St Mary's, Isles of Scilly. 2009

Illustration acknowledgments

The following individuals or organisations supplied photographs and illustrations, or gave permission for their use, which have greatly enhanced the content of this book, to whom I extend my grateful appreciation and thanks.

Cornwall & Isles of Scilly Maritime Archaeological Society (CISMAS) - both front and back cover photographs

David McBride, Underwater Cameraman (www.divescilly.com) - p32, 33, 34, 86, 93, 102

Kevin Camidge - 119

Kyne Gibson - p5, 10, 15, 36, 37, 57, 58, 73, 76, 78, 84, 85, 87, 90, 97, 105, 110, 125, 126, 128, 133, 137, 138, 142, 148, 149, 154, 168, 172

English Heritage - p117, 118

Harper's Weekly Joiurnal - p30

Rochester Town Hall - p18, 42

Elizabeth Slatter - p25

Royal Cornwall Gazette (Redruth Cornish Studies Library) - p26

Illustrated London News - p27, 1

Keith Austin - p31

National Maritime Museum, Greenwich - 39, 183, 190

Norwich City Museum - 40

Scillonian Diving Services - p46 (lower)

Braithwaite family - p50

Daily Telegraph (Paul Armiger) - p11, 44, 83

The Author's private collection - p6, 14, 16, 17, 22, 28, 29, 35, 41, 43, 45, 46 (upper and centre), 47, 48, 49, 51, 53, 54, 55, 56, 60, 61, 62, 63, 68, 69, 70, 71, 72, 74, 75, 81, 82, 86 (lower), 89, 91, 92, 96, 103, 107, 114, 115, 120, 121, 134, 135, 138 (Upper and middle), 140, 152, 158, 160, 163, 169, 171, 181, 186, 187, 188

Bibliography

Austin, K. *The Victorian Titanic, the loss of the Schiller in 1875* (2001)

Barber, R. *The Last Piece of England* (2002)

Baring-Gould, S. *Book of the West*, Vol.2. (1899)

Baring-Gould, S. *Cornish Characters & Strange Events* (1908)

Borlase, W. *Observations on the ancient and present state of the Isles of Scilly* (1756)

Boulay, J. du. *Wrecks of the Isles of Scilly* (1959)

Bowley, R.L. *Scilly at War* (2003)

Carew, R. *The Survey of Cornwall* (1602) reprinted in 1811

Chudleigh, D. *Bridge over Lyonesse*, (1989)

Colledge, J.J. *Ships of the Royal Navy*, Vol's 1 & 2 (1969)

Cooke, J.H. *The Shipwreck of Sir Cloudesley Shovell* (1883)

Courtney, L.C. *Guide to Penzance & its neighbourhood including the Isles of Scilly* (1845)

Dorrien-Smith, C. *Shipwrecks of the Isles of Scilly* (1949)

Dunbar, J. *The Lost Land - Underwater exploration in the Isles of Scilly* (1958)

Fagan, H.S. 'The Scilly isles', *Fraser's Magazine*, reprint

Gibson, A.& H. *The isles of Scilly* (1925)

Gill, C; Booker,F; Soper, T. *The Wreck of the Torrey Canyon*, Newton Abbot, (1967)

Grant, R.M. *U-Boats Destroyed* (1964)

Green, E. *Isles of Icris*, (1906)

Grigson, G. *The Scilly Isles* (1948)

Hardy, J. *Lighthouses, their History & Romance* (1895)

Harper, C.G. *The Cornish coast & Isles of Scilly* (1910)

Harris, S. *Sir Cloudesley Shovell - Stuart Admiral* (2001)

Harris, S. *Admiral Sir Cloudesley Shovell* (2003).

Heath, R. *A Natural & Historical Account of the Islands of Scilly* (1750) reprint 1967

Jellico, G.A. *A Landscape Charter of the isles of Scilly*

Jenkins, A.J. *Gigs & Cutters of the Isles of Scilly* (1975)

Kay, E. *Isles of Flowers* (1956)

Larn, R. & McBride, D. *The Cita, Scilly's own Whisky Galore wreck* (1997,1998 & 2009)

Larn, R.& B. *Shipwreck Index of the British Isles*, Vol.1 The West Country (1995)

Larn. R. & McBride, P. *Sir Clowdisley Shovell's Disaster in the Isles of Scilly* (1985)

Larn, R. & McBride, D. *A Diver Guide to the Isles of Scilly & North Cornwall* (2003)

Larn, R. *Cornish Shipwrecks - Vol.3. The Isles of Scilly* (1971, 1979, 1993, 2010)

Larn, R. (Editor), Ships, *Shipwrecks & Maritime Incidents around the Isles of Scilly* (1999)

Lewis, H.A. *St Martins, St Helens & Tean* (1900)

Llewellyn, S. *Emperor Smith - the Man who Built Scilly* (2005)

Mace, M. *HMS. Association - A Diver's Report* (1975)

Magalotti, L. *Travels of Cosom, the 3rd Grand Duke of Tuscany, through England & Wales in the reign of Charles II* (English translation 1821)

McBride, P. & Larn, R. *Admiral Shovell's Treasure & Shipwreck in the Isles of Scilly* (1999)

Mais, S.P.B. *Isles of the Islands* (1934)

Maybee, R. *Sixty-eight Years of Experience of the Scilly Islands*

Morris, R. *Island Treasure* (1969)

Morris, R. *Treasure Trove Islands*

Morris, R. *HMS Colossus* (1979)

Mothersole, J. *The Isles of Scilly* (1910)

Mumford, C. *Portrait of the Isles of Scilly* (1967)

Noall, C. *Cornish Lights & Shipwrecks* (1968)

Noall, C. & Farr, G. *Wreck & Rescue round the Cornish Coast* (Vol. 2 1965)

North, I.W. *A Week at the Isles of Scilly* (1850)

O'Neil, B.H. *Ancient Monuments of the Isles of Scilly* (1961)

Owen, J.G. *Faire Lyonesse* (1897)

Page, W. (Ed). *The Victoria History of Cornwall* (1906)

Quixley, R.C. *Antique Maps of Cornwall & the Isles of Scilly* (1966)

Rennell, J. *Observations on the Current to the West of Scilly* (1873)

Rogers, R. *Excavation of HMS. Association* (1969)

Smith, G.C. *The Extreme Misery of the Off-Islands* (1818)

Smith, G.C. *The Scilly isles & the Famine* (1828)

Smith, G.C. *The Cassiterides*(1863)

Stanbrook, E. *Bishop Rock Lighthouse* (2008)

Stevens, T. *Wreck of the Colossus - the find of a lifetime* (2007)

Stevens, T. & Cumming, E. *The Wreck of the Nancy* (2008)

Strike, F. *Cornish Shipwrecks* (1965)

Thurstan, P.C. *Cassiterides & Ictis, where are they?* (1909)

Tucker, B. *Concerning the formation of a safe roadstead at the isles of Scilly* (1810)

Tonkin, J.C. *The Homeland Guide for the Isles of Scilly* (1900)

Tonkin, J.& R. *Guide to the Isles of Scilly* (1887)

Tonkin, J. & Prescott, R. *Lyonesse, a Handbook for the isles of Scilly*

Troutbeck, J. *A Survey of the Ancient & Present State of the isles of Scilly* (1796)

White, W. *A Lononder's Walk to the Land's End, & a Tour of the Scillies* (1855)

Whitfield, H.J. *Scilly & its legends* (1852)

Williams, M. *Sunken Treasure* (1980)

Woodley, G.A. *A View of the Present State of the isles of Scilly* (1822)

Woodley, G. *A Narrative of the Loss of the steamer 'Thames' on the Rocks of Scilly*

.

Alphabetical index of shipwrecks on and around the Isles of Scilly

This index includes only ships which were lost on or around the Isles of Scilly. It does not include strandings which were subsequently re-floated and saved, nor vessels brought in as derelicts. Page numbers in italic denote illustrations, and the following abbreviations have been used to denote the type of vessel: Ships with no page reference are known to have been lost where stated but are not included in the text due to practical space limitations:

BR	Brig	**FR**	Full-rigged ship	**PC**	Pilot cutter
BN	Brigantine	**GA**	Galliot	**PD**	Paddle steamer
BQ	Barque	**KT**	Ketch	**PE**	Privateer
BE	Barquentine	**LC**	Landing Craft	**SL**	Sloop
CA	Cargo/passenger	**LU**	Lugger	**SM**	Smack
CM	Chasse-Maree	**HM**	Warship(sail)	**HMS**	Warship
SN	Snow	**CU**	Cutter	**SS**	Steamship
DA	Dandy	**TP**	Transport (sail)	**EI**	East Indiaman
TG	Tug	**EP**	East India Packet	**WI**	West Indiaman
FL	Fishing trawler, mfv	**FM**	Fishing trawler, ss	**MV**	Motor vessel
FS	Fishing vessel, sail	**PK**	Packet vessel	**SV**	Sailing vessel
YS	Pleasure yacht/sail	**YM**	Pleasure yach/motor	**BB**	Barge, motor

NB: HM relates to a sailing warship of any nation, HMS relates to an engine driven warship of any nationality, and not necessarily Her Majesty's Ship.

Ship Name	Type	Date lost	Location	Page
Active	SV	24.12.1804	Scillies	
Adeline	BR	30.01.1860	Isles of Scilly	
Adolphe	CM	01.12.1863	St Helen's	
Agnese	SV	05.01.1864	Offshore	179
Agnette	SV	31.07.1783	Isles of Scilly	
Aimee Maria	SV	03.03.1917	Offshore	
Aksai	SS	02.11.1875	White Island	146
Ala Charles	SC	06.06.1883	Seven Stones	
Albertine Beatrice	SV	15.06.1917	Offshore	
Albion	SV	10.01.1797	Scillies	
Alessandro il Grande	BR	01.01.1851	Tresco	
Alexander	SV	24.05.1786	St Mary's	
Alida	SC	16.02.1869	White Island	146

Ship Name	Type	Date lost	Location	Page
Alidia	SV	14.07.1869	Offshore	
Algonquin	SS	12.03.1917	Offshore	185
Ambassador	BR	12.06.1853	Seven Stones	165
Amelia	SC	16.11.1867	Offshore	
Amelia	FR	01.09.1810	Western Rocks	56
America	FR	02.02.1854	Seven Stones	165
Amethyst	BR	23.04.1851	Seven Stones	165
Andalusian	SS	12.03.1915	Offshore	182
Ann	SV	24.03.1789	Scillies	
Ann	BR	15.11.1807	Tresco	
Anna Margareta	GA	07.01.1852	St. Agnes	
Annie F.Conlon	SC	03.10.1917	St. Martin's	156
Ans	SC	06.12.1916	Offshore	
Anthony	BR	17.12.1838	Seven Stones	
Antonios	SS	08.12.1912	Western Rocks	46
Arcade	SN	01.01.1811	Scillies	
Ardencraig	FR	08.01.1911	Crim Rocks	60;60
Argentine	SS	01.04.1917	Offshore	185
Argo	SC	23.10.1880	Tean	143-144
Armenian	SS	28.06.1915	Offshore	184
Ason	SS	17.12.1916	Offshore	
Association	HM	22.10.1707	Western Rocks	9;11; 14; 17; 18; 23; 39-46; 46
Astillero	SS	17.02.1913	Offshore	
Atlantic	PC	22.01.1868	St. Mary's	
Atlantico	SC	30.09.1918	Offshore	189
Aurora	SV	11.12.1811	Seven Stones	
Aurora	BR	19.09.1860	Western Rocks	55; 59
Aurora	SV	31.12.1784	St. Helen's	
Award	FR	19.03.1861	Bryher	127
A.A. Raven	SS	14.03.1918	Offshore	
Bagdale	SS	02.06.1917	Offshore	185
Bandoeng	SS	22.02.1917	Offshore	
Bangalore	BQ	04.03.1881	Offshore	179
Barbadoes	SV	10.10.1816	Western Rocks	
Baron Erskine	SS	19.08.1915	Offshore	

Ship Name	Type	Date lost	Location	Page
Barreman	FR	09.07.1887	Seven Stones	168
Bathurst	SS	02.06.1917	Offshore 185	
Bassenthwaite	BR	07.04.1836	Broad Sound	64
Beechpark	SS	02.08.1917	Offshore	
Beemah	SS	27.04.1917	Offshore	
Belinda	CU	27.06.1854	Western Rocks	23
Belle Isle	SV	10.10.1766	Offshore	
Bernard de Percin	FL	16.01.1972	Offshore	
Bernardo	BQ	11.03.1888	Annet	88
Bertha	BQ	23.01.1879	Offshore	
Bertha	SC	29.01.1869	St. Martin's	
Betsey	SV	21.11.1819	Scillies	
Betsey	SM	01.02.1819	Offshore	
Betsey	CU	00.00.1827	Scillies	
Betsey	BR	24.12.1788	St. Mary's Sound	76
Betsey	SL	17.04.1806	Samson	
Betsey	SV	20.11.1737	Offshore	
Biscayneer	SV	13.01.1789	Western Rocks	
Blazer	TG	10.11.1918	St. Mary's	
Bohallard	BN	12.02.1899	Crow Bar	
Bolina	SC	12.01.1887	St. Agnes	72
Bohallard	BN	12.02.1899	St. Martin's	150
Bordelaise	SS	04.04.1874	The Hats	155
Borodino	BQ	07.02.1830	St. Mary's	105
Brave	HM	12.04.1805	Western Rocks	
Briardene	SS	01.12.1916	Offshore	
Brigand	PD	12.10.1842	Offshore	26; 27
Brighouse	SS	12.12.1887	Seven Stones	169
Brinkburn	SS	15.12.1898	Bryher	125-127; 125: 126
Britta	SS	06.12.1939	Offshore	
Brodfield	SS	13.11.1916	St. Mary's	99
Brothers	SC	22.01.1868	Seven Stones	
Brothers	SV	28.11.1769	Offshore	
Brothers	SV	09.04.1793	Scillies	
Buteshire	BQ	29.03.1911	Offshore	180-181; 181
Cadeby	SS	27.05.1915	Offshore	
Calliope	BQ	14.01.1865	Offshore	

Ship Name	Type	Date lost	Location	Page
Calliope	BR	30.10.1850	St. Mary's	
Camiola	SS	01.10.1892	Seven Stones	170
Cannebiere	BQ	24.10.1916	Offshore	
Carapanama	FR	01.01.1905	Offshore	180
Carbineer	HMS	18.05.1916	Western Rocks	58
Carmargo	SS	03.11.1893	Offshore	
Carnanton	SC	17.03.1867	Samson	
Caroline	SC	29.09.1848	Seven Stones	165
Caroline	SC	21.11.1868	St. Mary's	
Caroline	SV	07.05.1799	Scillies	
Castleford	SS	08.06.1887	Western Rocks	9; 56-57 *57-58*
Catharina Maria	SL	28.10.1827	Seven Stones	
Catherine	SC	08.02.1854	Offshore	178
Catherine Griffiths	BN	01.11.1875	Western Rocks	
Caucasian	SS	01.07.1915	Offshore	187
Cavalier	SS	13.12.1891	Offshore	177
Cecilia	SV	17.11.1824	Western Rocks	
Challenger	SC	21.11.1843	North Channel	64-65 156
Charles	BQ	05.01.1853	Offshore	
Charleston	SN	22.04.1765	Scillies	
Charlotte	BR	25.12.1848	Western Rocks	92
Charlotte Dunbar	SC	17.01.1881	St. Agnes	77
Charlotte & Molly	BR	20.11.1780	Bryher	
Charming Molly	BR	20.11.1780	Bryher	127
Chiswick	SS	05.02.1891	Seven Stones	169
Christian	SN	17.01.1780	Scillies	
Cita	MV	26.03.1997	St. Mary's	101-104; *102-103;* *107*
Cite de Verdun	FE	22.03.1925	Western Rocks	52
City of Bremen	SS	04.01.1915	Offshore	
City of Edinburgh	SV	16.10.1820	Crow Sound	
Cober	SS	21.08.1915	Offshore	182
Colossus	HM	10.12.1798	Samson	114-119 *114; 115;* *117;120;* *121*
Comet	SC	07.12.1828	St. Mary's	

Ship Name	Type	Date Lost	Location	Page
Commerce	SV	04.12.1830	Scillies	
Commerce	SV	03.11.1809	Scillies	
Conqueranr	HM	10.02.1781	Offshore	80
Cornelia	FR	04.04.1861	Offshore	
Cornish Girl	LU	09.06.1873	Gugh	
Courier	BR	19.01.1808	Scillies	
Craig Elvan	BQ	25.01.1898	Western Rocks	
Craven	SV	06.05.1757	St. Mary's	
Criccieth Castle	BR	09.02.1883	St. Mary's	
				98
Crown of Castile	SS	30.03.1915	Offshore	182
Cubana	BQ	25.04.1866	Seven Stones	166
Culmore	SS	07.05.1881	Bishop Rock	
Custos	FR	28.08.1856	Crim Rocks	59
Dauphine	SC	14.02.1856	St. Agnes	93
De Vedre	GA	02.11.1853	Scillies	
Decoy	DY	13.08.1904	Offshore	
Defiance	CU	05.11.1844	Samson	
Delaware	SS	0.12.1871	Mincarlo	122-124
Delphic	SS	10.08.1917	Offshore	187
Delta B.	FM	02.06.1915	Offshore	183
Deux Soeurs	SV	26.05.1838	Scillies	
Diamond	SC	30.10.1855	Offshore	178
Diana	SV	00.11.1738	Mincarlo	124
Diligence	SV	05.02.1740	Scillies	
Diomed	SS	22.08.1915	Offshore	182
Don Benito	SS	27.03.1917	Offshore	
Douglas	SV	04.10.1771	Scillies	
Douro	SN	28.01.1843	Western Rocks	56;56
Dowson	SV	04.01.1788	Scillies	
Draper	SV	19.09.1745	Scillies	
Dream	SS	05.03.1888	Offshore	179
Duck	SV	00.03.1807	Scillies	
Duke of Cornwall	BN	24.12.1786	St. Agnes	76
Duke of Cumberland	PK	17.05.1776	Offshore	
Duke of Cumberland	SV	17.02.1764	Scillies	
Duke of Cumberland	SN	25.12.1773	St.Helen's	143
Duke of Wellington	SC	19.11.1859	Offshore	

Ship Name	Type	Date Lost	Location	Page
Eagle	BN	05.06.1790	Western Rocks	92
Eagle	SV	07.12.1764	Scillies	
Eagle	HM	22.10.1707	Western Rocks	
Eagle	SC	18.01.1848	Offshore	58
Earl of Arran	CA	16.07.1872	Gt. Ganilly	148-150
Earl of Lonsdale	SS	08.06.1885	St. Agnes	78-79
				78
Edale	SS	01.05.1915	Offshore	
Eddystone	SV	03.10.1846	Tresco	
Edward	SV	09.11.1816	Scillies	
Eemland	SS	22.02.1917	Offshore	184
Elizabeth	SV	11.01.1788	Offshore	
Elizabeth	SV	18.06.1790	St. Martin's	144
Elizabeth	SV	15.03.1873	St. Agnes	93
Elizabeth	SV	29.10.1815	Scillies	
Elizabeth	SV	11.08.1852	North Channel	
Elizabeth	SV	27.07.1757	Seven Stones	
Elizabeth	SV	05.03.1786	Western Rocks	
Elizabeth Line	SV	27.12.1774	Scillies	
Embricos	SS	06.02.1892	White Island	145-146
Emilie	SC	18.09.1866	Seven Stones	165
Emma	SN	13.01.1843	Crow Sound	
Empire	SS	26.11.1860	Broad Sound	124
Endeavour	SV	00.00.1737	Scillies	
Endeavour	SV	00.10.1815	Seven Stones	
Endeavour	BR	03.03.1781	St. Helen's	
Enfant de Bretagne	FL	13.02.1977	Western Rocks	47
Erignac	SS	19.02.1892	Scillies	
Erik Rickmers	FR	25.10.1899	Scilly Rock	127-128
Erna Hagemeister	SV	19.02.1861	Scillies	
Esperance	BR	02.11.1801	Nut Rock	136-137
Essie	SC	24.01.1877	Offshore	
Euphemie	SC	02.12.1863	St. Helen's	
Europa	SV	22.03.1763	Scillies	
Europe	SS	01.05.1915	Offshore	182
Excelsior	BQ	27.11.1881	Crow Sound	145
Expedition	SV	11.12.1766	Scillies	
Experiment	HM	09.11.1828	Samson	
Express	BQ	15.12.1869	St. Mary's	106
E.R.I.	SC	30.01.1871	White Island	

Ship Name	Type	Date lost	Location	Page
Factory Girl	FR	02.12.1863	Offshore	
Fair Kathleen	SV	24.11.1852	Scillies	
Falkland	BQ	22.06.1901	Western Rocks	29
Fame	SV	04.02.1836	St. Agnes	
Fame	FS	27.04.1859	Seven Stones	165
Fanny	CV	22.10.1820	St. Mary's	
Fantee	MV	06.10.1949	Seven Stones	*169*;172
Felicity	SV	07.05.1773	St. Mary's	
Felix Guemole	BN	00.09.1889	Scillies	
Fiery Cross	BQ	03.07.1915	Offshore	185
Financier	SV	05.09.1783	Annet	87
Firebrand	HM	22.10.1707	Smith Sound	44; 79
Flaminian	SS	29.03.1915	Offshore	
Flink	BQ	18.03.1867	Scillies	
Florence	SS	08.12.1872	Offshore	
Floresta	BQ	14.02.1875	Seven Stones	167
Flossie	BR	23.10.1880	Offshore	
Fly	SV	02.12.1837	Samson	
Flying Fish	SV	00.00.1736	Scillies	
Foam	SC	16,04.1852	Offshore	178
Forester	HM	13.02.1883	St. Martin's	144
Fortune	SV	28.02.1759	Scillies	
Fortune	BR	12.02.1802	Seven Stones	164
Francisca	SV	07.02.1811	Scillies	
Frau Mini Petersen	SC	04.08.1911	Offshore	170
Frederick	SC	29.03.1878	Offshore	
Fredericus	SV	23.02.1783	Scillies	
Frere et Soeur	LU	12.03.1891	St. Mary's	104
Friar Tuck	FR	02.12.1863	St. Mary's	107
Fride	BR	06.08.1898	Offshore	
Friendly Emma	BR	05.01.1813	Offshore	
Friendship	FR	26.01.1758	Scillies	
Friendship	SV	09.12.1779	Scillies	
Furnace	SV	20.01.1758	Crow Sound	156
Gaasterland	SS	22.02.1917	Offshore	184
Gallaway	SV	26.07.1763	Seven Stones	
Galway Castle	SS	13.09.1918	Offshore	189
Gamet	BR	17.02.1795	Scillies	
Gauloise	BQ	15.01.1888	Eastern Isles	

Ship Name	Type	Date lost	Location	Page
Gem	SV	05.01.1867	Offshore	
Gem	CU	14.04.1874	St. Agnes	
Gem	SS	21.11.1881	St. Mary's	107
General Nott	BQ	02.03.1892	Offshore	179
General Roberts	FM	05.06.1906	Offshore	143
Georges	KT	12.01.1911	St. Mary's	77
Gift of God	SV	24.03.1636	Scillies	
Gilmore	BQ	12.04.1866	St. Martin's	147
Giustizia	SS	03.12.1916	Offshore	
Gladiator	SS	19.08.1915	Offshore	176
Gleaner	BR	08.05.1868	Offshore	
166				
Glory	BR	16.01.1780	Scillies	
Gomes IV	SS	09.08.1888	Great Ganilly	150-151
Good Intent	BN	00.12.1867	Eastern Isles	
Good Intent	SV	06.03.1809	St. Mary's	110
Good Intent	SV	25.11.1814	Scillies	
Gracia Divina	SV	25.10.1758	Western Rocks	
Granville	SV	06.12.1754	Scillies	
Grenada	SV	00.08.1810	Scillies	
Griffin	SV	00.00.1739	Scillies	
Grootzeesjk	SC	03.11.1864	Offshore	
Hampton	SV	00.12.1758	Scillies	
Hannah	SV	01.01.1740	Scillies	
Hannah Louisa	BR	22.02.1839	Annet	87
Happy Jenny	SV	00.12.1756	Scillies	
Harriet	SC	15.10.1886	St. Mary's	
Harriet	BR	24.03.1866	Offshore	179
Harriet & Ann	SV	22.12.1807	Offshore	
Harriot & John	SV	10.11.1810	Western Rocks	92
Hast	BN	11.04.1891	Offshore	179
Hathor	SS	02.12.1920	St. Agnes	85-86;86
Headlands	SS	12.03.1915	Offshore	182
Heather	FM	24.04.1917	Offshore	
Heathmore	SS	05.07.1897	Seven Stones	170
Hendon	BR	29.04.1877	Offshore	
Henrietta	SV	09.11.1816	Scillies	
Henrietta	CU	04.10.1794	Scillies	
Herald	TP	04.09.1814	Scillies	

Ship Name	Type	Date lost	Location	Page
Hero	SV	05.10.1821	Annet	87
Hesperus	SS	03.04.1917	Offshore	
Hester	BN	05.02.1722	Scillies	
Hind	HM	11.12.1668	Crim Rocks	63
Hitteroy	SS	02.12.1916	Offshore	
Hollandia	EI	13.07.1743	Broad Sound	63; 80-83 *81;82;83*
Homestead	SS	06.09.1920	Seven Stones	
Hope	SL	05.05.1814	Seven Stones	164
Hope	SN	12.11.1814	Scillies	
Hope	BR	06.09.1839	Western Rocks	
Hope	SV	00.07.1807	Scillies	
Hope	BR	19.01.1830	St. Martin's	
Hope	SV	10.11.1795	St. Mary's	
Horsa	BQ	04.04.1893	Offshore	146
Hound	Gig	10.07.1875	St. Mary's Roads	
Housatonic	SS	03.02.1917	Offshore	186
Huit Frères	BN	30.01.1869	Tresco	
Hunstanton	SS	04.04.1917	Offshore	185
Hunter	BR	24.02 1776	St. Mary's	
Hydra	BQ	06.02.1866	St. Agnes	93
Hydrangea	FM	15.06 1905	Seven Stones	170
Ida	FL	22.10.1910	Crow Sound	
Independenza	BQ	24.09.1881	St. Mary's	10;109
Indian City	SS	12.03.1915	Offshore	182
Indian Navigator	SS	02.01.1961	Offshore	191
Indiana	SC	18.03.1981	Offshore	
Industry	SV	30.04.1756	Scillies	
Isabella	SV	23.12.1817	Seven Stones	
Isabella & Ann	BR	02.01.1811	Scillies	
Isabo	SS	27.10.1927	Scilly Rock	130-131
Italia	SS	13.05.1917	St. Agnes	70 ;70 71;72; 101
Jacatra	SS	22.02.1917	Offshore	184
Jackson	BR	01.09.1815	Western Rocks	
Jacob Jones	HM	06.12.1917	Offshore	186

Ship Name	Type	Date lost	Location	Page
James	SV	00.03.1794	Scillies	
Jane Barry	SV	01.01.1740	Scillies	
Jane Ellen	BR	23.02.1840	St. Helen's	143
Jane Owen	SC	03.03.1889	Crow Bar	156
Jane Sophia	SC	20.08.1887	Seven Stones	168
Janus	SV	06.02.1787	St. Mary's Pool	108
Japanese Prince	SS	10.02.1917	Offshore	
Jason	PE	20.05.1781	Scillies	
Jean Gougy	FL	24.02.1970	Western Rocks	192
Jeanne Cordonnier	BQ	31.05.1917	Offshore	185
Jeune Celestine	SC	07.11.1867	Crow Sound	
Johanna	SV	20.04.1751	St. Agnes	77
John	SV	21.12.1820	Scillies	
John	SV	04.10.1816	Scillies	
John	SV	28.11.1820	Scillies	
John	SV	00.07.1645	Scillies	
John Esdaile	BQ	01.12.1845	St. Agnes	46
John Philips	FR	09.06.1872	Offshore	179
John & Ann	BR	29.01.1826	Tresco	136
John & Ann	SV	30.10.1769	Scillies	
John & Mary	BR	26.02.1812	Western Rocks	
Jonas Lie	SS	11.01.1945	Offshore	
Joseph	BR	18.11.1833	Seven Stones	164
Joseph	SV	02.05.1777	Scillies	
Joseph Howe	SV	06.11.1861	Offshore	
Joseph & Betsey	SV	21.01.1771	Sunker Rock(?)	
Julia	SV	31.12.1834	Tresco	
Julie	HM	10.02.1781	Offshore	80
Juno	BQ	10.11.1797	Eastern Isles	
J.K.A.	SC	11.11.1891	St. Martin's	150
K-5	HMS	20.01.1921	Offshore	183
Katherine	SV	00.09.1807	Rosevear	
Karolos	SS	12.01.1910	Offshore	
King Cadwallon	SS	22.07.1906	Eastern Isles	147-148
				148
Kong Sverre	BQ	21.08.1896	Western Rocks	65
La Bona Resolution	SV	15.02.1787	Scillies	
La Fratenite	BK	03.10.1916	Offshore	

Ship Name	Type	Date lost	Location	Page
L'Amilta	BR	25.02.1838	Tresco	
L'Authie	FM	11.10.1909	Western Rocks	
Madonna de Carmine	SV	14.07.1782	St. Helen's	
Madura	SS	18.10.1917	Offshore	
Magdeleine	FM	03.06.1906	Bartholomew Ledge	76; *76*
Maipu	BQ	27.07.1879	Bryher	131-132; *133*
Malta	SV	24.12.1835	St. Helen's	
Mando	MV	21.01.1955	St. Helen's	141-142 *142*
Mar Cor	SS	09.06.1917	Offshore	
Margaret	SV	26.10.1795	Scillies	
Margaret Thrasher	SV	10.01.1772	Scillies	
Margaret & Elizabeth	SV	01.04.1815	St. Mary's	
Margaret & Jane	BQ	22.11.1868	St. Mary's	
Margaret & Sarah	SV	00.00.1742	Scillies	
Maria	GA	26.01.1812	Tresco	137
Maria	SV	20.11.1840	Offshore	
Maria Clara	BR	30.12.1780	St. Mary's	
Maria Whitfield	SV	19.11.1858	Offshore	
Marie	SC	06.12.1916	Offshore	
Marigold	SV	00.00.1741	Scillies	
Marthe	SC	04.02.1917	Offshore	
Mary	CU	12.12.1816	Scillies	
Mary	SV	21.01.1788	Scillies	
Mary	SV	06.03.1807	Offshore	
Mary	SV	00.12.1721	Scillies	
Mary	SV	21.11.1819	Scillies	
Mary	SL	20.03.1819	Western Rocks	50
Mary Jane	SC	11.10.1876	Offshore	
Mary & Betsey	SL	12.12.1798	Scillies	
Mary & Eliza	SC	09.10.1844	St. Mary's Pool	108
Melantho	WI	13.01.1801	St. Mary's	
Mentor	SV	18.02.1861	Tresco	136
Mentor	BN	18.05.1856	Offshore	178
Mercurius	EI	19.01.1835	St. Mary's	110
Mercury	SV	21.05.1800	Scillies	
Mercury	SV	23.02.1791	St. Mary's	109
Mercury	SV	06.01.1797	Scillies	

Ship Name	Type	Date Lost	Location	Page
Mercury	SV	30.12.1767	St. Mary's	
Merlin	SC	21.02.1861	St. Mary's	
Mermaid	SV	30.12.1739	Crow Sound	156
Messenger	BR	28.10.1880	Skirt Island	144
Miarka	SC	09.01.1926	Offshore	
Minerva	SC	13.10.1836	Western Rocks	56
Minerve	BN	31.12.1881	St. Mary's	98
Minnehaha	FR	18.01.1874	St. Mary's	5:*10*;96 -98;*97*
Moel Rhiwan	BQ	13.03.1884	Offshore	
Molly	SV	11.02.1774	Seven Stones	
Monarch	HM	20.01.1925	Offshore	190-191: *190-192*
Monmouth	SV	27.02.1795	Scillies	
Montfort	SS	03.10.1918	Offshore	189
Mouette	SC	20.08.1896	Offshore	
Mysotis	SC	09.09.1916	Offshore	
Naiad	FR	15.12.1916	Offshore	
Nancy	BR	04.01.1809	St. Helen's	
Nancy	SV	05.09.1783	Annet	
Nancy	SV	00.00.1743	Samson	
Nancy	SV	08.02.1799	Scillies	
Nancy	EI	26.02.1784	Western Rocks	47-50
Nancy	SV	09.03.1742	Tresco	136
Nascent	SS	25.08.1917	Offshore	
Nellie	BN	26.03.1886	Western Rocks	83; 179
Nelson	BQ	07.10.1870	Seven Stones	166-167
Neptune	SV	25.04.1755	Scillies	
Nerina	BR	18.11.1840	St. Mary's	100-101
New Friends	SV	02.11.1812	Offshore	
New Jane	SL	08.01.1828	Western Rocks	
New York	BR	00.00.1782	St. Mary's	108
Ngaroma	SS	08.08.1942	Seven Stones	
Nickerie	BQ	21.11.1843	Western Rocks	51
Nimrod	SV	17.01.1775	Offshore	
Niord	SS	13.03.1892	Offshore	
Noel	FL	20.09.1946	Offshore	
Noel Raphael	BR	23.03.1867	Seven Stones	
Noorderdijk	SS	22.02.1917	Offshore	184

Ship Name	Type	Date lost	Location	Page
Normanna	SS	22.02.1917	Offshore	
Nostra Senora de Muriel	SV	00.10.1760	Scillies	
Nugget	SS	31.07.1915	Offshore	104
Nyanza	LU	26.05.1898	Western Rocks	57
Nymph	BR	23.11.1809	Samson	
Ocean	SN	04.01.1829	Western Rocks	
Ocean Belle	SC	29.11.1896	Offshore	
Ocean Queen	BQ	17.05.1865	Offshore	179
Oldenburger	BR	24.01.1783	Tresco	
Olive	SV	12.02.1819	Seven Stones	
Optimist	SC	00.03.1922	Offshore	189
Orion	SV	24.03.1810	Samson	
Osiris	BQ	29.05.1838	Western Rocks	58
Osvetirel	BQ	14.07.1860	Maiden Bower	124
Otto	BN	06.12.1869	St. Mary's Roads	119
Oxus	FR	31.08.1869	Seven Stones	166
Pacquebot de Cayenne	BQ	27.11.1838	Crow Sound	151
Padstow	SV	24.12.1804	Little Ganinick	151-155
Palinurus	BQ	27.12.1848	White Island	147
Palmgrove	SS	22.08.1915	Offshore	182
Palmos	SC	07.04.1897	Offshore	
Parame	BQ	26.10.1899	Scilly Rock	
Patrie	BR	17.03.1867	Offshore	179
Pauline	SC	18.02.1861	Crow Sound	156
Pelham	SS	13.06.1915	Offshore	
Perseus	SV	27.01.1810	Samson	
Persic	SS	08.09.1918	Offshore	187
Perseverance	BR	14.11.1805	Seven Stones	
	164			
Perseverance	SV	17.01.1815	Scillies	
Pheasant	BR	16.01.1780	Scillies	
Phoenix	SC	06.01.1785	Scillies	
Phoenix	SV	08.08.1745	Scillies	
Phoenix	EI	11.01.1680	Western Rocks	53
Phoenix	HM	22.10.1707	Tresco	133-136
Phosphor	SS	13.07.1904	Offshore	180
Phyllis Anne	FM	29.04.1909	Offshore	
Pierre L'Abbe	SC	25.05.1912	Bryher	

Ship Name	Type	Date lost	Location	Page
Pincher	HMS	24.07.1918	Seven Stones	171-172
Plaminian	SS	29.03.1915	Offshore	182
Plato	SS	29.02.1892	Offshore	179-180
Plenty	SC	03.12.1840	Eastern Isles	
Plump	CU	30.12.1885	Samson	
Plympton	SS	14.08.1909	St. Agnes	15; 84-85; *84*
Poleire	MV	15.04.1970	Tresco	138-139; *138; 140*
Porth	SM	10.03.1891	Annet	88
Pretty Peggy	SV	12.03.1759	Scillies	
Pride	BR	00.08.1898	Offshore	180
Primos	BQ	24.06.1871	Seven Stones	167
Primrose	HM	13.03.1656	Seven Stones	163
Prinses Maria	EI	25.01.1686	Western Rocks	53
Prosper	BR	01.10.1829	Crow Sound	
Prosperous	CU	27.03.1836	Scillies	
Providence	CM	03.07.1854	St. Mary's	
Providence	EI	13.02.1833	Crow Sound	
Providencia	BR	02.10.1821	Annet	87
Providentia Divina	SV	13.09.1782	Western Rocks	58
Punjab	BQ	14.09.1860	Seven Stones	165
Punta	SS	22.07.1955	Seven Stones	172
Quatre Freres et Marie	BN	14.12.1868	Tresco	
Queen Charlotte	BR	27.01.1815	Scilly Rock	127
Quicksilver	FR	30.05.1804	Crow Sound	156
Raglan	SS	00.00.1882	Offshore	179
Rarau	FL	29.09.1976	Seven Stones	*171; 172; 173*
Recovery	BR	02.06.1795	St. Mary's	
Renown	BR	16.04.1852	St. Mary's Roads	
Restormel	SS	19.08 1915	Offshore	
Revenge	SV	30.11.1674	Seven Stones	
Reward	BR	06.11.1810	Seven Stones	164
Richard	SN	13.01.1814	Scillies	
Richard Davey	YM	25.04.1973	Tresco	
Richard Warbrick	SC	30.01.1882	Seven Stones	
Rio Mondego	SV	01.09.1918	Offshore	189

Ship Name	Type	Date lost	Location	Page
River Lune	BQ	27.07.1879	Muncoy Neck	*87*; 88 131
Romney	HM	22.10 1707	Western Rocks	
Rosa Tacchini	BQ	23.11.1872	Tresco	137
Rosaire	BR	26.02.1879	Seven Stones	168
Rosamund	BN	07.01.1886	Offshore	179
Roscius	SN	09.01.1815	Scillies	
Rosherville	BR	03.03.1855	St. Mary's Roads	105
Rothesay	SS	05.03.1916	Offshore	
Roxburgh Castle	SS	13.03.1891	Offshore	179
Royal Oak	EI	18.01.1665	Western Rocks	25
Ruby	BE	04.01.1917	Offshore	
Ruel	SS	21.08.1915	Offshore	182
Runter	SV	19.11.1809	Scillies	
Ruperra	SS	29.07.1903	Offshore	180
Sackville	SV	00.00.1832	St. Mary's Sound	
Sadi Carnot	SV	04.09.1917	Offshore	
Sado	SS	20.04.1870	Western Rocks	56; 59
Sainte Marie	BE	07.04.1916	Offshore	
Sally	SN	14.01.1769	St. Mary's	
Salmon	SC	15.01.1871	St. Mary's Roads	
Salvor	LC	13.10.1968	Offshore	
Samara	SS	19.08.1915	Offshore	
Santisimo Trinidade	SV	05.11.1781	St. Martin's	
Sarah	SC	19.03.1865	Offshore	
Sarah	SC	02.04.1870	Western Rocks	
Sarah	SC	27.01.1853	St. Martin's	155
Sarah & Emma	BN	20.05.1863	Seven Stones	
Schiller	SS	07.05.1875	Western Rocks	*16:30: 31-38*
Scipio	SV	22.12.1758	Scillies	
Scotia	BR	22.05.1863	Offshore	
Sea Flower	SV	24.02.1748	Scillies	
Sea Nymph	SV	13.03.1815	St. Mary's	
Seahorse	SV	19.12.1766	Scillies	
Seapoint	SS	28.12.1917	Seven Stones	
Serica	SS	24.11.1893	St. Mary's	*110*;111
Setiembre	SS	26.03.1911	The Hats	155
Shamrock	BB	15.07.1908	St. Mary's	

SHIP NAME	TYPE	DATE LOST	LOCATION	PAGE
Tamer	BR	15.11.1807	Tresco	
Tancred	BR	04.04.1848	Seven Stones	
Tanared	BR	04.04.1848	Offshore	178
Telxinoi	BR	17.02.1872	Crow Bar	156
Terwagout	HM	03.11.1788	Scillies	
Thames	SS	04.01.1841	Western Rocks	*53;53; 54-55; 55;59*
The Hugh	SV	13.06.1809	St. Mary's	
Thelma	SV	00.00.1748	Scillies	
Thedorick	BR	04.09.1839	Western Rocks	25
Theris	SV	29.10.1799	Scillies	
Thomas	GA	06.02.1776	St. Mary's	
Thomas W. Lawson	SC	15.12.1907	Annet	88-92; *89; 90 91;92*
Thomas & Sally	BR	16.12.1812	Scillies	
Thomas & William	SL	30.01.1801	Scillies	
Thornliebank	FR	28.11.1913	Western Rocks	*61; 61 -62*
Three Sisters	SV	15.04.1777	Scillies	
Ticina	BQ	30.12.1869	St.Mary's	106
Toanui	TG	11.06.1913	Seven Stones	171
Tobasco	BE	24.03.1879	St.Martin's	
Toledo	SS	20.08.1898	North Channel	122
Torrey Canyon	SS	18.03.1967	Seven Stones	141; 158-162; *160*
Tralee Trader	MV	19.12.1971	Seven Stones	
Trignac	SS	19.02.1891	Offshore	170
Triron	BR	16.04.1874	Offshore	179
Triton	BR	13.05.1802	Offshore	178
Triumph	SV	09.10.1736	St.Mary's	109
Triumph	SV	07.02.1776	Scillies	
Tryal	BR	31.08.1780	Crow Sound	151
Tudor	SV	08.02.1867	Scillies	
Turquoise	SS	31.07.1915	Offshore	104
Twee Gebroders	GA	14.02.1838	Scillies	
Twee Sodskende	GA	09.09.1827	Offshore	164

Ship Name	Type	Date lost	Location	Page
Unidentified	SV	00.00.1700	Scillies	
"	SV	07.06.1788	Western Rocks	46
"	LU	06.11.1871	St. Mary's	
"	SV	00.00.1667	Scillies	
"	SV	23.10.1820	Crow Sound	
"	SV	21.02.1812	Western Rocks	65
"	SS	10.10.1890	Seven Stones	
"	SV	00.00.1793	St.Mary's	106
"	SV	13.09.1686	Scillies	
"	SN	10.11.1759	Scillies	
"	SV	00.00.1743	Bryher	
"	SL	27.02.1795	Scillies	
"	SV	00.00.1764	St.Agnes	77; 84
"	SV	21.02.1675	Scillies	
"	SV	00.00.1737	St.Agnes	71
"	HM	14.01.1780	Western Rocks	
"	SV	00.00.1752	Western Rocks	47
"	SV	09.12.1782	Scillies	
"	SV	00.00.1616	Offshore	
"	BR	24.01.1792	Scillies	
"	SC	16.01.1826	Seven Stones	164
"	SV	00.00.1760	Western Rocks	
"	BR	00.05.1789	Scillies	
"	SL	23.10.1820	St.Mary's	
"	PE	10.12.1798	Scillies	
"	TP	25.05.1807	Seven Stones	
"	PE	27.12.1810	Scillies	
"	SV	00.00.1750	Western Rocks	46
"	CU	04.04.1791	Western Rocks	65
"	SM	08.03.1833	Seven Stones	
"	SV	14.06.1743	St.Mary's	
"	BR	09.10.1844	St.Martin's	
"	BN	03.02.1873	Seven Stones	167
"	SV	00.00.1762	Western Rocks	47
"	SV	00.00.1730	Western Rocks	47
"	SV	08.12.1775	Offshore	
"	SV	00.12.1832	Western Rocks	
"	SV	00.01.1796	Western Rocks	
"	SV	00.04.1737	Tresco	
"	CU	05.01.1818	Offshore	

Ship Name	Type	Date lost	Location	Page
Unidentified	HM	00.00.1805	St.Agnes	
"	SV	29.07.1849	Offshore	
"	SV	04.12.1777	St.Mary's	106
"	HM	10.05.1651	St.Mary's	
"	HM	19.10.1707	Seven Stones	
"	SV	01.10.1782	Scillies	
"	BR	29.04.1865	Offshore	
"	SV	29.03.1852	Crow Sound	
"	SV	07.02.1783	Scillies	
"	SV	00.00.1771	St.Mary's	100
"	SV	00.00.1764	Western Rocks	
"	SV	00.00.1771	Gugh	71
"	SV	00.00.1555	Bartholomew Ledge	75; 74-5
"	SV	18.08.1740	Scillies	
"	SV	00.00.1720	St.Agnes	70
"	SL	12.01.1827	Scillies	
"	SC	02.04.1841	St.Agnes	93
"	SV	28.05.1765	Scillies	
"	SV	00.00.1681	St.Agnes	
"	BQ	13.09.1884	Seven Stones	
"	SV	00.00.1679	Western Rocks	
"	SV	22.12.1667	Scillies	
"	SV	15.02.1814	Western Rocks	
"	SV	14.09.1785	Scillies	
"	SV	13.01.1849	Western Rocks	
"	SV	28.04.1738	St.Mary's	98
"	SV	31.10.1797	Scillies	
"	GA	16.10.1774	Offshore	
"	SV	19.10.1795	Scillies	
"	BR	02.01.1788	St.Agnes	
"	SV	25.11.1783	St.Helen's	
"	SL	16.12.1832	Western Rocks	
"	WI	22.10.1810	Scillies	
"	SV	00.00.1784	Bryher	47
"	SV	00.10.1817	Offshore	
"	SV	21.08.1670	Scillies	
"	SC	28.02.1840	Seven Stones	
"	SV	00.11.1829	Western Rocks	65
"	SV	00.00.1767	Scillies	
"	GA	00.00.1764	St.Agnes	

Ship Name	Type	Date lost	Location	Page
Unidentified	SV	22.05.1789	Western Rocks	
"	SV	07.11.1785	Scillies	
"	SC	00.04.1871	Bryher	
"	SV	00.00.1305	Tresco	
"	TP	18.11.1689	St.Mary's	
"	SV	00.00.1733	Melledgan	92
"	SV	00.00.1753	Porth Killier	
"	HM	00.00.1800	Offshore	
"	BR	13.09.1884	Seven Stones	168
"	BR	23.03.1866	Offshore	179
Union	SN	28.01.1820	St Helen's	
Unity	SV	27.02.1795	Scillies	
Unity	BR	20.11.1807	Scillies	
U-27	U-Boat	19.08.1915	Offshore	
U-247	U-Boat	01.09.1944	Offshore	188
U-480	U-Boat	24.02.1945	Offshore	30 -31
U-1209	U-Boat	18.12.1944	Offshore	189
UC-19	U-Boat	28.11 1916	Offshore	188
Valentine & Helene	BQ	02.03.1892	Offshore	180
Valuna	BR	01.06.1857	St. Agnes	83
Velox	SC	21.03.1857	Bryher	
Venetian	SV	02.11.1758	Scillies	
Venus	FL	08.09.1969	Offshore	192
Venus	SV	04.05.1764	Offshore	
Venus de Isles	FL	01.09.1975	St.Martin's	
Vesper	SC	01.05.1844	St.Mary's	111
Vesper	PD	19.01.1867	Offshore	179
Victoria	SC	14.02.1838	Crow Sound	
Vigilancia	SS	01.04.1917	Offshore	185
Vigilant	DA	05.11.1865	Bryher	
Viking	CU	01.03.1905	St.Mary's	109
Ville de la Rochelle	SS	12.02.1875	Seven Stones	
Vine	SV	09.02.1796	Western Rocks	
Virginia de Craman	LU	09.12.1806	Western Rocks	
Volmer	SS	26.12.1912	Offshore	
Voluna	BR	01.06.1857	St.Agnes	
Waterloo	CU	25.12.1840	Offshore	178
Weddel	BR	04.02.1775	Tresco	

A Graveyard of Shipwrecks?

Historically, numerous writers have credited the Isles of Scilly as having the greatest number of shipwrecks anywhere in the British Isles - which is simply not true. As with any stretch of coast, the total number of shipping losses that can be credited can only be those that have been recorded in some sort of publication or documentation in the past. Local or provincial newspapers have been around since roughly 1830, and in the West Country exceptionally Farley's *Exeter Journal* since1723. These have all recorded shipwrecks to varying degrees, and are a prime research source. Prior to that there were several London papers which spasmodically recording shipping losses back to the early 1600's. These of course pre-date Lloyd's List as well as the extensive Admiralty Wreck Returns, Board of Trade Wreck Returns and Victorian publications such as the *Shipwrecked Mariner's Journal* of the late Victorian era.

Prior to the 1600's the only reference to shipwrecks is to be found in hand-written correspondence, letters passing between gentry or officials, since the average person did not have the ability or need to write letters, being mostly il-literate. Going back further still into the Middle Ages correspondence was even sparser and sometimes written in Latin, and of course there was no central repos-itory for documentation. If letters were retained, it was frequently in damp musty private cellars, quickly becoming illegible and attacked by vermin, after which they were either destroyed or sold to book binders.

The Isles of Scilly have belonged to the Duchy of Cornwall since the 1300's, and any reference to early shipwrecks would have been communicated to London in writing by the resident Governor or Duchy Agent. Hence Duchy archives held at Buckingham Gate may be a rich source of research material, but regrettably public access is not encouraged. All this means that whilst the preceding list of 770 recorded shipping losses around Scilly is definitive going back to about 1740, prior to that is virtually a 'black hole' still, and is likely to remain that way for the foreseeable future.

When my wife Bridget and I compiled seven volumes of the *Lloyd's Shipwreck Index of the British Isles*, an undertaking that recorded some 50,000 ship losses around the United Kingdom, seeking a simple method whereby shipwreck density for any one county could be quantified and compared with others, we counted up the total losses and divided it by the length of coastline in miles. The results for the West Country were astonishing to say the least:

North Devon has seen 8.25 wrecks per mile of coast.

Lundy Island	26.6
North Cornwall	26
South Cornwall	20
South Devon	15.9

Comparing similar statistics to the East coast of Gt. Britain:

Suffolk	25
Norfolk	25.6
Yorkshire	16
County Durham	44 (the highest loss rate in the country)

Where does the Isles of Scilly feature, supposedly, according to some, as having the greatest number of shipwrecks in the British Isles? 770 wrecks in 100 miles of coastline equates to 7.7 losses per mile of coast, a relatively modest number. As percentages and totals of 770 (which includes a huge number lost offshore), various geographic features indicate the following:

Shipwrecks known to have taken place but with no exact location:	= 140 (18.2%)
" " offshore	= 205 (26.6%)
" " St. Martins & White Island	= 40 (5.2%)
" " St. Mary's & Roads	= 98 (12.7%)
" " Seven Stones	= 76 (9.9%)
" " Western Rocks	= 97 (12.6%)
" " Tresco	= 24 (3.1%)
" " St. Agnes & Gugh	= 37 (4.8%)
" " Annet	= 8 (1%)
" " Samson	= 13 (1.7%)
" " Bryher	= 19 (2.5%)
" " St. Helens & Tean	= 14 (1.8%)

General Index